SAM STERN'S
COOKERY
COURSE

FOR
STUDENTS IN THE KITCHEN

photography by
Chris Terry

Quadrille
PUBLISHING

Cooking has to be one of the greatest pleasures of all time; it's creative, it's fun, it's relaxing and it's social. It's the ideal excuse for getting mates and family round. It's also an ideal activity on purely selfish grounds. Cooking for yourself means you get to make informed choices about what you eat. When you're feeling greedy you can indulge (but in a good way). When you're training for a marathon or just want to get yourself fit you can cook and eat to take greater care of yourself. It saves loads of time: yes, a great home cook meal can be thrown together from scratch in less time than it takes to take delivery of a pizza. And those long slow cook recipes are the perfect opportunity to do something chilling while your roast is sizzling away in a very low oven. But if you're just starting out of course it can feel daunting. So think of *Virgin to Veteran* as a personal masterclass. I'm not a professional chef but I've been a passionate cook since I can remember. I've cooked in all kinds of kitchens (at home, at uni, all over the place) and I cook every meal from scratch as I totally believe that you are what you eat and that every meal you eat has to earn its place on your plate. So I've structured the book to be relevant, (only foods you'd really want to eat) comprehensive (I've pulled together loads of key information in the introductions to each chapter) and easy to follow. You'll find each recipe moves logically through every step you'll need to take. It encourages you to be creative. And it starts with a guide to setting up a workable kitchen – a place where you can bang on the music and get into cooking with confidence.

SAM

KITCHEN SETUP

THE KNIFE SET Knives are like an extension of your arm: you need them close to your board. I'm right handed so that's where I put my knife block. Use the appropriate one for the job (p9). Don't store them in the drawer – it ruins the blades and it's dangerous. Keep them in a block or on a wall-mounted magnetic strip, or in a chef's roll instead.

SEASONINGS Sometimes I'll put these on a tray, sometimes they'll be grouped together. Clear a space to put any appropriate oils, vinegars, spices, dried herbs, a lemon, salt and pepper.

THE TIMER Check you've got a reliable timer available: bang it on the work top where you can't miss it, set the timing function on your oven, or set your mobile; if you're wandering off when something tasty's cooking you don't want to forget it.

SETTING UP YOUR BASE KITCHEN

Go into any kitchen shop and there are thousands of bits of equipment begging 'buy me'. Who needs them? You don't. What you do need is an organised space, the right bits for the job, a workable fridge and smartly stocked shelves and cupboards. Get this lot sorted and get yourself cooking...

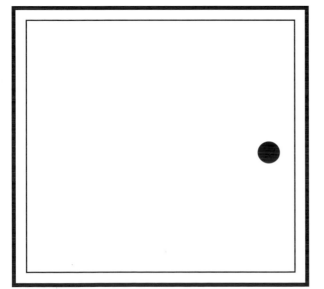

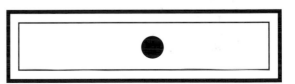

THE WORK TOP Ideally you want 80 x 80cm free space on your work top – basically the reach of your arm all round. You'll be doing all your prepping here, so it needs to be clear of clutter. If there's a power point near that's good.

THE CHOPPING BOARD It's not glamorous but a good board anchors your cooking. It'll help you master fast, precise cutting and won't ruin your knives (cheap plastic ones do). Get two. A tight grained wooden one (2.5 5cm thick) for all your vegetable work and a plastic one to use for prepping raw fish and meat.

KITCHEN SCALES For me these have to be digital, but it's your choice (p8). Have them handy – especially for baking where you will be needing to measure absolutely everything.

TOOLS OF THE TRADE

HARDWARE ESSENTIALS

These are the hand tools I find myself using all the time. Get them cheap from any specialist kitchen store. Rather than lose them in drawers, I stick them in pots and sit them by my board then shift them across to the hob when I'm working there.

WOODEN SPOONS For turning/beating/creaming/mixing. Long cool handles won't burn your hands and the ends won't melt. Hand-wash.

METAL SPOONS For measuring and baking. Don't use them in pans, they'll scratch.

LONG METAL SKEWER For testing steak/roasts/chops for doneness. Cheap and it works.

SLOTTED SPOON For draining and lifting food out of oil/liquids/stir-fries.

BALLOON WHISK For whipping cream/meringue/egg whites etc. Helps make the smoothest of sauces.

TONGS For quick and easy turning, shifting meat and other slippery things in and out of hot pans or lifting spaghetti onto dishes. A key tool in your arsenal.

SPATULA Use to turn food. Made in metal and nylon (for non-stick pans) their wide, slotted head and off-set angle is ideal for turning and shifting.

FISH SLICE Designed to slide easily under a whole bit of fish so you can turn it neatly (the solid head helps). Use for wide food like chicken schnitzel or small roasts.

THIN SPATULA Slide under biscuits to release from the tin or use to ice cakes. It's long, narrow and very thin, so perfect for lifting food like steaks to check for doneness.

RUBBER SPATULA Has flexibility and at least one rounded tip to retrieve all the mix from the cake bowl/sauce from the pan.

POTATO RICER A giant garlic press for spuds. Inexpensive. Makes the best, driest mash.

LADLE For moving soups and other liquids (eg. crêpe mix/eggs for omelette) into or out of the pan.

PEELER Use to peel spuds and other veg. Cuts carrots/courgette/cucumber into ribbons; makes chocolate curls/parmesan shavings.

MICRO-PLANE GRATER For fine grating hard cheese/citrus zest.

GARLIC CRUSHER What it suggests. Does it fast. Alternatively, use a chef's knife (p9).

SILICONE BRUSH Nifty. Use to brush egg-wash/glaze on pastry; grease tins/dishes/soufflé dishes; brush oil onto food; re-apply a marinade.

HARDWARE DRAWER

Some gear here you could improvise...

ROLLING PIN For rolling out pastry/thinning meats and crushing dry ingredients (or use a clean wine bottle instead).

TWEEZERS For nipping bones out of fish (if using eyebrow tweezers sterilise them).

COOKIE CUTTERS For biscuits/scones/big ravioli (or use a paring knife/thin glass). Can also be used as cook's rings.

CERAMIC BAKING BEANS For baking tarts blind (or use dried butter beans/rice).

APPLE CORER Neat and fast (or cut around the core with a paring knife).

COOK'S RINGS Shape rice/salad/rosti other cheap eats to create height. Looks impressive.

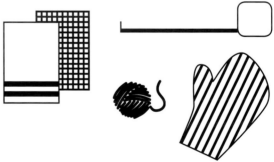

SOFTWARE DRAWER

Bits you'll take for granted but are so useful (often essential). I always keep a thick tea towel handy for shifting things fast, hanging on to small or slippery dishes that oven gloves won't hold, protecting my hands against hot handles and mopping mess/spills.

TEA TOWELS For blotting salad leaves/covering dough; wiping hands; protecting.

OVEN GLOVES Get them thick enough and check your hands can move in them.

KITCHEN PAPER Draining fried food/chips; drying veg and salad; wiping pans out.

TAPE MEASURE For measuring the base of cake and tart tins for accurate baking.

GREASEPROOF/BAKING PAPER For lining tins; cooking food in paper.

CLING FILM Covering and wrapping; thinning meats; perfect shaped poached eggs.

STRING Measuring tins; tying a bouquet garni, cuffing chicken legs.

FOIL For protecting food during cooking; wrapping; protecting a resting roast; cooking food in foil parcels.

FREEZER BAGS Come in all sizes. Get labels for freezer and use a freezer pen.

MUSLIN Cheap cloth used to make cheese; fine straining liquid for jellies.

PIPING BAG For decorating cakes; shaping meringue; piping mash.

ON THE SHELF (or in the cupboard)

Some of your hardest working items, bowls especially.

MIXING BOWLS 1 x 4 litre and 3 smaller for stacking: Pyrex is less likely to scratch than plastic (essential if using to whisk egg whites) or to absorb smells: use it for mixing/freezing/reheating/melting chocolate/making sauces over hot water.

MEASURING JUGS For measuring/mixing liquids, controlled pouring for sauces/mayo.

COLANDER For draining anything. Use as a fruit bowl or over pan as a steamer.

SIEVE For sifting flours etc. for baking/draining vegetables. Use to purée fruit.

BOX GRATER For grating cheese/vegetables etc.

PESTLE AND MORTAR For bashing marinades/smashing spices.

MINCER For mincing your own meat. Makes a radical difference.

PASTA MACHINE Reasonably cheap and gives impressive results.

GET HOOKED
hang your pots and pans for space, time, accessibility.

POTS AND PANS

Poor pans won't do your techniques proud: if you're buying new you want a good surface, a weight to suit your hand and metal handles so you can fry and bake. Thicker bases mean your food is less likely to burn and you'll keep command and control. Non-stick are easier to use but don't last as long.

LIDDED SAUTÉ PAN For sautés (high-heat frying/tossing food) and stews/sauces.

GRIDDLE PAN Pan-grills fast and healthier than frying. Like an indoor BBQ.

OVENPROOF FRYING PAN Metal handled. For fry-bake recipes and standard fry.

PASTA PAN Needs to be big. Convert to a steamer/use for stocks.

MEDIUM SAUCEPAN For making soups/sauces, boiling potatoes.

SMALL SAUCEPAN For cooking eggs, small amounts of vegetables or heating milk.

WOK For stir-fries, also good for deep-frying but it'll need a flat base.

CRÊPE PAN Easy in and out for pancakes and good for flatbread.

OMELETTE PAN Neat 15cm pan: just the right size and multi-tasks.

DISHES

Don't go mad: see how few you can get away with: raid pro-kitchen stores for value.

CASSEROLE DISH Get the size to suit your needs. I like using wider ones.

LARGE SHALLOW BAKING DISH For bakes/lasagne/roasting vegetables.

RAMEKINS For prep storage/puddings/soufflés/baked eggs.

MUGS, CUPS, PLATES AND BOWLS Use your usual stuff for mixing, prepping and serving.

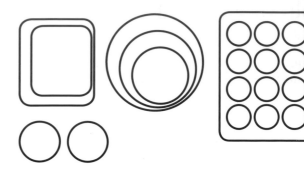

PLUG-INS

You can do pretty much everything in the kitchen by hand but there are times when it's good to get a machine to share the effort...

KETTLE For tea/boiling up water to pour into pan for vegetables/making up stock.
STICK BLENDER Blends soups/hummus/breadcrumbs/sauces.
ELECTRIC HAND MIXER For mixing and whisking cakes/eggs/sauces.
FREE-STANDING MIXER Brilliant for mixing bread/pizza dough/cake mixes.
PROCESSOR Does a bit of everything. Best for mixing pastry.
BLENDER Fast and very efficient. Cool food a bit before using and never over-fill.
DEEP-FAT FRYER A safer way to deal with deep-fry.
ICE-CREAM MACHINE Opens up the world of homemade ice-cream. I love mine.

TINS AND THINGS

No rules here, except get a roasting tin that's thick enough to use on your hob and thick baking sheets which don't buckle in the heat for pizza.

ROASTING TINS Get one big enough to take a chicken plus vegetables and a smaller one.
YORKSHIRE PUDDING TIN 4 individual holes, or use a muffin tin or smaller roasting tin.
TART TINS Get bigger (23cm) and individual (10cm) for sweet and savoury tarts/quiche.
LOAF TINS For bread/loaf-shaped cake/tea breads. Get a 450g or 900g one.
BAKING SHEETS For pizza/biscuits/scones/finishing/reheating food/catching drips.
CAKE TINS Get 1 x 22cm round tin for proper cakes, 2 x 18cm for sponge cakes.
SPRING-FORM CHEESECAKE TIN Spring-form means the cake is easily released.
COOLING RACK Avoid the base of new baking getting damp: get a higher one or elevate what you've got.

GETTING THE MEASURE

Accurate measuring gives you a confident base to work from when you're starting out. It's about getting the balance of ingredients right. Having a carrot-heavy casserole for example is not a disaster, but exact measurement is more crucial in baking. If the amount of raising agent's wrong or the egg/fat/flour ratio is out your cake may not be as light as it could be. Use metric/imperial, cups, spoons, US cup measurements, old-school scales with weights, electronic jobs with loads of extras like thermometer, timer, whatever – as long as it's easy to read, fits into your space and is above all accurate. Once you're fully into it, you'll find you can start to judge your measurements by eye. Recipes are written in a mix of measurements: check online for conversions for dry weight and liquid volumes, or use an app or an oven magnet instead.

✚ EMERGENCY ROOM

FIRE BLANKET Keep one handy just in case; throw over a burning pan if it's safe (never use water and don't try to pick the pan up and run with it).

MOBILE Call for help if there's a real problem; better safe than sorry.

PLASTERS For small nicks; happens to the best of us but take care.

COLD WATER For very minor burns; hold under cold running water. For worse; call for help.

CUTTING THINGS

A good-quality knife makes all the difference in the kitchen. It should be balanced in your hand, not too heavy, razor sharp and with a good grip. Don't think you need to be getting the most expensive: some Japanese hand-made beauties are highly desirable but maybe something to work up to. A reasonably priced stainless steel knife with a fully forged reinforced blade is easily found on the high street.

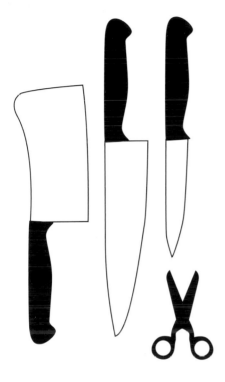

THE ONES FOR THE JOB

CHEF'S KNIFE A multi-purpose broad blade. Good for precision cutting/dicing/slicing/chopping/cubing/light butchery.
PARING KNIFE A small short-handled blade useful for smaller jobs. Use to trim and prepare vegetables/fruit/cheese.
BREAD KNIFE A serrated blade for doing the obvious effortlessly. Also good for cutting butternut squash/pineapple/aubergines.
CARVING KNIFE A long, thin blade perfect for carving neat, wafer-thin slices of meat.
FILLETING KNIFE A long, thin, flexible blade. The give in the blade lets you work cleanly to lift raw fish off the bone.
BONING KNIFE A long, narrow slightly curved blade with a sharp tip. Only used for boning meat, so only needed if you're into butchery.
CLEAVER A big, heavy knife with a very broad blade. Use for heavy jobs (e.g. chopping through ribs/bone) which would damage other blades.
SCISSORS Endlessly useful. Use to gut and trim fish; butterfly small chicken; snip string/chives/bacon. Get a good strong pair from a specialist kitchen shop.
BLUNT KITCHEN KNIFE Use to run around the edge of tins to loosen your baking.

CUTTING RULES

• Check your knife is sharp enough – treat it to the steel if not.

• Check your hand and the knife handle aren't greasy.

• Always chop on your board.

• If doing a lot of knife work, sit a damp tea towel under your board to keep it steady.

• Grip the knife well: put it comfortably in your hand; sit your thumb to the side of the handle, never on top of it.

• Wash knives by hand and dry immediately.

KNIFE SHARPENING

Keep your blades in best shape and your knives will last: more importantly you'll get maximum performance out of them and they'll be safer (blunt knives slip). Use a steel – a rod of high-carbon steel on a handle – on all non-serrated blades for longevity, safety and sharp techniques. Do it every time you use your knife so it never blunts in the first place. If in doubt, ask your friendly butcher for an impromptu lesson.

1 Hold the steel comfortably in one hand. Point it up and away from you. Check your hand is safely behind the guard.

2 Take the knife in your other hand and cross the steel and blade just above their respective handles.

3 Firmly slide the knife at a 20 degree angle along the steel so its edge is honed from its base to tip. Repeat the process on the other side. Do it a few times until you're happy with the outcome. Wash the knife before using.

HEATING THINGS

THE OVEN

It's your best friend for baking, roasting, pan-baking, simple reheating; so, get to know it and then work with it. Fact is, every one is different. Gas or electric: fan-assisted or not? That's just the start of it. Work out what sort of beast yours is and then work with it.

THE GRILL

An under-rated part of your arsenal: use for cooking steaks, chops, whole fish and fillets, kebabs, finishing omelettes, gratins, cooking bacon. Slide the grill pan and rack to the right position for high, medium or slow-cook. Preheat to high; reduce to a temperature you judge appropriate. Brush prepped food lightly with oil (too much oil or a heavy marinade may flare up, so take care). Use oven gloves to slide the tray in and out. Grill food both sides until done: turn kebabs a few times. Grilling sends oil out into the atmosphere so use the extractor fan, open window or consider griddling food then oven baking. Pros: grilling is healthy, the fat drains away. It can taste delicious (think in-door BBQ). Cons: food can dry out so watch it.

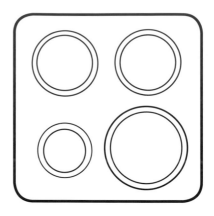

THE HOB

The fast action station where you'll be developing your fundamental skills: griddling, frying, browning to seal and develop flavour, sautéing, reducing, stirring, whisking, adding, adjusting, seasoning, tasting things: cooking. So, keep tools, seasonings, oils, ingredients close by; get comfortable with using the right ring on the hob for the job and the pan; learn to adjust the heat through a recipe to get best results. Try switching between hob, grill and oven to achieve different results: pan-fry quickly then bake finish: start the omelette in the pan and finish under the grill: mix and match.

OVEN *Rules*

USE THE TOP SHELF for quicker cooking/higher temperature dishes, middle for medium and bottom for lower temperature/slower cooking dishes.

SET THE RACKS before you preheat.

ALWAYS PREHEAT THE OVEN at the right stage of your recipe.

CHECK THE TEMPERATURE IS REACHED before you put the food in.

If you're using a fan-assisted oven, **SET IT FOR 20°C LESS** than specified.

DON'T USE FAN-ASSISTED FOR BREAD (it disturbs the dough).

DON'T OPEN THE DOOR during cooking unless you have to.

CHECK FOR DONENESS if you need to towards the end of cooking.

OPEN AND CLOSE THE OVEN DOOR SLOWLY and gently to avoid air disturbance.

USE THE TIMER but don't trust it; it's only a machine.

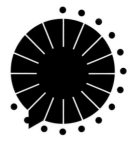

Temperatures

Knowing how to shift from one temperature system to another means you can interpret any recipe with confidence. The recipes here give celsius and gas mark measures – for other systems check online.

COOLING THINGS

FRIDGE ETIQUETTE

• Check the temperature: just below 5°C is safe.
• Don't over-fill it: it'll stop the air-flow and alter the temperature.
• Sit smaller packs at the front so you can see to the back.
• Use old stuff before new: First In–First Out is the rule.
• Cool hot food down before storing it.
• Wrap things well to store: use storage boxes for stacking.
• Don't be a slave to sell-by dates: smell, touch, use your judgement.
• Dishes such as curry/stews/casseroles benefit from chilling for a day or two.
• Save time: rise dough in the fridge overnight: chill batter for breakfast pancakes.
• Wash it with soapy water: sprays taint flavours.
• Check individual chapters for fridge rules on specific ingredients.
• Defrost frozen food in the fridge overnight.

SHELF LIFE – *what goes where...*

TOP SHELVES: soft cheese, yoghurt, cooked meats, cream, butter, hummus etc.

MIDDLE SHELF: covered leftovers

LOWER MIDDLE SHELF: covered and in-pack raw meats and fish

BOTTOM SHELF: Well-covered and in-pack raw poultry on plates

SALAD DRAWERS: Veg/salad leaves and hard cheeses

DOORS: relishes, pickles, sauces, ketchup, juices, milk, white wine

THE FREEZER

Something interesting happens when you start to cook: you get to love bits of equipment you've previously frozen out. Your freezer becomes less a graveyard for peas and ice-cream, more an addictive resource; time-saver; cash-cow. Freeze the following things and all's good: homemade ready-meals like chilli, casseroles, stews, meat and vegetable burgers, pies, pasta dishes, soups, tomato and meat sauces, pizza bases. Store by-products of your efforts like stocks, pastry, leftover egg whites and wine in ice-cube trays. Bang in frozen vegetables, berries, frozen fish and prawns; freeze a whole emergency chicken: freeze bits of the bird (thighs, legs, breasts, wings) a steak and a chop or two; homemade ice-cream.

HOW TO Freeze stuff

• Check your items to freeze are properly cold.
• Set freezer to fast freeze: a quicker freeze means better results.
• Wrap food to be frozen up well in cling film to protect against the arctic cold.
• Label the bags or boxes before you fill them.
• Free-standing bags are easy to pour/spoon food into.
• Freeze small bits of leftover sauce/gravy in ice-cube trays.
• Don't over-fill freezer bags/boxes: two-thirds full is good.
• Fish is hard to freeze at home: best to buy already frozen.
• For easy access later, individually wrap steaks/burgers/chops in cling film before putting in freezer bags.
• Freeze cakes and scones cooked (reheat the scones): freeze fruit pies uncooked and reheat.
• Don't freeze anything that's been frozen then thawed out.
• Don't cook raw food from frozen.

STORING THINGS

THE STORE CUPBOARD

A revelation: when testing recipes for this book I was spending ages looking for the right dried herb. I've got dozens of pots and, eventually, I organised them alphabetically. I reckon it saved me minutes every day. It's an extreme example, but fact is when you can see what you've got you're going to use it; a storage space isn't just a load of shelves full of random things: looking at it should inspire you.

OILS Have a huge influence on your cooking. Some add positive flavour (olive, sesame, walnut); some are healthy (olive, rapeseed), some are brilliant for frying and using at higher temperatures (groundnut/sunflower/vegetable). Use the right one for the job but other than that it's down to taste. Store in a cooler, darker place in your cupboard as oils do go off.

VINEGAR Not just for chips. Use white, red, cider, balsamic and malt. Their acidity can make or break a salad dressing, add depth to a stew or sauce; raspberry adds a fruity note, tarragon is chic, Chinese wine lifts things.

SEASONINGS Sea salt is brilliant as it gives texture and bursts of flavour; grind it into cooking for even distribution, just keep it off the table. Black pepper is best freshly ground. Use lemon, lime, vinegars.

SPICES AND DRIED HERBS I keep a good few in as they're the fastest and easiest way to transform basic ingredients. Use in rubs and marinades, and sprinkle in different combinations; see what suits.

STOCK CUBES Keep good ones in for emergencies. Bear in mind the stock will be saltier than homemade, so adjust seasoning.

FLAVOURINGS AND TOP SAUCES Keep English and Dijon mustard for dressings/sauces/mash; Worcester and anchovy sauces for a beefy touch to meat dishes; oyster, soy, hoisin, red bean paste, sweet chilli, Thai fish sauce, for Chinese/Thai; harrisa paste for a spicy kick to marinades; mint jelly/sauce for lamb; horseradish,

ketchup, brown sauce, passata, tamarind paste and lime juice for the rest.

CANS AND JARS No kitchen's complete without tomatoes, chickpeas, butter beans, kidney beans, cannellini beans, sweetcorn, coconut milk, olives, capers, anchovies, jalapenos and sundried tomatoes.

DRIED BREADCRUMBS Panko are best. Make your own (p201) or buy from Chinese stores.

DRIED PASTA Chuck spaghetti, linguine and penne in the cupboard and dinner's always in.

SWEET THINGS Keep in runny honey for balancing sweet/sour in a sauce or stew, adding to marinades/yoghurt, drizzling over ice-cream, cake glazing; redcurrant jelly for sweetening meat jus with citrus for an instant gravy; golden and maple syrup, black treacle, raspberry jam and fig relish for the rest.

BAKING My baking cupboard features dried yeast, baking powder, bicarbonate of soda, plain and self-raising flour, bread flour (white and wholemeal), cornflour, cocoa, oats, dried fruits, nuts, seeds, cocoa, 70% chocolate, crystallised ginger, custard powder, leaf gelatine for setting jellies, caster/granulated/demerara sugar and vanilla. See p198–199 for more details.

TEA BAGS AND COFFEE For cooking and drinking.

DRY CIDER AND RED AND WHITE WINE (Sauvignon's good).

STORE LORE

- Use up old stuff before you buy new.
- Keep jars labelled and labels facing forward.
- Keep shorter things to the front of shelves.
- Organise ingredients to type: so, baking things in one area, oils and vinegars together, spices and dried herbs, pastas, noodles, rice and other grains together, cans together, etc. Make it geographic.

COOKING THINGS

And so it begins: we've sorted out the kitchen, now for the recipes. Just a few points to remember...

 Make sure to **READ EACH RECIPE THROUGH** before you start so you won't miss a vital step like 'the day before' or a key ingredient.

 Consider **'MISE EN PLACE'** as part of your prep.

 DON'T WORRY IF YOU MAKE A MISTAKE: some of the best discoveries happen when you're going wrong; getting round it is half the fun.

 Once you've got the techniques sorted **EXPERIMENT** with a dish.

 Expect that **THE SAME DISH WILL TASTE DIFFERENT EVERY TIME** you cook it even if you've followed the recipe to the letter; that's the joy of it.

 It's probably **BETTER NOT TO TRY SOMETHING FOR THE FIRST TIME** when you've got a load of people round, unless you're learning together.

 Think about how you can **SAVE ENERGY** (and cash) as you cook: cover pans with lids; boil a kettle and pour into the pan for your green vegetables; cook enough for more than one meal – it costs less to reheat the second one than cook another.

 If you're cooking for loads of people, **TRY PREPPING AND EVEN COOKING MUCH OF IT AHEAD**, so you can enjoy yourself.

 Don't forget you can **RECYCLE THINGS**: roast up potato peelings in oil and salt; turn stale bread into breadcrumbs; defrosted frozen egg whites are better than standard for whisking/holding air for meringues and soufflés: grate up any dried cheese bits for a sauce: turn excess pasta into a bake or throw it into a frittata; fry cooked noodles up like a pancake.

 Don't just throw them into a pan, **ENGAGE WITH YOUR INGREDIENTS** at each stage of the process; smell when something's ready; see how raw or cooked through it is: touch it for doneness; listen to its water simmering or boiling; the oil sizzling or spluttering; it's all telling you something a book can't.

 TASTE... Have a few teaspoons handy so you can dig in and judge the balance in a dish; it's key to seasoning and building your palate.

 KEEP IT BALANCED on the plate: you are what you eat.

 MAKE IT LOOK BEAUTIFUL, even if it's only a snack.

 ENJOY – you're in it for a lifetime.

MISE EN PLACE

means 'everything in its place'. It involves getting out all the ingredients needed for your dish/dishes and the equipment and organising it around your worktop; doing all the preliminary work such as slicing, beating, sifting or whatever and putting all the individual elements into neat containers ready for cooking.

Vegetables
AND SALAD

The Vegetable (salad and otherwise); source of essential nutrition and magnificent eating. My own special relationship with these guys began back in the day when I saw what they meant to my vegetarian sisters. But let's get this straight, vegetables and salads aren't just for vegetarians – they're an essential part of your cooking repertoire. Here's where the knives come in to play: plenty of chopping and slicing required. Seasoning needs to be just so to bring out the best in a veg, especially when you're aiming for beautiful simplicity. It's all about enhancing their textures and flavours, learning not to mask them. On the other hand there are times when you need your veg present in a purely secondary role – subtly flavouring a rich chicken stock, punching some sort of character into a sauce or sorting out the base for a lovely casserole. Get down with the skill-set in this chapter and you're equipped for most of your savoury recipes. Enjoy….

FRESH, FRESH, FRESH
WHAT TO LOOK FOR

POTATOES Should be firm, plump, unblemished, dry: don't cook or buy any with green patches (they're toxic) or shoots ('eyes'): check bags aren't sweaty or smell fishy.

CARROTS, PARSNIPS, TURNIPS, SWEDE, BEETROOT, CELERIAC Get firm, plump root vegetables without shrivelling, spots or signs of damage.

GREEN BEANS/PEAS Look for bright green, firm snappy pods free of browning.

LEAFY GREENS Avoid any with yellowing leaves/heads (on broccoli) or dried stalks.

MUSHROOMS Good ones have a bloom, smell fresh and look typical to variety.

CELERY, CHICORY, ASPARAGUS Should smell fresh, be firm, have tightly packed heads.

TOMATOES, PEPPERS, AVOCADOS, AUBERGINE Buy firm, shiny, heavy examples. Odd shapes are fine but no bruising.

ONIONS, SHALLOTS, GARLIC Go for firm, plump fresh smelling characters.

SALAD LEAVES Fresh look just picked, packed with life and brightly coloured (no wilting).

WHERE TO BUY
Getting your hands dirty

LOCAL MARKET You can touch, smell to check quality; buy loose in amounts to suit; check which days your stall of choice is there; establish a relationship.

VEGETABLE STORE Find a route home which passes a good one with a fast turn-over.

SPECIALITY VEGETABLES Find exotic and unusual veg at good prices in Chinese, Caribbean and Middle-Eastern stores.

HEALTH AND ORGANIC STORES You can pay extra for organic food (no pesticides) and it can be healthier but check for food-miles – a complex issue. Local is good if fresh.

SUPERMARKET Essentials through to organics available. Loose foods are usually cheaper and you can touch/smell them. Always use the fresh test. Check air-miles.

OUT OF THE FRIDGE

Potatoes: remove plastic packaging and store in a cool, dark place. Floury varieties can last months in a sack/paper bag; waxy types need using in a few days.

Onions: last for months kept in a cool, dry place.

Tomatoes: store in the kitchen at room temperature.

Chillies: store in the kitchen or freeze and use from frozen.

Garlic: can last for six months. Keep away from other foods.

Cress: in the plastic box it comes in: water it.

• • • • • • • • • • • • • • • • •

Nuisance Neighbours

If your veg are going off before they should it could be that they are ethylene sensitive (most veg and leaves are). This natural gas is created by tomatoes, pears, melons (and more) so keep them apart.

• • • • • • • • • • • • • • • • •

IN THE FRIDGE

Mushrooms: store in a paper bag in the warmest bit of the fridge to avoid freezing.

Spinach: store in a plastic bag away from the back; it freezes easily.

Cucumber: store in the warmest part of the fridge or in the kitchen

Beetroot: put fresh roots unwrapped in the salad drawer: chilled vac-packs last ages.

Beans/Cabbage: store in plastic bags.

Carrots: last a few weeks without losing nutrients. Store in plastic bags.

Leaves: highly perishable. Store in plastic bags in the salad drawer for a week.

Asparagus: wrap damp kitchen paper around roots or stand in a jar with a little water in the fridge; lasts a few days.

Watercress: store bunches in a jar as above: or in plastic pack.

JUST TENDER...
VEGETABLE COOKING TIMES

Use your eye and a sharp knife. It's hard to be accurate as there are so many variables – use your judgement.

MAKE VEGETABLE STOCK

Wash and chop the following: 2 large onions, 1 stick celery, 1 large leek, 3 carrots, some fresh parsley or coriander if you have any, 3 cloves garlic. Dump into a pan with 2.3 litres water, 1 teaspoon salt, a few black peppercorns, a piece of scrubbed lemon peel and juice. Bring to the boil. Reduce the heat. Simmer, half covered for at least 30 minutes or until reduced by a third. Strain through a sieve. Use or chill.

VEGETABLE AND SALAD NUTRITION

Never under-estimate a vegetable – it's a powerhouse of nutrients.

ANTI-OXIDANTS

ARE UNIQUE TO PLANTS, mopping up harmful free radicals which could otherwise cause diabetes, certain cancers, cardiovascular disease or a weakened immune system. VEGETABLES CONTAIN SOLUBLE → **FIBRE** key to maintaining a healthy digestive system. Eating them raw/steamed (in particular cabbage/leafy greens/broccoli) helps fight diabetes, reduces cholesterol and makes you look and feel sharper. VEGETABLES ARE A GREAT SOURCE OF ESSENTIAL COMPLEX **CARBOHYDRATES** which convert to glucose and provide us with energy. LEAFY GREENS, SPINACH AND BROCCOLI ARE RICH IN

IRON

athletes benefit from the *Chromium* IN POTATOES AND GREENS AND THE

POTASSIUM

in asparagus and tomatoes. **VITAMINS** are present in different strengths and combinations, so mix and match and you're getting everything you need.

THE VEG PLOT
What's on offer?

ASPARAGUS Grassy, sexy, extravagant. Trim the woody stem; steam/griddle/boil: eat with butter/parmesan/hollandaise or dunk in a boiled egg. It's delicious, nutritious and packed with folate.

AUBERGINE Decadent, smoky, silky, almost meaty when cooked. Bake/griddle and use in curries, stir-fries, pasta, Middle-Eastern dishes. It drinks oil. De-gorge to remove the bitter juices and reduce oil absorption.

········ **HOW TO...** ········
De-gorge aubergine
Sprinkle slices with fine salt: leave to weep for 30 minutes. Rinse under a cold tap. Dry thoroughly.

AVOCADO Buttery, creamy flesh. Blitz it up for guacamole; slice and chop it into salads. Rich in vitamin E (good for skin and hair).

BEANS The long thin ones (French and runner) and the plump podded ones (broad beans) are all fast to cook and can be teamed with just about anything. Briefly boil/steam and toss in fast flavourings: chopped tomatoes/oil/garlic/chilli/a bit of butter, sour cream. Fling into salads, curry, Middle-Eastern dishes.

BEETROOT Earthy sweetness in a hard root. Roast whole or in chunks or boil: adds a chic note to risottos, salads. Get it vacuum-packed to save time. It's a super-food.

BROCCOLI Robust, mustardy taste. Cook briefly (stir-fry or fast boil/steam); eat raw dipped in oil or hummus; bang into cheese sauce; roast in oil/garlic/cumin.

BUTTERNUT SQUASH Sweet and versatile. Roast with oil and garlic; steam/boil/griddle then mash as a side or purée for soups/risottos; add to pies, stews, casseroles.

CABBAGE Sexy when cooked for crispness. Shred, blanch then stir-fry with oyster/soy sauce; lightly toss shredded red/white in dressing or mayo for salads.

CARROTS Sweet, cheap glorious super-food. Best raw in strips with dips/grated into salads; cut into ribbons or matchsticks for stir-fries; boiled/steamed for crushing, mashing; in soups, stews, curries, roast and casseroles for fullest flavour.

CAULIFLOWER Star of cauliflower cheese. Bang into curries/stews; make soups; roast; break into florets and steam/boil briefly; fry in tempura batter. Roast in oil, garlic, chilli and cumin.

CELERIAC Knobbly root tasting of celery. Add to standard/parsnip mash.

CELERY Gives a raw, slightly earthy crunch to accompany cheese/dips/hummus. A star in caponata and adds a useful, anonymous note to stocks, stews and sauces.

CHICORY Chic, crisp, slightly bitter leaves. Good for salads; dipped and scooped into hummus; roasted around a chicken; wrapped in ham and baked in cheese sauce.

CHILLIES Spicy goodness all the way. Green are usually hotter than red, smaller fiercer than large. Use in curries, stir-fries, soup, salad and marinades. Wash your hands after handling.

········ **HOW TO...** ········
Deseed chillies
Capsaicin (the heat in chillies) is mostly found in the seeds and membrane. If you like fire on your tongue, just slice or dice. To remove the seeds and leave the membrane: cut off the stem, roll the chilli vigorously between your palms and shake the loosened seeds out. To remove both: cut the chilli lengthways, trim the end and scrape out with the tip of a knife or spoon.

CORN Sweet: strip silks and leaves. Boil till tender. Treat it to butter/spices/lemon/chilli; slice the kernels for relish.

COURGETTES Can be bland, but that's the challenge. Contrast with chilli or garlic; use in a rich tomato sauce or ratatouille; get crisp on a BBQ/griddle.

CUCUMBER Deliciously cool and all about texture. Grate for dips and fritters; slice thinly for sweet and sour pickle; chop into half-moons for stir-fries.

GARLIC Like culinary highlighter it opens other flavours up. Use liberally across your repertoire but in measured amounts for each individual dish.

HOW TO...
Crush garlic

Break as many cloves as needed off the head. Lay them flat on a board. Lay the flat of a chef's/other large knife on top. Press down to crush. Remove the skin. Cut out any green shoot. Crush to a paste with the tip of the knife and add a bit of fine salt.

GINGER Unglamorous root with a chic lemon tang. Peel and grate for marinades and sauces; blitz for curry paste; slice into matchsticks for stir-fries; slice it for stocks.

LEEKS Sweet onion-light taste and soft texture; wash to remove grit. Slice to melt into stews/soups/tarts/pies. Cut into julienne strips to cook slowly in butter as a side.

MUSHROOMS Earthy to bland with a variety of textures; griddle or stuff whole field/portobello mushrooms. Slice, sauté or stir-fry white/chestnut mushrooms. Exotic, wild and Asian mushrooms are more expensive but you don't need as many. Add to stews/soups.

ONIONS Kitchen workhorses. Use shallots (delicate and sweet) for dressings/sautés/raw/salads; red (refreshing) for salsas/dips/salads/onion jam/roasting; white (sweet) for risotto/tarts/stuffing/baking; brown (stronger) for regular cooking; whole baby in casseroles; spring in salads/stir-fries/champ.

PAK CHOI/BOK CHOI Sweet and nutty with a faintly bitter edge. Strip down, slice and stir-fry in sesame oil with garlic/soy; steam whole; slice into soups. Ridiculously nutritious.

PARSNIPS Earthy sweetness which caramelises when roasted. Boil and bang into mash; fling into stews/soups/casseroles.

PEAS Like quick-cook sweets with a grassy edge. Boil fast or steam. Team with mint and butter. Use for soups. Add to stir-fries, risottos; toss raw into salads.

PEPPERS Colour coded for ripeness – green taste grassier, yellow/orange/red move to sweetness. Eat raw; roast for salads; stuff and roast.

HOW TO...
Roast peppers for salad

Preheat the oven to 230°C/Gas 8. Sit whole peppers on foil in a roasting tin. Roast for 30–40 minutes, turning once, or until soft and blistered. Chuck into a freezer bag. After 20 minutes, remove. Strip the skin off; remove seeds; slice flesh. Add oil.

POTATOES Choose your type. Firm, waxy jobs (Jersey Royals, Charlottes) are brilliant for potato salad/curry; floury (Maris Pipers, King Edwards) are perfect for chips/mash/roasts/frying/baking.

RADISH Chic, crisp and peppery. Slice into salads; dip in oil/salt; eat with sashimi.

SPINACH Healthy with an iron tang. Baby leaves give an edge to salads; wilt large leaves and toss in lemon/garlic/butter or use in classic pasta dishes/with eggs or fish/on pizza. It reduces alarmingly.

SPROUTS Can taste good. Trim, shred and stir-fry with garlic; boil briefly and finish in butter with garlic and bacon/chopped chestnuts/flaked almonds.

SWEDE Warm, comforting and sweet. Boil and mash and sex up with cream and spices; roast; dice for a Cornish pasty.

SWEET POTATOES Rich, sweet and nutritious. Peel and make into soup; bake whole; mash; throw into curries or stews; roast or griddle in chunks. Make tasty wedges.

TOMATOES Don't get ripped off – too many perfect looking tomatoes are tasteless! Buy loose and sniff (look for a peppery whiff from the vine). Use cherry and vine tomatoes for salads; beef for slicing and stuffing; canned for cooking.

HOW TO...
Skin a tomato

Cut a cross into the base of each fruit with a sharp knife. Bang them into a bowl and submerge in boiling water for a minute. Drain and cover immediately in cold water. Peel the skin off with your fingers, starting from the cross where it's loosened.

TURNIPS Sophisticated tasting white golf balls. Slice for stir-fries/stews; eat raw.

WATERCRESS Super-food with a tart taste. Strip any tough stems and use in soups/tarts/sauces/salads/egg sandwiches or as garnish.

VEG CUTTER
KNIFE TECHNIQUE

Do this on a strong board using a sharp knife. Using a pivot action, raise the knife over your chosen vegetable and slice down, working across the vegetable and holding it down on your board with the other hand.

CHOP Cut simply into fine/large pieces as your recipe needs.

STRIPS (JULIENNE) Cut into thin slices. Stack a few of these up, then cut into thin strips.

DICE Cut into even slices. Stack a few; cut lengthways into sticks and across again into even dice.

ROUNDS Cut across your chosen veg to make thick, round slices.

HANGING ON TO THE GOOD BITS (and flavour) HERE'S HOW

—leave the peel on your potatoes & carrots as it's home to fibre and vitamins—nutrients fade with age so buy small amounts of veg a time and use immediately—cut with a sharp knife as a blunt one damages cells—cook as soon as your veg are prepped—don't soak vegetables – the nutrients leak out—steam if appropriate—cook for the minimum amount of time possible—use minimal water—serve immediately—

Salad Rules

■ Salad leaves bruise easily: treat them gently.

■ Wash them well in cold water: check for grit and living things.

■ Blot them softly to dry: wet leaves won't hold dressing.

■ Use a salad spinner if you've got the room: they're cheap.

■ Chill leaves for 30 minutes before eating to crisp up.

■ Create a dressing to suit your style of leaf.

■ Crisp leaves (Romaine hearts, Cos, iceberg) carry creamy and oily dressings.

■ Soft leaves work best with oil-based dressing.

■ Leaves have character: bitter, sweet, mild, spiky, soft, explosive – check them out.

THE LETTUCE LIST

BUTTERHEAD: soft loose leaves with a sweet delicate taste. Easy eating.

LAMB'S LETTUCE: Mild and delicate. Mix for contrast; good for neat heaping.

PEA SHOOTS: sweet, good-looking and moist. A good edible garnish.

CRESS: tiny, peppery and nutritious. Keep on the windowsill (and trim the roots).

RED OAK: Big, sweet loose red-edged leaves. Likes a bold dressing.

ICEBERG: Fresh, mild, crisp lettuce with tight, structured leaves. Tear or shred just before using in sandwiches/burgers/ salads/tortillas or use to wrap hot/cold fillings.

ROMAINE/COS/ LITTLE GEM: crisp, fresh, long leaves. Use for Caesar salad.

LOLLO ROSSO: red, bold leaves (no heart) with a nutty taste.

ROCKET: dark green and peppery leaves. Staple of Italian cooking and side salads.

HERB HANDLER

A sweet way to radically alter flavour and transform a dish.

STORAGE Store big bunches of herbs from the market in cups or jars. Potted herbs need watering regularly. Packets of fresh herbs (expensive) should be stored in the fridge.

PREPPING Fresh herbs: Tear leafy herbs or shred them with a knife. Finely chop the leaves of coarse herbs. Snip chives with scissors. Bashing in a pestle and mortar strengthens taste. Dried herbs: are stronger. Use 1 teaspoon of dried herb to every 2 teaspoons of fresh.

BASIL Spicy yet fresh and a bit grassy – think subdued mint. Make pesto (p172), add to tomatoes/pizza (at the end of cooking if you can). Grow in a pot. Never used dried.

BAY Deep, dark and aromatic. Use whole fresh or dried sparingly in a bouquet garni to flavour a stew, pie, casserole or bread sauce. Keep a bay tree.

CHIVES Sweet hint of onion. Snip with scissors and use in fast cooking or add at the end. A tasty garnish.

CORIANDER Bright, fresh and warm with a hint of citrus. Use the leaves, stems and roots to liven up marinades/dull meats/curries/stir-fries/tex-mex/chilli.

DILL Grassy and sharp feathery stalk. Use with fish/eggs/potato, adding at the end of cooking.

LEMONGRASS Lemony and bright. Bash to bruise well then chop very finely. Use for curries. Ready-chopped frozen stalks are a good fast option.

MINT Bright and lively – think chewing gum. Use with lamb/peas/potatoes or cover with boiling water to make into tea.

OREGANO Woody. Use fresh or dice judiciously and add to pizzas/courgettes/marinades.

PARSLEY Grassy, fresh, flat-leafed or curly. Chop finely over potatoes; works with other herbs, white fish and over most things. Always use fresh.

ROSEMARY Woody: good for lamb/pork/beef/chicken/BBQ foods. Shove whole sprigs up a roast chicken; chop finely and add to bread dough. Use fresh only.

SAGE Dark woodsy: best with pork, sausages, duck, darker meats, stuffing, cheese, pasta.

TARRAGON Hints of aniseed; brilliantly enhances chicken/mushrooms/egg/fish dishes; works in sauces/butters/tarts/soups. Use French tarragon only.

THYME Bittersweet and beautiful. Use with meats/pizza/pasta.

MAKE A BOUQUET GARNI

Sit a sprig of rosemary, 10 peppercorns and 10 crushed cardamom pods on a piece of muslin. Pull it up and tie a bit of string round it tightly.

FRIENDS

GREENS

BROCCOLI: ANCHOVY, BEEF, OYSTER SAUCE, SOY, CHEESE, CHILLI, CUMIN, GARLIC **SPINACH:** CHEESE, EGGS, PASTA, NUTMEG, TOMATO **CABBAGE:** BACON, BLACK PEPPER, GARLIC, GINGER, HAM, LEMON, PORK, POTATO

ROOTS

POTATOES: BEETROOT, BUTTER, GARLIC, HARD AND BLUE CHEESES, FISH, LEMON, MEAT, MUSTARD, NUTMEG, ONION, PARSLEY, ROSEMARY **BEETROOT:** BLUE CHEESE, EGG, FETA, GOAT'S CHEESE, HARD CHEESE, OILY FISH, ORANGE, WALNUTS **PARSNIP:** CURRY POWDER, HONEY, LEMON, NUTMEG, PORK, POTATO **CARROT:** BUTTER, CARDAMOM, LEMON, ORANGE, STAR ANISE

MUSHROOMS

BACON, BLUE CHEESE, EGG, CREAM, GARLIC, PARMESAN, POTATO, TARRAGON

BEANS AND PEAS

BEANS: BUTTER, CUMIN, GARLIC, TOMATO SAUCE **PEAS:** BACON, BEEF, BUTTER, CHICKEN, CHILLI, EGGS, LAMB, MINT, PARMESAN, PORK, RICE, WHITE FISH

PEA CHILLI, AND MINT SOUP

HEALTHY   FAST

FEEDS 2

This super-smooth soup makes for a simple punchy lunch or a sofa cuppa soup – the mix of salty and sweet does it. If you're not a bacon fan, make croutons (p29).

INGREDIENTS

4 shallots
1 green chilli
2 garlic cloves, peeled
40g butter
salt and pepper
500ml chicken/vegetable stock
   (p49/p15)
400g frozen peas
½ tsp granulated sugar
10 small mint leaves
   (or quantity to taste)
4 streaky bacon rashers (optional)
25ml single cream/yoghurt (optional)

········· TIME SAVER ·········

This recipe's fast to make but if time's a real issue make it the night before. Cool, cover with cling film and chill until needed.

PREP Peel and finely dice the shallots on a board using a chef's, paring or filleting knife. De-seed and finely dice the chilli. Crush the garlic.

Put a large saucepan on to heat. Add the butter. Once it foams, add the shallot, garlic, chilli and a tiny pinch of salt. Stir and reduce the heat to low. Pop the lid onto the pan and let the mix sweat very gently without colouring until it softens up. It'll take at least 5 minutes. Don't rush – if you burn the mix it'll get bitter and you'll need to start again.

Meantime, pour the stock into another pan and put it on the hob to heat. Once the shallots have sweated down, add the hot stock and stir well. Add the peas and sugar and season lightly with salt and pepper. Bring the mix to the boil, then reduce the heat and simmer gently for 5–6 minutes.

COOK Remove from the heat and add the mint. Now either tip the soup carefully into a food processor and whiz until really smooth, or blitz everything together in the pan using a stick blender. If it's not absolutely smooth, put the soup through a fine sieve (texture matters with this one). Taste and adjust the seasoning. Keep warm.

If you want bacon with your soup, set the grill to high. Lay the streaky rashers on the rack and cook for 2–3 minutes per side, till crispy. Rest on kitchen paper.

PLATE Pour the soup into a warm bowl or mug. Crumble the bacon on top if using, swirl over a bit of cream or yoghurt if you like, or leave plain. Enjoy with bread and butter.

CARROT SOUP

HEALTHY

FEEDS 4

INGREDIENTS

1 medium onion
700g carrots
200g floury potatoes
   (e.g. Maris Piper/King Edward)
25g piece of fresh ginger
2 garlic cloves
1 tbsp olive oil
½ tbsp butter
salt and pepper
1 star anise
juice of ½ a lime
1 litre vegetable stock (p15)
a good handful of coriander

—— BONUS BITE ——
LEEK AND CHEESE SOUP

Wash and thinly slice 700g leeks. Add them to the sweated onion and potato base as before and cook very slowly under a cartouche for 10 minutes. (Leeks turn bitter if browned at all so keep the heat low). Add a handful of torn flat-leaf parsley, 1 litre vegetable/chicken stock and 2 tsp mustard. Simmer for 30 minutes. Cool then blitz in batches with a handful of grated cheddar. Stir in 3 tbsp milk. Serve with crumbled bacon bits and/or croutons (p29).

Subtle Asian flavours make this a bit of a soup hero. Sweat the vegetables slowly to release their potential and don't let them brown up. This recipe demonstrates a vegetable soup formula by the way. Use onion/potato/other vegetables/stock in these proportions to create your own variations depending on what's in season.

PREP Slice the onion in two. Peel and chop it with a sharp chef's knife. Wash, dry and trim the ends away from the carrots. Peel with a knife or peeler and slice into 2.5cm rounds. Peel the potatoes over a sink using a peeler or knife. Dunk under the cold tap as you go to wash surface dirt away. Dry and chop into small pieces.

Peel the ginger with a sharp knife. Grate it finely. Peel and crush the garlic.

COOK Put a large pan on to heat. Heat the oil and butter. Add the onion and a pinch of salt. Sweat gently on low for 5–10 minutes until soft not coloured, stirring occasionally.

Add the ginger and star anise. Stir and cook for 2 minutes. Add the carrot and potatoes, stirring, and cook over a very low heat for 10 minutes with the lid on. If you've got a bit of greaseproof paper or a butter wrapper, lay it directly onto the vegetables and put the lid back on (this paper, or 'cartouche' helps retain moisture as the mix cooks). Don't let the vegetables catch or brown up.

Remove the paper. Stir. Add the lime juice and pour in the stock. Tear in most of the coriander – reserving a few leaves for garnish – and season to taste. Bring to the boil. Reduce and simmer on very low heat for 30–40 minutes, or until the carrots are soft (test with a knife).

Cool for 5 minutes. Fish out the star anise. Blitz till smooth with a stick blender in the pan, or leave to cool for 5 minutes before blitzing in a blender/processor in batches. Taste and adjust the seasoning, by adding a bit more lime juice if it needs a lift.

PLATE Pour the soup into warmed bowls and top with torn coriander. Serve with croutons (p29) and small wedges of lime for squeezing.

MUSHROOM AND TARRAGON SOUP

FEEDS 4

Using specific herbs can transform ingredients; here tarragon works its magic to create a soup that's earthy with a twist of aniseed.

INGREDIENTS

*350g mix of portobello
   and chestnut mushrooms
3 shallots, peeled
2 garlic cloves, peeled
1 tbsp butter
a splash of olive oil
a few fresh tarragon leaves
850ml chicken/vegetable stock
   (p49/p15)
salt and pepper
3–4 tbsp double cream/crème fraîche*

—— CHANGE IT UP ——

Replace the tarragon with flat-leaf parsley and add a pinch of nutmeg before serving.

PREP Rub the mushrooms with a bit of barely damp kitchen paper to clean. Don't wash them. Chop or tear them roughly. Dice the shallots and crush the garlic.

COOK Melt the butter and oil in a large pan on a low heat. Fry the shallots gently for 5 minutes, stirring with a wooden spoon, until soft and colourless. Add the garlic, most of the tarragon and all the mushrooms and stir well. Cook gently for 10 minutes with the pan covered, checking and stirring the mix occasionally.

Add the stock. Increase the heat to boil then reduce to simmer on a gentle heat in the covered pan for 15 minutes. Season with salt and pepper and add the remaining tarragon.

Leave to cool for 5 minutes. Add a tablespoon or two of cream or crème fraîche. Pour the soup into a blender in batches and blitz until smooth. Taste and adjust the seasoning to suit your palate, adding more cream/crème fraîche if you like.

PLATE Reheat the soup very gently. Pour it into bowls and enjoy with some good buttery toast, cut into soldiers for dipping.

BONUS BITE

BLITZED SPICED CAULIFLOWER SOUP

Break a medium-sized cauliflower into florets. Fry off a chopped large onion with 1 crushed garlic clove, ½ tsp each of cumin, turmeric, garam masala and dried chilli flakes in a little oil. Stir in the florets and sweat under a cartouche for 10 minutes, or till soft without colouring. Add 110g ground almonds, 1 litre vegetable/chicken stock and season to taste. Simmer for 15 minutes. Cool. Add a little lemon juice, taste and adjust the seasoning if necessary. Blitz in batches. Top with torn basil leaves and flaked almonds.

BRUSCHETTA

HEALTHY FAST **FEEDS 2**

Italian for great-tasting stuff on toast. Here are three sweet toppings which work whether you're cooking for yourself or the masses. Check out the carpaccio toppings on p83 – they also work really well here.

INGREDIENTS

1 garlic clove
4 x 2.5cm thick bread slices
(ciabatta/French stick/country loaf)
a little olive oil

PREP Cut the garlic clove in half widthways. Make your topping of choice (see below).

COOK Put a griddle pan onto a high heat. Brush the bread lightly with oil. Griddle for a minute or two on each side till crisp and marked up.

PLATE Rub each bit of bread with the cut garlic clove before spooning over your chosen topping.

—— BONUS BITES ——
MUSHROOM AND TARRAGON TARTS
Make up the mushroom topping (see opposite) adding a pinch of dried or chopped tarragon. Spread on a base of thinly rolled bought all-butter puff pastry cut into large circles or as you like. Bake for 20 minutes at 200°C/Gas 6 or till the base is crisp.

—— CHANGE IT UP ——
Try rubbing the bread with a lemon or fresh rosemary/basil leaves instead of garlic.

—— TOPPINGS ——

1 BROAD BEAN AND WENSLEYDALE
Put a pan of water on to heat with a good pinch of salt. Bring to the boil. Add 110g broad beans (fresh or frozen) and simmer for 5–6 minutes till tender (test one). Drain into a colander. Cool under running water. Remove and discard their outer skins. Toss into a bowl. Add 30g roughly crumbled Wensleydale cheese, 3 tsp olive oil and 2 tsp lemon juice. Roughly mash the mix with a fork, leaving some good chunks. Taste and season lightly, adjusting the oil and lemon if needed.

2 TOMATO AND BLACK OLIVE
Slice 8–12 good-quality cherry or baby plum tomatoes in half lengthwise, slice in half again and tip into a bowl. Chop 6 black olives (if the stones are still in, remove them first by cutting round using a small, sharp knife) and add to the bowl with half a diced shallot. Add 1 tbsp oil, a pinch each of salt and sugar, a little black pepper and a few rocket or basil leaves, if you like, and mix well.

3 HOT MIXED MUSHROOMS
Clean 350g mixed mushrooms (e.g. portobello, chestnut or oyster) with kitchen paper, trim if needed and slice into 1cm thick pieces. Put a heavy-bottomed medium frying pan over a medium heat with 50g butter and a drop or two of oil. Add a finely diced shallot and 1 crushed garlic clove and cook, stirring for a minute or two. Add a small glass of white wine and bring to the boil. Lower to a simmer and add the mushrooms and a small pinch of dried thyme. Cook, stirring, for 2–3 minutes, until the mushrooms are soft but still holding their shape. Season to taste. Remove from the heat, stir through 1½ tbsp double cream/crème fraîche and squeeze over a little lemon juice.

PUNCHY CHICORY WATERCRESS, BACON, AVOCADO
IN A HONEY MUSTARD DRESSING

HEALTHY

FEEDS 2

A good dressing pulls ingredients together. Add the oil slowly so it emulsifies. Here's a great little salad that's open to a range of other ingredient options. So go ahead and build it up. Follow the salad rules (p18) and you'll be laughing.

INGREDIENTS

2 big handfuls of watercress
a head of chicory (endive)
2 streaky bacon rashers
1 avocado
juice of ¼ a small lemon
HONEY MUSTARD DRESSING
½ tsp runny honey
1 tsp Dijon mustard
1 tbsp white wine vinegar
3 tbsp extra virgin olive oil
½ small shallot, peeled
salt and pepper

—— CHANGE IT UP ——

1. Add baby spinach to the salad for extra nutrients. **2.** Switch the avocado for regular pear, sliced and tossed in lemon juice, and use walnut dressing (p33). **3.** Switch the bacon for crumbled goat's cheese, stilton or roquefort and add caramelised walnuts (p194). **4.** For a simple green salad, leave out the bacon and avocado.

PREP Wash and dry the watercress. Discard any woody stems. Sit the chicory on a board, trim the end or just strip the leaves off. Wash and dry them well. Leave whole, tear into bits or mix it up – your choice.

Make the dressing: put the honey and mustard into a small bowl. Using a spoon or mini-balloon whisk, beat the vinegar in gradually until creamy. Add the oil drop by drop, then in a trickle, beating as you go, so it emulsifies. Slice the shallot thinly and stir it in. Dip a leaf in to taste so you can adjust the seasoning and balance of acidity if you need to. Set aside.

Preheat the grill to high. Lay the bacon on the rack in the pan. Cook for 2 minutes. Turn with tongs or a fork. Repeat till cooked (don't burn it). Transfer to kitchen paper. Sit your avocado on a board. Cut it in half by slicing horizontally through the skin and flesh till you hit the stone. Rotate the fruit as you hold the knife in place. Hold both halves of the fruit and twist in opposite directions to separate. Leave the stone in the half you're not using, rub the flesh with lemon and wrap in cling film: save this for guacamole (p75) . Scoop the flesh from the other half with a spoon, slice it and toss in lemon juice.

Toss the leaves and dressing together with your fingers, judging it so you don't use too much, yet every leaf is coated.

PLATE Bang the dressed leaves onto plates or into a bowl. Add the avocado and crumble over the crisp bacon.

MILD LETTUCE SALAD WITH RADISH, CUCUMBER, CRESS, CHEESE AND CLASSIC FRENCH DRESSING

`HEALTHY`   FEEDS 2

Salad is all about textures, contrasts and excellent dressing: toss this one or any basic green leaf side salad in a classic French vinaigrette to transform it.

INGREDIENTS

½ a soft lettuce (like butterhead)
6 radishes
1 x 10cm length of cucumber
3–4 snips of cress from a box
50–75g manchego/gruyère/cheddar
    cheese (optional)
FRENCH DRESSING
1 tbsp white wine vinegar
salt and black pepper
3 tbsp extra virgin olive oil

PREP Pull as many leaves as you need off the lettuce (don't cut it as it bruises and the rest won't last as long). Wash and dry it well. Wash, dry, trim and slice the radishes, mixing your slicing style (rounds and lengths) if you like. Run a fork down the length of your piece of cucumber to score the edges for looks, then slice thinly. Snip the cress with scissors. Wash and leave to drain in a sieve. Slice the cheese into matchsticks, if using.

For the dressing: spoon the vinegar into a small bowl with a good pinch of salt and a few grindings of pepper. Whisk/beat the oil in drop by drop for an emulsion. Toss everything except the cress in the dressing using your fingers.

PLATE Heap into a bowl or onto plates. Scatter the cress on top.

——— CHANGE IT UP ———

Try teaming this salad with cherry tomatoes, sliced hard-boiled eggs and ham, or a very good pork pie with cold roasted meats and hard cheeses.

A CLASSIC PEPPERY ROCKET SIDE SALAD WITH BALSAMIC DRESSING

`HEALTHY`   FEEDS 2

Your classic rocket side salad in a sharp, dark dressing. Mix it up by shaving over parmesan or adding croutons (opposite), toasted pine nuts or cherry tomatoes. If making this – or any – salad to go, pack the dressing in a pot and dress just before eating.

INGREDIENTS

2 big handfuls of rocket
BALSAMIC DRESSING
a pinch of salt
a pinch of sugar
1 tsp balsamic vinegar
1 tbsp extra virgin olive oil
1 tbsp light olive/groundnut/
    sunflower oil

PREP Wash the rocket leaves in a sieve or colander under cold running water. Handle them lightly as they easily spoil and bruise. Get them really dry by patting on a tea towel or kitchen paper or use a spinner. They'll hold their dressing better, it's not diluted and you'll use less.

Make the dressing: beat the salt, sugar and balsamic together in a bowl. Add the oils in drop by drop, beating as you go so the dressing emulsifies naturally. Taste and adjust the seasoning and balance of acidity to suit your palate.

Toss the rocket and dressing together with your fingers, judging it so you don't use too much, yet every leaf is coated.

PLATE Lift and arrange the dressed leaves on plates/bowls.

CRISP CAESAR SALAD

HEALTHY

FEEDS 2

Here's a lighter alternative to a standard Caesar. Have it plain or throw in your choice of crunchy additions (vegetarians – use non-rennet cheese). Make your own croutons: they're way tastier than bought-ins.

INGREDIENTS

a head of Cos/1 large Romaine heart/
  2 Little Gem lettuces

CAESAR DRESSING

2 tbsp plain yoghurt
2 tbsp mayonnaise (p153)
10g parmesan, plus extra to finish
1 tsp lemon juice
3 drops of Worcester sauce
a little black pepper

ADDITIONS

4 streaky bacon rashers
a handful of pine nuts
a handful of croutons of your choice

PREP

Strip all or a good number of whole leaves from your chosen lettuce variety. Wash and dry them carefully and put in the fridge to crisp for 30 minutes.

Make the dressing: mix the yoghurt and mayo in a bowl. Finely grate the cheese and stir in. Add the lemon juice, Worcester sauce and pepper to season (the cheese provides salt). Taste and adjust to suit your palate.

BACON: Preheat the grill. Lay the bacon on the pan and grill for 2 minutes. Turn with tongs. Grill till cooked. Don't burn. Cool on kitchen paper to crisp up.
PINE NUTS: Put a dry frying pan on to heat. Add the nuts. Shuffle or toss them so they toast evenly for 2–3 minutes, or until pale gold. **CROUTONS:** prep as per your chosen recipe.

Tear and toss the leaves into a bowl with some of the dressing. Turn to coat.

PLATE

Pile into bowls. Top with the croutons, pine nuts, and crumbled bacon. Shave or grate over some extra parmesan to finish.

—— CHANGE IT UP ——

For a chicken Caesar salad, top with two sliced griddled chicken breasts (p51). For a walnut Caesar, sprinkle with caramelised walnuts (p194) and chopped dates.

TIPS

1. Stale bread or baguette makes ideal croutons (it may well cook a bit faster, so keep checking it). **2.** Stale bagels make the crunchiest croutons.

TO GO WITH

CROUTONS

Preheat an oven to 180°C/Gas 4. Using a serrated knife, cut 3 thick slices from a loaf of bread. Slice off the crusts. Cut the remaining bread into even fingers then cubes. Toss in a thin coating of olive oil and a bit of sea salt. Bake on a tray for 10 minutes or until crisp.

PEPPER CROUTONS

Bash ¼ tsp peppercorns in a pestle and mortar or with the end of a rolling pin. Toss in a bowl with the oil and bread. Bake as above.

GARLIC AND CHEESE CROUTONS

Mix a crushed garlic clove with a bit of olive oil and a little bit of freshly grated parmesan or other cheese. Coat the bread cubes and bake as above.

LENTIL SALAD
THREE WAYS

FEEDS 2

I love these little salads. Team your lentils with smoked fish and bacon, sausage and caramelised onion or a good sharp cheese. Toss them in a tasty dressing: make it look extraordinary.

INGREDIENTS

110g Puy lentils
250ml vegetable stock (p15)
80ml white wine
salt and pepper

TOPPINGS

1 *50g smoked salmon*
1 small avocado
juice of ¼ a small lemon
2 bacon rashers
a small handful of fresh dill
1 x honey mustard dressing (p26)

2 *1 brown onion*
2 tbsp olive/groundnut oil
1 tsp butter
1–2 good-quality chipolatas
1 x honey mustard dressing (p26)

3 *75g Lancashire/feta/goat's cheese*
1 shallot
a handful of pea shoots/soft lettuce leaves
1 x walnut dressing (p33)

PREP Wash the lentils in a sieve under running water. Pour the stock and wine into a pan. Bring it to the boil. Add the lentils and a touch of salt. Reduce the heat and simmer for 15–20 minutes until the lentils are tender, but still holding their shape. Be vigilant, as they can turn to mush in an instant.

Meantime, make the dressing to match your topping and set it aside.

Test the lentils for doneness. Drain them into a sieve and leave to cool for a minute, then tip into a bowl and toss with a tablespoon or two of dressing, tasting to judge the amount.

1 Chop the salmon into thin strips. Cut the avocado in half. Remove the stone and peel. Chop and toss in lemon juice. Grill the bacon until crispy. Sit it on kitchen paper. Chop the dill.

2 Peel and thinly slice the onion. Heat half the oil and butter in a pan. Cook the onion over a very low heat for 20–30 minutes, until soft and caramelised. Add the chipolatas to a separate small pan with the remaining oil and fry over a low heat for 10 minutes, turning, until done.

3 Crumble the cheese and peel and slice the shallot.

PLATE Stir the lentils and taste to see if they need more dressing or seasoning.

1 Mix the dill into the lentils. Pile on the salmon, avocado and bacon. Grind a bit of black pepper over the lot and serve with a handful of green leaves and a dollop of sour cream on the side.

2 Mix some of the onion into the lentils. Arrange slices of sausage and the rest of the onion on top. Stir a little mustard through a few dollops of sour cream and serve on the side with a few dill pickles.

3 Scatter the cheese, shallot and leaves over the lentil base. Drizzle over the walnut dressing and serve with some good crusty bread.

CREAMY THREE BEAN AND ALMOND SALAD

 HEALTHY   FAST   FEEDS 3-4

Beans can be so boring, but I'd never do that to you. Every mouthful here is a contrast of texture and flavour. The dressing is delicious.

INGREDIENTS

1 x 450g can of cannellini beans
salt and pepper
110g frozen broad beans
200g French beans
a handful of flaked almonds

DRESSING

1 tsp Dijon mustard
a big squeeze of lime juice
3 tbsp chopped coriander
4–6 tbsp crème fraîche
a pinch of caster sugar

PREP Tip the can of beans into a sieve or colander. Leave to drain and dry a bit.

COOK Boil up a pan of water. Add a pinch of salt. Tip in the broad beans and cook for 4 minutes or till tender. Drain into a colander. Refresh under cold running water. Set aside for a bit to cool and dry. Now, remove and discard the tough outer skins. Find the bit of spare skin on the edge of the bean and squeeze it – the innards should pop out easily. Put them into a bowl and set aside.

Boil a second pan of lightly salted water. Wash and trim the fine beans. Boil for 5 minutes or a little longer until tender but not overcooked (you want some bite).

Drain and hold under cold water to crisp them up again and hold their colour.

Mix all the elements for the dressing in a bowl. Taste it and adjust the seasoning to suit your palate.

Tip all the beans into a bowl. Add the flaked almonds and stir in your dressing.

PLATE Shift the beans to a clean bowl or plate. Enjoy with other salads and bread, or team with my leek tart (p170), egg and bacon tart (p169), or griddled lamb/chicken.

PLOUGHMAN'S STYLE BEAN AND CELERY SALAD

HEALTHY   FAST

FEEDS 2 (on the side)

INGREDIENTS

120g canned red kidney beans
3 sticks celery
a handful of sultanas
2 crisp apples
a squeeze of lemon juice
110g mature cheddar
a handful of pea shoots/lamb's lettuce/
  other soft salad leaves
WALNUT DRESSING
2 tsp Dijon mustard
a pinch of caster sugar
a pinch of salt
2 tbsp white wine vinegar
6 tbsp walnut oil

Very little effort for a great tasting plate: use good sharp apples for a taste contrast. Who doesn't love a ploughman's?

PREP Make the dressing: put the mustard, sugar and salt into a small bowl. Beat the vinegar in gradually until creamy. Add the oil drop by drop, then in a trickle, beating as you go, so it emulsifies.

Drain the beans into a sieve or colander. Set aside.

Wash, string and slice the celery.

Remove the cores of the apples with a corer or cut them into quarters and scoop the pips out with a sharp knife. Chop them into large bite-sized pieces. Toss them in lemon juice to stop discolouration.

Cut the cheese into bite-sized cubes. Toss the beans, celery, sultanas and apple in a bowl with 2–3 tablespoons of your dressing. Taste and adjust the seasoning.

PLATE Pile it onto your plates. Top with the leaves and cheese. Serve alongside a plate of cold ham or roast pork or team with a big, buttered baked potato.

—— CHANGE IT UP ——

1. Switch the walnut dressing for honey mustard dressing (p26). **2.** Use gruyère/Lancashire/Wensleydale cheese in place of cheddar. **3.** Tear in a few pieces of salami. **4.** Replace the cheese with bite-sized chunks of freshly cooked pork sausage. **5.** Make it fruity by adding some chopped dates, dried figs, chopped pear, whole grapes or chopped orange.

✶✶✶✶ CASH SAVER ✶✶✶✶
Replace 2 tbsp of the (pricey) walnut oil with the same quantity of groundnut oil instead.

CRISP POLENTA
AND TOMATO
CAPONATA SALAD

FEEDS 4

Crisp, soft, hot and cold: this one's so good. The salad's cooked ahead of time, which gives the flavours time to develop. Fry off the polenta discs at the last minute for a real contrast in temperatures and textures.

INGREDIENTS

2 glossy aubergines
sea salt and black pepper
450g fresh tomatoes
3 sticks celery
1 onion
2 garlic cloves
50g dried apricots
4 tbsp olive oil
1½ tsp red harissa paste
60g black olives
1½ tsp capers
1 tbsp caster sugar
4 tbsp white wine/sherry vinegar
a handful of chopped flat-leaf parsley
POLENTA
600ml water
150g fast-cook polenta
a few pinches of dried oregano
25g butter
a handful of freshly grated parmesan
olive oil, for shallow-frying

TIP
When sprinkling salt on a dish, do so from a height so it covers the food lightly and evenly

——— CHANGE IT UP ———
1. Switch the parmesan for cheddar. 2. Serve the polenta discs with bolognaise (p85) or an easy tomato sauce (p176).

PREP Trim the aubergine stalks and slice into thick rounds with a serrated/bread knife. Sprinkle both sides lightly with fine sea salt and leave for 30 minutes to draw out any juices. Wipe the slices on kitchen paper and chop into bite-sized pieces.

Skin the tomatoes (p17) and cut into thick slices vertically. Wash, dry, then strip any stringy bits away from the celery. Slice it thinly. Peel, halve and slice the onion. Peel and crush the garlic. Finely chop the apricots.

COOK Heat the oil in a large frying pan/shallow casserole dish. Fry the vegetables in turn so their flavours stay separate. Start with the aubergines (fry and stir for 10 minutes or until soft, brown and cooked through). Transfer to a plate with a slotted spoon. Lower the heat and fry the celery for a few minutes. Spoon it out and set aside on the plate.

Fry the onions very gently for 5–10 minutes until soft, not coloured. Then add the garlic, harissa paste, apricots, tomatoes, olives and capers. Let the mix boil then reduce and simmer on a very low heat for 15 minutes.

Stir in the sugar and vinegar. Simmer till sticky for 10 minutes, then bang the aubergines and celery back in the pan, add the parsley and stir well. Adjust the balance of sweet and sour to taste (adding a little more sugar or vinegar as necessary). Tip into a dish to cool as you make the polenta.

Polenta: Measure the water into a pan. Cover and bring to the boil. In a bowl, mix the polenta and oregano. Season with salt and pepper. Shove the mix into the boiling water in one go, beating furiously with a wooden spoon for 5 minutes as it splutters and spits. Beat in the butter and cheese. Pour into a 20 x 20 x 2cm oiled tin and leave to cool. (If you find yourself with extra polenta, pour it into another tin, cool it, cut it out and freeze it for later.)

Cut rounds of cooled, set polenta with a 9cm cookie cutter or wine glass. Shallow-fry in olive oil for 3 minutes a side or till cooked through and beautifully crispy.

PLATE Sit the polenta on plates, pile on your salad and serve (this is a good-to-go-by-itself dish, so doesn't really need accompanying with anything).

TOMATOES MARINATED IN LIME JUICE AND HONEY WITH SALTED MOZZARELLA

HEALTHY

FEEDS 2

The tomato is a wonderful beast when it's at its best (in season). When it's not it can do with help and that's when interesting seasonings, herbs and ingredient combinations really make the most of it.

INGREDIENTS

3 good-sized best ripe vine tomatoes
2 tbsp fruity extra-virgin olive oil,
  plus extra for serving
1–2 tsp runny honey
sea salt and black pepper
juice of ½–1 lime (to taste)
a small handful of coriander leaves
1 x 125g ball of good mozzarella

PREP Wash and dry the tomatoes. Remove the stem. Working on a board, use a sharp vegetable knife or a serrated blade to slice them thinly horizontally. Shift the tomato slices over to a shallow dish or plate to marinate and pour over any juices that may have escaped while slicing.

Mix the oil, honey, a little pepper and lime juice together and drizzle over the tomatoes. Wash, blot and tear the coriander. Scatter over the lot and leave for twenty minutes to an hour to marinate. Baste the tomatoes (spooning the marinade juices over them) just before serving.

Slice the mozzarella just before plating.

PLATE Spoon the tomatoes onto a fresh dish/plates or leave as they are. Arrange the cheese on top and treat it to a few drops of oil and a couple of pinches of sea salt flakes to taste. Have some warm bread in the oven ready to mop up the juices.

> **TIP**
> When using tomatoes raw in a dish like this, make sure they are at room temperature to enjoy their flavour and texture at their best.

ROASTED TOMATO SALAD IN A TIN

HEALTHY

FEEDS 2

Slow roasting transforms average tomatoes into sweet beauties. Dip your bread in the tin to soak up the juices.

INGREDIENTS

4 large vine tomatoes
1 garlic clove
salt (or celery salt) and black pepper
a few pinches of dried oregano
olive oil

PREP Preheat the oven to 220°C/Gas 7. Boil a kettle.

Skin the tomatoes (p17). Sit them on a board. Slice each one across into halves horizontally. Fit them cut-side up into an oiled shallow enamel tin/dish in a single layer. Cut the garlic clove in half widthways and use to rub over the tomato tops. Sprinkle with oregano and salt or celery salt and drizzle with oil.

COOK Roast for 10 minutes. Reduce the temperature to 180°C/Gas 4 and cook for a further 40 minutes, or until soft and almost caramelised. Leave to cool.

PLATE Share from the tin and enjoy with warm bread and cheese.

— **BONUS BITE** —
OVEN-DRIED TOMATOES
Set the oven at 120°C/Gas ½. Halve the tomatoes. Leave in their skins and roll in oil, seasoning, dried or fresh herbs. Bake on trays for 6 hours until reduced and shrivelled. Remove. Bang into clean jars. Add olive oil to cover and keep in the fridge for up to 6 months. Eat with salads.

RETRO BEEF TOMATOES FILLED WITH A CHOICE OF SALADS

HEALTHY   FEEDS 2

Don't take this dish too seriously: food needs its comedy moments. Stuff your beef tomatoes with micro-salads. Prepping them this way heightens the flavours.

INGREDIENTS

2 large beef or very large vine tomatoes
a pinch of salt
GREEK SALAD FILLING
50–60g feta cheese
a pinch of dried oregano
a pinch of chilli flakes
2 tsp olive oil
2 tsp lemon juice
10 black olives
1 x 5cm piece cucumber
1 shallot
2 crisp chilled iceberg lettuce leaves
1–2 tsp red wine vinegar
PRAWN COCKTAIL FILLING
4 tbsp mayo or yoghurt/mayo mix
1 tbsp tomato ketchup
1 tsp lemon juice
1 garlic clove, peeled and crushed
salt and pepper
4 cherry tomatoes
8 small cooked prawns, shelled (p134)
12 large, whole cooked prawns
a large crisp iceberg lettuce leaf, torn into pieces
a sprinkle of paprika

PREP Use a sharp chef's knife to slice the tops off the tomatoes to create lids. Hollow out the tomatoes with a teaspoon, scraping down to the shell. Rub salt around the insides. Invert on a rack to drain their moisture.

GREEK SALAD FILLING: Drain the feta if it comes in liquid. Pat dry on kitchen paper and dice into tiny cubes. Mix the oregano, chilli flakes, oil and lemon juice in a bowl to make a marinade and sit the feta in it to flavour up. Dice the olives (pit them first if they have stones). Peel, halve, deseed and finely dice the cucumber. Peel and slice the shallot. Shake moisture out of the tomatoes. Sit them up. Line each one with a torn iceberg leaf, letting it come over the top (a rough finish is good). Use a teaspoon to layer it with a bit of marinated feta, diced olive and cucumber. Repeat, finishing with a pile of feta. Add a few drops of red wine vinegar and scatter over the shallot slices to finish.

PRAWN COCKTAIL FILLING: Mix the mayo, ketchup, lemon juice, garlic, salt and pepper together in a bowl to make a Marie Rose sauce. Dice the cherry tomatoes and small prawns. Spoon a bit of sauce into the base of each tomato, then alternate layers of diced prawns, diced tomato and sauce, finishing with sauce. Wedge pieces of lettuce creatively down the sides of the tomatoes, alternating with whole prawns which you can hook over the tops so they're looking out. Add more sauce and a sprinkling of paprika over the top to finish.

PLATE Prop the tomato lids back on if they go. Eat the Greek salad tomatoes with warm, soft pittas and the prawn cocktail tomatoes with brown bread and butter.

—— CHANGE IT UP ——

1. For a caprese salad, cover a plate with overlapping layers of sliced vine/beef tomato, mozzarella, and whole basil leaves. Drizzle with good olive oil. Sprinkle with sea salt. **2.** For a simple tomato salad, mix together a little caster sugar, black pepper, crushed sea salt, olive oil, lemon juice and torn basil. Drizzle over sliced tomatoes.
3. For an everyday tomato and shallot salad, chop or slice a handful of vine or beef tomatoes and toss in French dressing (p28) with diced/sliced shallot or red onion.

COURGETTE AND
FETA FRITTERS WITH HUMMUS AND MEZZE BITS

FEEDS 3-4

INGREDIENTS

450g courgettes
salt and black pepper
1 large egg
110g feta cheese
3 spring onions (white and green)
4 tbsp plain white flour
2 tbsp chopped fresh dill
a pinch of dried mint
a small pinch of smoked paprika
groundnut oil with a dash of olive oil,
    for shallow-frying

—— CHANGE IT UP ——

1. For yoghurt hummus, stir in 1–2 tbsp of plain or Greek yoghurt to regular hummus to taste. **2.** For coriander and lemon hummus, blitz in a little fresh coriander and 1 tsp lemon zest with the chickpeas. **3.** For parsley and sundried tomato hummus, add a little flat-leaf parsley and a few sundried tomatoes before blitzing.

Make these delicious fritters the star attraction of a mezze plate. Mix it up with home-marinated olives (cheaper and better than shop-bought), easy tzatziki, good punchy hummus, spectacular smoky aubergine dip and wrap it up with steaming hot flatbreads.

PREP Wash, dry then grate the courgettes coarsely onto a board. Tip them into a bowl with a few pinches of fine salt. Mix and leave to sweat for 15 minutes.

Meantime, beat the egg with a fork. Crumble the feta cheese roughly. Bunch the spring onions together on a board, trim the roots then slice across thinly.

Tip the courgettes into a colander/sieve to drain. Squeeze them with your hands to remove moisture, then put half into the centre of a tea towel. Pull it round them then twist and squeeze. (You need to remove as much moisture as possible so the fritters aren't wet). Repeat with the rest.

Tip the dried courgette into a large dry bowl. Mix in the flour, spring onion, dill, mint, paprika and feta cheese and season with salt and pepper. Add the egg gradually, stirring, until evenly distributed.

COOK Put a medium frying pan on to heat and add enough oil to cover the base of the pan. Test the heat of the oil – it's hot enough when it can brown a breadcrumb in 10 seconds. Carefully add the fritter mix a tablespoon at a time. Cook for 2–3 minutes per side or till golden (check with a spatula). Turn very gently as these guys aren't robust. Set aside on kitchen paper.

PLATE Sprinkle with salt. Serve hot with mezze bits: lemon and garlic marinated olives, aubergine dip, cucumber tzatziki, hummus and coriander flatbreads.

TURN OVER
FOR MEZZE BITS

TO GO WITH

HUMMUS

Tip a 400g can of chickpeas into a sieve over a bowl, saving the water. By machine: Pulse the chickpeas till fine as wet sand in a processor. Add water from the can (2 tbsp), 2 tbsp tahini paste, 3 tbsp lemon juice, 4 garlic cloves and salt. Blitz to a smooth paste then start to trickle 100ml olive oil in through the funnel. Stop before it's all in. Sample for taste and texture, adjusting lemon/salt as necessary. Add a little more oil or add water for a much lighter mix. Taste and adjust again. By hand: Use a stick blender or mash the same ingredients together. Spoon the hummus into a bowl and drizzle olive oil over the surface. Sprinkle over a little paprika and a few pine nuts/chopped coriander leaves if you like to finish.

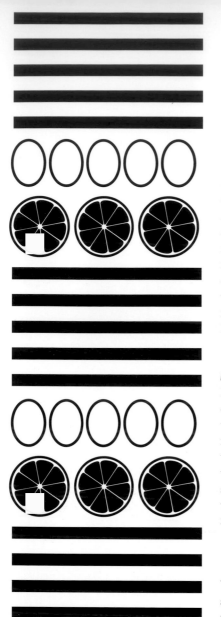

LEMON AND GARLIC MARINATED OLIVES

Slice the top and base off a medium lemon and sit on a board. Using a sharp or serrated knife, cut down the curve of the fruit to remove the peel and pith. Lay the bare fruit on its side. Hold it firmly with one hand as you cut down along the inside of each of the segment lines to the centre of the fruit until neat wedges of membrane-free lemon can be removed easily. Cut each one into three. Tip 3 thinly sliced garlic cloves and a pot each of black and green olives into a bowl that can take them snugly in a layer. Add the lemon. Sprinkle with 1 tsp dried oregano and cover with fruity extra virgin olive oil. Leave to marinate in the fridge, covered, for a few hours at least (preferably 24 hours). Return to room temperature before serving.

AUBERGINE DIP

Preheat the oven to 200°C/Gas 6. Wash and dry 2 medium aubergines. Roast on a baking tray for 30 minutes until blackened, soft and collapsing. Or hold them over a gas flame on a fork to blacken and smoke for a few minutes before finishing in the oven. Cool for 5 minutes. Slit them open. Spoon and scrape the flesh free and discard the skins. Squeeze the flesh gently to remove some of the juices. Drop it into a processor (or use a stick blender). Add half a chopped shallot, a garlic clove, the juice of 1 lemon, 2 tbsp extra virgin olive oil and 1 tbsp chopped flat-leaf parsley. Blitz till smooth. Season lightly. Cool and cover. Serve in a bowl for spreading/dipping.

CUCUMBER TZATZIKI

Wash and dry ½ a cucumber. Grate it thickly and put in a colander. Let it drain a little and squeeze out a bit of the water with kitchen paper. Bang 300ml thick Greek yoghurt, 1 tbsp finely chopped mint (or a pinch of dried mint/dill), 2 tsp olive oil, 1 tsp lemon juice, a crushed clove of garlic and a pinch of caster sugar into a large bowl. Season to taste. Stir in the cucumber. Eat now or chill.

CORIANDER FLATBREADS

Combine 50ml boiling water/100ml cold water in a jug. Sift 250g white bread flour into a bowl, adding 1½ tsp cumin seeds and a few fresh coriander leaves. Mix the water in gradually, using a fork or your hand until it integrates into a smooth (not sticky) ball. Divide equally into 4 on a lightly floured board. Roll one piece out into a very thin circle. Fold it in half and then half again before rolling it out very thinly again. Cover with a tea towel and repeat with the other pieces. Put a crêpe pan or large flat frying pan on to a very high heat for 3 minutes. Add the first flatbread. Cook for 1–2 minutes per side or until puffed and charred. Remove. Brush with a bit of oil and sprinkle with a little coarse salt. Eat immediately. Repeat with the remaining flatbreads.

BUTTERNUT SQUASH FALAFEL-STYLE FRITTERS

HEALTHY

FEEDS 3

Butternut squash takes on a more exotic identity in this one, teaming up with cheap and nutritious chickpeas and spices for an extravagant tasting, festival-style fritter.

INGREDIENTS

400g butternut squash
2 tbsp olive oil
a pinch of dried cumin
salt and black pepper
a pinch of chilli flakes
1 x 450g can of chickpeas
3 spring onions
60g cheddar
a small handful of fresh coriander
a pinch of ground ginger
a pinch of dried oregano
60g white breadcrumbs made
  from stale bread (p201)
a pinch of dried mint
a squeeze of lime juice
4–5 tbsp white or gram flour,
  for coating
groundnut oil with a dash of olive oil,
  for shallow-frying

PREP Preheat the oven to 200°C/Gas 6. Using a sawing action, cut into your squash with a bread knife. Scoop out any seeds with a spoon and chop into large, fairly equal pieces, keeping the skins on. Sit on a baking tray and roll in olive oil to coat. Sprinkle with cumin, salt and chilli flakes and roast for 20 minutes, or until the flesh is tender. Remove and leave to cool, then scoop the flesh from the skins (these can be discarded). Blitz into a purée in a blender, put in a large bowl and set aside.

Drain the chickpeas into a sieve. Dry them with a tea towel or on kitchen paper, then tip into a bowl and mash roughly, leaving some almost whole for texture. Finely chop the spring onions. Finely grate the cheddar and tear the coriander roughly.

Mix a good big pinch of ginger (as much as you can get between thumb and forefinger) and one of oregano into the squash purée. Throw in the chickpeas, breadcrumbs, cheese, spring onion, mint, lime juice and coriander. Mix well with a fork. Taste to check it's well seasoned. The mix should be firm, not sloppy.

Coat the fritters, scatter a bit of flour over a large plate. Damp en your hando. Scoop up tablespoons of the mix and shape into fritters then roll them in the flour to coat. Chill for 30 minutes at least. Preheat the oven to 180°C/Gas 4.

COOK Pour enough groundnut oil into a wok to about 1cm depth, adding a dash of olive oil. When it's hot enough to crisp a breadcrumb to a count of 10, add the fritters. Cook for 2 minutes per side (without over-browning) then transfer to a baking tray and finish in the oven for 10 minutes.

PLATE Serve these up on a pile of couscous or tabbouleh (p128) with a plate of lightly griddled vegetables, or bang them into pittas with leaves and hummus (p38). Save any extra for a lunch box.

SWEET POTATO AND BLACKEYE BEAN BURGER

FEEDS 4

INGREDIENTS

400g sweet potato
2 tsp dried oregano
1 tsp ground cumin
salt and black pepper
1–2 tbsp olive oil, for coating
1 x 400g can of blackeye beans
50g crustless fresh white bread
a good handful of torn coriander
juice of ½ a lime
¼ tsp smoked paprika
*4 homemade (p82) or shop-bought
 burger buns*
EXTRAS
lime mayo (p45)
sweetcorn salsa (opposite)
guacamole (p75)
grated cheddar
shredded iceberg lettuce leaves

TIP
Why ruin a burger with bad bread? Try making your own buns (p82).

This Mexican-inspired gourmet vegetable burger is full of spicy flavours which ping off all over the place. It's delicious.

PREP Preheat the oven to 180°C/Gas 4. Peel the sweet potatoes and cut into 1cm slices. Chuck them onto a baking tray and sprinkle with oregano, cumin, salt and pepper. Toss them in olive oil and roast for 30 minutes, or until soft and golden (test with a knife at 20 minutes). Remove. Tip them into a bowl and mash to a smooth paste. Leave to cool.

Meantime, drain the beans into a sieve. Shake them dry. Tip them into a bowl. Mash roughly with a fork. Blitz the bread to crumbs (p201). Mix the mashed beans, breadcrumbs, coriander, lime juice smoked paprika and some salt and pepper into the sweet potato mash. Divide and shape into 4 flat burgers with your hands. Chill for 10 minutes. Make your mayo, salsa and guacamole.

Slice the burger buns across and grill or toast lightly. Set aside.

COOK Put a frying pan on a medium-high heat. Fry the burgers for 5 minutes per side or till golden, crispy and hot all though, regulating the heat so they don't burn. (Alternatively, fry for a minute each side to seal the burger before finishing in a hot oven for 10 minutes.)

PLATE Stack the warm buns with lime mayo, sweetcorn salsa, the burgers and guacamole before finishing with the cheddar and lettuce. Serve with tortilla crisps, spiced sweet potato wedges (p82) or a healthy salad.

TO GO WITH

SWEETCORN SALSA

Drain a 250g can of sweetcorn into a bowl. Squeeze over the juice of 1 fat lime, add 1–2 tbsp runny honey and stir together. Throw in 2 tbsp chopped coriander, ½ a deseeded, finely diced chilli (p16) and 1 small finely diced red onion. Stir together and season to taste. Set aside for the flavours to develop until needed and stir before using.

AUBERGINE AND GOAT'S CHEESE BURGER WITH OLIVE MAYO AND TOMATO

FEEDS 2

INGREDIENTS

2 x 1cm firm goat's cheese rounds

1 egg

4–5 tbsp plain white flour, for coating

a handful of panko/panko-style breadcrumbs (p201)

salt and black pepper

1 small aubergine

2–3 tbsp olive oil

a pinch of dried thyme

2 homemade (p82) or shop-bought burger buns

2–4 sunblush/sundried tomatoes

a handful of soft green leaves

groundnut oil, for shallow-frying

OLIVE MAYO

1 tbsp mayonnaise (p153)

a few chopped black olives or 1 tsp olive tapenade

There's a Mediterranean vibe going on here: this burger's fresh, zingy and totally satisfying. Don't be tempted to buy standard breadcrumbs – they're no good here. Get a pack of light tasty panko breadcrumbs from your Asian supermarket or make your own (p201) instead – they're easy.

PREP Coat the cheese: Beat the egg and tip it into a bowl. Put your flour and breadcrumbs onto separate plates. Season the flour lightly with salt and pepper. Toss the cheese discs one at a time into the flour, turning to coat well. Dip the floured discs into the beaten egg (making sure to cover) then toss and turn in the breadcrumbs. Dunk them back into the egg and finally into the crumbs. Refrigerate on a plate for at least 30 minutes.

Meantime, slice the aubergine into 1cm discs using a sharp knife/bread knife. Sit the pieces in a colander and sprinkle with a little salt to draw out any bitterness. After 20 minutes, wipe off any moisture then brush sparingly with olive oil and a sprinkle of thyme. Heat the remaining olive oil in a large pan. Add the slices and fry for 1–2 minutes per side, until well browned and soft. Drain on kitchen paper and set aside in a warm place.

Prep your mayo by mixing it with the chopped olives/tapenade in a bowl. Set aside.

Slice the burger buns across and grill or toast lightly. Spread with mayo. Add a couple of slices of aubergine, a sunblush or sundried tomato, then top with a few of the green leaves and the remaining aubergine.

COOK Pour groundnut oil into a small shallow frying pan so it's around 1 cm deep. If you have a cooking thermometer, heat the oil to around 180°C. Otherwise, drop a breadcrumb in and count to 10. If it's crisp and lightly golden after this time, the oil is ready.

Gently place the crumbed cheese discs in the oil. Cook for 1–2 minutes per side, turning carefully using a spatula, until they're hot and soft inside, crisp and golden outside. Sit them briefly on kitchen paper.

PLATE Bang the hot cheese discs on top of the aubergine. Top with leaves. Leave open with the lids leaning jauntily against the stack. Eat with chips and some dressed leaves.

SMOTHERED GARLIC AND TARRAGON PORTOBELLO MUSHROOM BURGER WITH LIME MAYO

FAST

FEEDS 2

You definitely don't miss the meat with this gorgeous combination of flavours. So good that I've had them for breakfast. Not baking your own buns? Ciabatta rolls are excellent for soaking up the juices.

INGREDIENTS

1 garlic clove
a few fresh tarragon leaves
    (or a pinch of dried)
2 tsp softened butter
2 fat portobello mushrooms
a glug of olive oil
salt and black pepper
a handful of fresh green leaves
    (rocket/spinach)
2 homemade (p82) or shop-bought
    burger buns
LIME MAYO
3 tbsp mayonnaise (p153)
juice of ½–1 lime

PREP Peel and crush the garlic and finely chop the tarragon. Add to the butter in a bowl and cream together with the back of a spoon. Brush the heads of the mushrooms with kitchen paper if they need cleaning. Don't wash them. Cut off the stalks. Smear the whole of each mushroom with a generous coating of olive oil.

Make up the lime mayo by mixing up regular mayonnaise with a good squeeze of fresh lime juice to taste. Get it nice and sharp to contrast with the burger.

COOK Heat a griddle pan. Once hot, put the mushrooms bottom-side down to cook for 5 minutes. Turn them over. Smear a teaspoon of the butter mix over each and cook for another 5 minutes, or until soft. (Thin mushrooms may take less time so keep your eye on them). Season. Meantime, lightly toast or grill your burger buns separately.

PLATE Stack both bottom halves of the toasted rolls with lime mayo and green leaves and top with the mushrooms.

TIP
If you have a roomy pan, try griddling the buns in it with the mushrooms rather than toasting them separately. This way they'll absorb some of the lovely mushroom juices.

—— BONUS BITE ——
BACON AND CHEESE MUSHROOM BURGER
Brush the mushrooms with oil and griddle as above. Grill 2 bacon rashers and chop roughly. Grate some cheddar cheese. Top the mushrooms with both the bacon and cheese and place under a preheated grill until the cheese is melting and bubbling hot. Bang into toasted rolls and serve with ketchup and iceberg lettuce.

Chicken

Chicken has done me a great service over the years. A proper roast dinner was the first meal I ever cooked and since then Mrs Chicken and I haven't looked back; I've eaten and cooked loads of it. And for good reason; a good chicken is irresistible. As with other meats (perhaps even more so with chicken) it's all about bagging the best bird you can get. The arguments are well rehearsed: using free-range organic and other well looked after chicken is the key to fuller flavour, and it's humane. The birds get to lead happier lives and you get a meat that's lower in fat, nutritionally superior and way tastier. From the cook's point of view a chicken's a gracious bird – the meat is beautiful when simply cooked but it permits the addition of a huge number of flavours that can take your skills and your palate travelling anywhere. Enjoy…

TALKING CHICKEN BITS

BREAST (OFF THE BONE) Makes for a great simple fast cook (thin it out) and has very low fat content without skin. Cook with care to avoid chewiness or cook with skin for the flavour and then remove if it's an issue. Perfect for stir-fry, skewers, escalope, griddling, schnitzel, pan-fries, casseroles.

WING A tender, juicy, flavoursome and very cheap cut, perfect for sharing and parties (or just pigging out on) – my favourite bit.

THIGH Carries more fat so has deeper flavour and is less likely to dry out than breast meat. It's also cheaper which makes it a top buy. Cook it bone-in (best) or off. Sauté or bake it then get in there with your fingers or whack it into stews and casseroles. Tender and juicy.

BREAST ON THE BONE Cooking on the bone imparts a beautiful juicy sweetness – sear off then slow roast or casserole.

LEG Made up of the thigh and the drumstick, this part of the chicken is great for a really tasty budget feed. Treat it like a small roast or use in casseroles.

DRUMSTICK Ideal for mucky eating. Slather in your choice of marinade, bake, grill or start in the oven then bang on the BBQ for summer eating. Good in stews.

OYSTER A right little gem, tucked under the bird at the end of the leg. It's the tenderest part of the chicken – chef's treat.

CHICKEN LIVERS Trim, season and fry in a little butter and oil. Bang them on salads or griddled bread and use them for pâté.

WHOLE BIRD Roast in the oven or shoot in to a pot-roast with stock, vegetables and seasoning.

GIBLETS Inner bits stored in a plastic bag in some whole birds. Use for stock.

POUSSIN A mini-chicken great for one person. It's low on taste but takes flavours well. Roast, spatchcock, griddle or grill it.

— BUY IT - STASH IT —

Flight time from **STORE TO FRIDGE** shouldn't be more than **3 HOURS MAX**. Bang it into the fridge in the original packaging unless it has giblets inside (it'll say on the label). Remove these at once and keep separately. Store naked chicken, loosely covered, on a plate. **PLACE IT WELL AWAY FROM OTHER FOODS** – especially cooked food. Fresh meat lasts up to **2 DAYS**. Top organic birds from the butcher can last **4 DAYS**. Follow sell-by labels.

CHICKEN COSMETICS

Appearance counts. If buying a whole bird, look for one that's fat, well-rounded, and neatly shaped. Its skin wants to be creamy and pretty uniformly smooth. Avoid anything with tears, marks, stubble or marks from freezer burn. Check the packaging too. It should be unscathed. Press before you buy: a properly stored bird should feel cold. Take it home in separate wrap.

WHAT'S THE BEST BIRD?
Cutting through the jargon

Be canny and work out where the chicken's from and what sort of quality you're getting. It's all about reading the labels and interpreting them (or asking your butcher).

STANDARD These guys have very little room to move. They grow unnaturally fast, and are often loaded with hormones and antibiotics. Stress affects the quality and flavour of the meat. It's cheaper, but cruel? There's no distinctive labelling.

HIGHER WELFARE INDOOR-REARED Means less-intensive rearing with a better environment leading to better life and better flavour.

FREE-RANGE The birds are allowed to roam outdoors and have a longer, more natural life. The label may specify the farm and farmer. It's more expensive.

ORGANIC Same as free-range but fed organic feed so fewer chemicals involved – never a bad thing. If money's tight, consider getting a cheaper cut of this more expensive bird or only eating organic free-range but less often.

CORN-FED Fed on maize, these guys should be clearly labelled and slightly juicer with a more intense flavour, but check where they've come from.

ᴡᴡᴡᴡᴡᴡ *Scare Tactics* ᴡᴡᴡᴡᴡᴡ

Keep it clean and you won't wind up in the emergency room. Wash your hands after handling raw chicken and scrub your utensils to avoid contamination. Chicken should be freshly fragrant, by the way. If the inevitable smell from the wrapping doesn't disappear in seconds, ditch the bird.

FRIENDS AVOCADO, BACON, BLUE CHEESE, CAESAR DRESSING, CHILLI, CORIANDER, CRANBERRY JELLY, CREAM, CRÈME FRAÎCHE, CHICORY, COCONUT MILK, FETA, FISH SAUCE, GARLIC, GINGER, ICEBERG LETTUCE, LEMON, LEMONGRASS, LIME, MARJORAM, MAYO, MUSTARD, OREGANO, OYSTER SAUCE, PAPRIKA, PARMESAN, PEANUT, POTATOES, REDCURRANT JELLY, ROSEMARY, SAGE, SEA SALT, SOY SAUCE, TARRAGON, THYME, TOMATO KETCHUP, WALNUT, WATERCRESS, WINE

CHICKEN NUTRITION

BRILLIANT FOR:

PROTEIN

Builds muscles and cells and helps with repair and general body maintenance.

Tryptophan

An essential amino acid which allows the release of the cheer-you-up happy hormone SEROTONIN

IRON

FOUND IN THE DARK MEAT AND LIVER HELPS CARRY OXYGEN THROUGH the bloodstream, fights anaemia and helps you think straight.

VITAMIN B6

Produces insulin for stability, helps with PMT (*I'm told*) AND PROTECTS AGAINST CARDIOVASCULAR DISEASE.

ZINC

STRENGTHENS THE IMMUNE SYSTEM, helping fight off colds, infections etc.

CALCIUM

WORKS TO STRENGTHEN TEETH AND BONES.

FATTY ACIDS

in the bird help to LOWER CHOLESTEROL, helping your heart out, while the

LACK OF FAT

(in the white meat in particular) makes chicken the popular choice for anyone with health concerns or weight watching.

TRUSSING

Binding a whole chicken's bits together with string means it doesn't flap about during cooking. It holds any stuffing in and neatens it. I don't bother to do it with a smaller bird and many come pre-tied anyway. However, if you're going for a bigger chicken and where presentation matters, it's worth a go.

Spatchcocking

Opening the bird up by cutting out the backbone then griddling or grilling it whole means faster even cooking – it's really easy, try it (p63)

JOINTING

Take a whole chicken and divide it up into its component parts. Ideal for economical eating as it's much cheaper than buying everything separately. Cut into 8 using a sharpened filleting or other good knife with a bit of a flex to it.

1. Place the bird flat on board with the breast facing up and legs towards you.

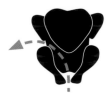

2. Cut through skin between leg and breast following the line of the carcass to keep maximum meat.

3. Push and twist to break leg out of socket.
4. Turn bird on side and cut round the oyster so it stays attached to the leg, taking it all off in one piece.

5. Sit the chicken back up. Find the backbone with your finger and cut along the edge of the left side all along it.
6. Use long, clean slices to follow the shape of the ribcage round and cut the breast meat off neatly including the wing.

7. Remove the wings from the breasts. Snip the tips and discard. Repeat on the other side.

CHICKEN TRICK

Velveting chicken stir-fry Chinese-style like this keeps it tender.
1. Slice skinless breast into strips across the grain.
2. Bang in a bowl with a smooth mix of egg white and cornflour.

3. Add sesame and veg oil to a hot wok to heat. Add meat.
4. Toss and turn on medium/hot flame for 4–5 minutes or till cooked.
5. Use as is or add sauce. Bang on noodles or use with whatever.

APPROXIMATE COOKING TIMES

Here's a very rough idea for chicken cooking times but you'll need to test your meat for doneness – chicken has to be cooked right through (overcooking ruins it).

WHOLE ROAST CHICKEN: 20 minutes per 450g + an extra 20 minutes at 180°C/ Gas 4.

ROAST CHICKEN LEG: 35–40 minutes at 180°C/ Gas 4.

CHICKEN BREAST (BONELESS): pan-fry for 2 minutes each side or until golden then bang in the oven at 180°C/Gas 4 for 8–10 minutes depending on the size of the breast.

DRUMSTICKS: slash, marinade then roast in the oven for 40 minutes at 200°C/Gas 6.

A CHICKEN STOCK (*or three*)

Stock's your best friend. Use it as the base for soups, risottos, sauces, casseroles. Here are a few different ways of making it.

LAST-MINUTE FIX VERSION Mix a good chicken stock cube with boiling water. It won't taste nearly as good as proper homemade stuff and may be salty, so remember that as you're seasoning your dish.

EMERGENCY VERSION Bang a few slashed chicken wings or small joints into a pan with an onion, carrot, a bit of celery, a few peppercorns and some salt. Cover with lots of water then boil for 30 minutes and strain. Discard the bits. Makes a light but very useful stock.

POST-ROAST CHICKEN VERSION Tip the chicken carcass with any spare meat and gravy, an onion, carrot, whatever herbs you have to hand and some seasoning into a large pan with lots of water. Boil then simmer it for an hour. Strain and discard the bits. Chill to use the next day (it lasts 4 days in the fridge) or freeze in small containers for stock shots when cold or in pour-in storage bags. This makes a top stock and a great soup base.

IS IT DONE YET?

Sometimes, timings don't do it. To know for sure whether your chicken's cooked use these methods.

SIGHT TEST

Cut into the meat to check it's white all through (no pink). See if the juices run clear. Put a skewer into the bird at the thickest part and catch any juice that comes out with a teaspoon. Good to go if not pink.

Touch test

Push a metal skewer into the thickest part. Count to 5 and remove. If it's burning to the touch, it's done.

MEAT THERMOMETER NEEDS TO READ...

74°C minimum

A COUPLE OF CLASSIC MARINADES

PIRI-PIRI

Make this classic high-street chicken sauce as hot as you like by playing with the chillies. For a good base, deseed and chop 4 hot red chillies (or keep seeds for heat). Bang in a pan with 4 fat garlic cloves, 1½ tbsp paprika, 1 tsp salt, 1 tsp dried oregano, lemon juice to taste and 6 tbsp oil. Heat very gently for 5 minutes without browning the garlic. Remove. Blitz. Cool. Slap over your chicken.

YOGHURT RUB

Mix a bit of natural yoghurt with harissa paste, garlic, lemon juice, oil, cumin, fresh coriander, cinnamon, salt and pepper. Rub into skinless breasts or chunks for skewers.

BUTTERFLIED GRIDDLED
HERB CHICKEN
WITH ZINGY TOMATO GREEN BEANS

FEEDS 2

Fresh, tasty and quicker than any ready-meal: butterfly your bird for even cooking and griddle it for a BBQ effect all-year-round.

INGREDIENTS

*2 plump boneless, skinless chicken
   breasts*
1 tbsp olive oil
*a handful of torn fresh herbs
   (coriander/oregano/rosemary/
   thyme/marjoram)*
2 garlic cloves, peeled and crushed
salt and pepper
grated zest and juice of 1 lemon
*a few slices of coarse bread, for
   griddling*
*a dollop of hummus
   (shop-bought or homemade, p38)*
ZINGY TOMATO GREEN BEANS
200g fine green beans, trimmed
1 tbsp olive oil
1 garlic clove, peeled and diced
6 cherry tomatoes, halved

**** CASH SAVER ****
Buy and use skinless chicken thigh fillets.
Open them up then roll them out with a
rolling pin. Griddle for a bit longer.

—— CHANGE IT UP ——

For mustard and honey butterflies, marinade
the chicken in a mix of 2 tbsp white wine
vinegar, 1 crushed garlic clove, 2 tsp dried
herbs (oregano/thyme/rosemary) 1 tsp
honey and 3 tsp each of Dijon mustard and
olive oil. Cook as above, adding lemon juice
and sea salt.

PREP Butterfly the chicken: first, take a look at the bottom of the chicken breasts. If they have tenders attached (mini-fillets) slice them off to cook separately. Sit the breasts on a board, smooth sides up. Using a sharp chef's knife held parallel to the board, slice cleanly sideways through the centres of each one but NOT all the way through. Leave a hinge. Open each breast out into one thinner piece like a book. Lay the first butterfly between two pieces of cling film. Flatten it some more by hitting it with the flat of your hand or by rolling and bashing it with a rolling pin. Take care not to rip it. Transfer to a plate. Repeat with the second piece. Add any tenders.

Make the marinade: Mix the oil, herbs, garlic, pepper, lemon zest and half of the juice in a bowl. Tip it over the chicken and rub in. Set aside.

Blanch the beans in a pan of boiling water for 2 minutes or till *al dente* (bite one to test). Tip them into a colander held under running cold water for 30 seconds to fix the colour and texture. Set aside to drain.

COOK Heat a griddle pan till almost smoking hot. Slap the butterflies down. Leave them to cook for 2 minutes, pressing down a bit with your spatula, until golden brown. Flip. Repeat for 2 minutes or until cooked (test with a knife: the flesh should be white, not pink). Remove to a plate. Sprinkle with salt and remaining lemon juice. Griddle the bread on the pan till crisp and marked each side.

Finish the beans: heat the olive oil in a frying pan. Add the diced garlic and cook for a few seconds but don't brown it up. Add the beans, turning, and cook for a minute or two. Add the tomatoes, turning, and cook for a further minute until warmed through.

PLATE Pile the beans and tomato artistically onto your plates. Sit the butterfly at a jaunty angle. Add a dollop of hummus and hot bread. Sit on the sofa and enjoy.

BONUS BITES

HERBED CHICKEN SKEWERS
Chop the non-butterflied meat into bite-sized chunks. Add your marinade. Thread onto metal or pre-soaked wooden skewers. Cook under a hot grill, turning, till white all through and still juicy. Eat on rice or in warmed pittas with salad.

CHICKEN FAJITAS
Thin meat as above before cutting into long thin strips. Add 2 tsp paprika, 1 crushed garlic clove and a squeeze of lemon. Pan-fry quickly before banging into warmed tortillas with guacamole (p75), grated cheddar, sliced red onion and shredded iceberg lettuce.

SCHNITZEL WITH A TWIST

FAST

FEEDS 1

INGREDIENTS

1 large boneless, skinless chicken breast
¾ tbsp olive oil
a knob of butter

TOPPING
1 plump shallot, peeled and diced
2 tsp olive oil
1 tsp chopped sage
15g crumbled blue cheese

COATING
50g plain white flour, seasoned
1 small egg
2 slices of white bread, crusts removed

TIP

Make loads if you've crowds heading round.
Mix and match the topping options.

·········· **TIME SAVER** ··········

Use a jar of panko breadcrumbs instead of
making your own.

—— **CHANGE IT UP** ——

1. For garlic, cream cheese and Parma ham
schnitzel, soften 1–2 tbsp cream cheese in
a bowl. Smear a little over the top of the
thinned meat. Lay on a slice of Parma ham,
smear over the remaining cheese and coat
and cook as before.
2. For banana and ham schnitzel, butterfly
the breast (p51) and lay in a slice of ham and
half a mashed banana. Close it up. Coat and
cook in the pan or fry and bake in the oven
at 200°C/Gas 6.

*These gorgeous hot chicken sandwiches are crisp on the outside and
ooze with a tasty herb and blue cheese centre. If that topping's not to
your taste, head for the garlic cream cheese or Parma ham and banana
options. Plain schnitzel, meanwhile, is a classic fast-food favourite: if
that's what you're after, thin the chicken, skip the topping, coat and fry.*

PREP Thin the chicken breast: Place it between sheets of clingfilm or
greaseproof paper on a board and roll or bash it with a rolling pin
until it's about 3cm thick. Set aside.

Make the topping: fry the shallot very gently in the oil in a small pan over
low heat for a few minutes until soft. Tip it into a bowl. Add the sage and blue
cheese and mix until smooth. Cool for 2 minutes. Spread the mix over the top
of the chicken breast, using your hands to encourage it to stick. Set aside.

Organise the coating: spread the flour over a plate. Crack the egg onto a second
plate and beat with a fork. Roughly tear the bread and blitz it to rough crumbs
in a processor/blender or with a stick blender. Sprinkle onto a third plate.

Very carefully, place the topped chicken in the flour (bottom first). To coat the
top, flick flour over the meat and pat it on to cover the cheese mix. Or turn the
whole thing very carefully. Then, with care, dip it into the egg, flicking again
for a good sticky covering. Finally, sit it in the breadcrumbs, flicking or turning
to coat it completely. Cook it now or chill until you need it.

COOK Preheat the oven to 180°C/Gas 4. Put an ovenproof pan onto
medium/high heat. Add the oil and butter. When it's frothing,
carefully add the schnitzel. Fry for 3 minutes, or until golden. Use a wide
spatula and in one smooth movement turn it carefully. Fry for another
3 minutes (check and adjust the heat to ensure it doesn't burn at any point).
Shove the pan into the oven for 5 minutes to finish off. Remove. Check it's
cooked through (test with a knife). Sprinkle with sea salt.

PLATE Serve with chunks of lemon. Team with a crisp salad and shallow-
fry chips (p78) or spaghetti with easy tomato sauce (p176).

BONUS BITES

CHICKEN FINGERS
Cut the thinned breast into long slices with a sharp chef's knife. Coat in flour, egg and crumbs
as above. Fry in oil and butter till cooked through or for a minute per side before finishing in the
oven at 200°C/Gas 6 till white all through.
CHICKEN KIEV
Slice into the side of the breast to create a pocket. Stuff it with well-chilled garlic butter.
Seal with a couple of toothpicks before coating as above, frying then finishing in the oven
for 15 minutes or until cooked through.

CRISPY CHICKEN WINGS AND DIPS

FAST

FEEDS 6-8

These little beauties are perfect for sharing and dipping. Wings are the sweetest bits of the bird. If you're treating yourself, just reduce the quantities. Choose a cooking style to suit your event: oven-bake, griddle, grill or BBQ.

INGREDIENTS

*900g chicken wings
(whole or pre-butchered)
2–3 tbsp olive oil
a light sprinkling of paprika/smoked
paprika (optional)
salt and pepper*

PREP If you've bought whole wings (still wing-shaped), trim them. Cut off the tips at the end joint with kitchen scissors or a sharp knife at an angle. Discard or use for stock. Find the remaining joint by flexing the wing. Cut cleanly through it at an angle into two. Dry these pieces on kitchen paper, then tip into a large bowl. Coat with the olive oil, sprinkle over the paprika (use it if you're making plain wings) and grind over a little pepper. Chill in the fridge while you make your chosen dip or cook now and enjoy plain.

COOK OVEN: Preheat the oven to 220°C/Gas 7. Bang the wings onto a rack over a baking tray/roasting tin. Cook for 20–30 minutes till golden and crispy. GRIDDLE: Put the griddle onto medium/high heat. Slap the wings (and extractor fan) on. Cook for 10–15 minutes, turning and pressing with a spatula sometimes. Finish under a very hot grill for a few seconds if you like. GRILL: Turn regularly for 10–15 minutes. BBQ: Place the wings directly over medium coals, turning frequently until golden (10–15 minutes). To check for doneness, cut to the bone to make sure there's no redness.

PLATE Lightly salt the wings and pile onto a big plate; serve with dips in bowls and let everyone help themselves.

**** CASH SAVER ****

For a cheap solo or shared meal, pile chicken wings onto bowls of basmati or sticky rice, drizzle with one of the dips below and serve with stir-fried greens.

········· **TIME SAVER** ·········

Prep the wings and the dipping sauces a few hours ahead.

—— **CHANGE IT UP** ——

Marinate the wings in olive oil, lemon juice and rind, crushed garlic and cayenne pepper. Oven-bake as before then toss in chopped parsley/coriander.

DIPS

1 THAI BOUNTY
Mix a 40g piece of grated, creamed coconut with 4 tbsp boiling water till it looks like toothpaste. Mix together with 2 tbsp fish sauce, 2 tbsp soy sauce, 1 tbsp tamarind paste, 3 tsp caster sugar, 1 chopped small red chilli, a 2cm piece of bruised, finely chopped lemongrass and a little fresh coriander.

2 SICHUAN
Deseed and slice 1 large red chilli and thinly slice 2 spring onions. Mix together with 2 crushed garlic cloves, 1 tbsp sesame oil, 3 tbsp low-salt soy sauce, 2 tsp mirin/rice vinegar, ¾ tsp brown sugar and lots of torn fresh coriander. Tip into a food processor or use a stick blender and blitz to a thick liquid.

3 TERIYAKI
Mix together 2 tsp grated fresh ginger, 8 tbsp soy sauce, 3 tbsp Chinese rice wine, 4 tbsp rice vinegar, ½ tbsp caster sugar and a good squeeze of lemon juice.

4 SCORCHING DIJON
Mix together 4 tbsp white balsamic vinegar, 2 tbsp dried oregano, 6 tsp Dijon mustard, 1 chopped red chilli and a pinch each of salt and sugar. Squeeze a little lime juice onto the chicken wings before adding to this dip.

A SIMPLE ROAST
CHICKEN (AND BITS)

HEALTHY   FEEDS 6

INGREDIENTS
THE BIRD
1 x 2–2.2kg good-quality chicken,
    giblets removed
salt and black pepper
1 small eating apple/1 lemon
a small handful of fresh herbs
    (sage/tarragon/rosemary/thyme)
a knob of butter
a squeeze or two of lemon juice
2 tbsp olive oil
a good sprinkling of dried herbs
    (oregano/tarragon/marjoram/
    rosemary/thyme)
5–8 unsmoked streaky bacon rashers
    (or sufficient to cover breast)
250ml chicken stock/water/white wine/
    cider

✴✴✴✴ CASH SAVER ✴✴✴✴

For a cheaper roast for two, bang 2 large
chicken legs or a poussin (small bird) into
an ovenproof frying pan/dish/tin. Add
chopped root veg. Sprinkle with a few dried
herbs, scatter over some sliced garlic and
season. Squeeze over a bit of lemon juice
and drizzle with olive oil before roasting as
above for 40 minutes to 1 hour.

You can't beat a roast bird; it's one of the all time greats. But don't restrict it to weekends – any night can be a roast night. Stuff it the no-fuss way with fruit and herbs, or flavour it up with my sweet sage and onion stuffing. This one multi-tasks: cook it in the bird or in a separate dish so it crisps up (it makes a great meal in its own right).

PREP Remove the chicken from the fridge an hour before cooking so it returns to room temperature. Check the weight to calculate cooking time (p49). Preheat the oven to 180°C/Gas 4.

Sprinkle a little salt and pepper into the cavity, then push the fruit, fresh herbs and butter inside. Larger birds may be sold trussed (legs tied) in which case you'll need to undo it, add the bits and re-truss it. If going for the weekend option, push a few tablespoons of cooled sage and onion stuffing (p56) into the cavity. But don't pack it in as it slows the cooking process. Cook any extra separately in a dish alongside the chicken.

Sit the bird, breast up, in a large roasting tin. Squeeze a little lemon juice over it then brush or drizzle with olive oil. Sprinkle over the dried herbs and a little salt and pepper.

COOK Put the tin into the oven. Watch the top of your bird as it doesn't want to get too brown. A third of the way into the cooking time, remove from the oven. Spoon the juices over the breast. Lay the bacon rashers over the breast in a single layer to cover and protect it. Return to the oven.

Once your calculated cooking time has elapsed, remove the chicken from the oven. Test for doneness (p49). Transfer to a plate and leave to rest in a warm place for 10–15 minutes. To make the gravy: place the tin directly onto the hob. Add stock or your liquid of choice to the juices along with those from the chicken plate. Stir and scrape the mix with a wooden spoon. Let it boil to reduce a bit. When you're happy with the consistency, add lemon juice and taste for seasoning.

PLATE Cut any trussing string, sharpen your steel and carve the chicken at the table, sharing out the white and dark meat, crisp bacon and stuffing, if using. Bang your chosen veg into bowls and gravy into a jug. Fight over the wishbone and enjoy…

SWEET SAGE AND ONION STUFFING

Blitz 75g crustless white bread in a processor for 2 seconds to make crumbs. Tip them into a bowl with the grated zest of ½ lemon and 4 chopped sage leaves. Slit 3 pork and apple sausages along their sides. Cut the meat into rough chunks (discarding the skins). Add to the bowl. Fry a finely diced medium onion in 1 tbsp butter on medium heat until soft. Mix evenly into the stuffing with 1 tbsp brandy/cider. Spoon into an 18 x 12cm greased ovenproof dish. Bake for 30–40 minutes (put it in the oven 20 minutes before the bird is due to come out) or till crisping up and browning on top. Let it rest for 5 minutes. Spoon or carve it out.

A GREEN VEGETABLE PLATE

Put a steamer of water on to boil or set a colander or sieve into the top of a saucepan of boiling water. Break a head or two of broccoli into florets, trim the ends off a handful of green beans and wash both vegetables well. Put the broccoli in the steamer and cook for 5 minutes, then add the beans and cook for a further 5 minutes. Drain, then chuck into a dish – adding salt, butter and lemon juice if you like.

BITS

ROAST POTATOES

Parboil 1.5kg peeled floury white potatoes for 10 minutes. Drain. Bang them back into the pan. Shuffle over the heat for a few seconds to dry and ruffle their edges for a crisper finish. Add to the tin with the bird along with a pinch of salt and ½ lemon, cut into chunks. You may need a drop more oil. While the chicken is resting, turn the oven up to 220ºC/Gas 7 and bang the spuds back in to cook for a further 10–15 minutes, till golden and crispy.

A ROAST ROOT VEGETABLE PLATE

Peel and chop a mix of carrots/parsnips/ sweet potato/butternut squash/beetroot into chunks. Cut 2 red/white onions into quarters and slice the tops off 2 heads of garlic. Drizzle the lot in olive oil, salt, lemon juice and sprinkle over a pinch dried oregano. Bang onto a baking tray to roast 20 minutes before the bird comes out. Cook for another 10–15 minutes or till soft and starting to caramelise.

FAST TANDOORI-STYLE ROAST WITH ONIONS

FEEDS 4

INGREDIENTS

1 x 1.3kg chicken
3 large onions, peeled and thinly sliced
300ml chicken stock (p49)
sea salt
a handful of coriander leaves, torn
MARINADE
175ml natural yoghurt
5 garlic cloves, crushed
50g fresh ginger, peeled and grated
2 tbsp paprika
2 tbsp lemon juice
2 tbsp groundnut/vegetable/
    sunflower oil
1 tsp garam masala
1 tsp chilli powder/cayenne pepper
1 tsp ground turmeric
1 tsp ground cumin
½ tsp cinnamon
1 tbsp tomato purée/ketchup
50g cheddar, grated
½ tsp black pepper
1 tsp salt

TIP

Chicken wings, skinless breasts, chopped
breast meat (for skewers), drumsticks,
poussins and even lamb chops taste amazing
in this marinade: just adjust your cooking
method and timings to suit the ingredient.

·········· TIME SAVER ··········
In place of the spices listed, blend 4 tbsp
good tandoori/tikka paste with the yoghurt,
lemon juice, cheddar, garlic and leave to
marinate as above.

Roast chicken goes to Bollywood – and why not? Eat as it is or make this one the star of a curry banquet.

PREP Mix the marinade ingredients together in a bowl. Spoon and rub over the chicken so it's completely coated. Chill on a plate for a few hours, or overnight. Return to room temperature before cooking.

COOK Preheat the oven to 220°C/Gas 7. Put the chicken in a roasting tin. Surround with the onions and add half of the stock. Cook for 20 minutes. Add remaining stock and baste the chicken. Cook for a further 20 minutes before checking for doneness (p49). Give it longer if you need to.

PLATE Leave to rest on a plate for 10 minutes. Sprinkle with sea salt. Carve or tear the bird onto plates, pile on the onions and fresh coriander. Enjoy with honey mint raita (p130), lemon chunks, mango chutney, naan bread (p130), rice and crisp shredded lettuce.

BONUS BITES

SUMMER ROAST CHICKEN ON COUSCOUS WITH ROASTED VEGETABLES AND FETA CHEESE
Mix 50g soft butter with finely chopped mint, crushed garlic and lemon rind. Taking a whole chicken, gently release the skin over the breast, working your fingers in from the edge of the cavity to create space. Spread the butter over the top of the chicken then pull the skin back into place over it. Drizzle with oil. Roast in an oven preheated to 180°C/Gas 4 for 20 minutes per 450g plus an extra 20 minutes until cooked. Leave till warm. Carve or chop into pieces. Throw onto a plate of cooled couscous with crumbled feta, roasted root vegetables and a dressing of yoghurt and crushed garlic.

ROAST POUSSIN IN WINE, CREAM & TARRAGON
Preheat the oven to 190°C/Gas 5. Mix 50g soft butter with a few handfuls of finely chopped tarragon and use to stuff and coat the outsides of 2 poussins. Roast in a tin with 1 large glass of white wine for 30–40 minutes until tender. Remove. Stir a bit more tarragon, 4 tbsp crème fraîche and 1 tsp mustard into the gravy and bring to the boil and stir. Pour over the birds.

ROAST CHICKEN LEFTOVERS

Remember, there's more to life than a plain cold chicken sandwich (although it is good). Check out these other tasty ways with leftover roast chicken.

1 ROAST CHICKEN AND STUFFING SANDWICH

Spread slices of good bread with mayo/butter, cranberry sauce, sliced chicken and cold cooked stuffing. Classic.

2 TANDOORI WRAP

Fry off cooked potato chunks in diced shallot, butter, a pinch or two of curry powder, lemon juice and a bit of torn coriander. Cool. Pile into warmed wraps with cold tandoori chicken, yoghurt mixed with crushed garlic, cucumber batons, thinly sliced red onion and tomato, mango chutney and more fresh coriander.

3 CHICKEN AND VEGETABLE SOUP

Make a homemade stock (p49). Boil then reduce to a simmer. Add finely diced carrot, sliced green or broad beans and chopped asparagus. Simmer until tender. Add a little finely shredded cold chicken. Season to taste with salt, pepper, lemon juice and scatter over finely chopped parsley or tarragon to finish.

4 CHICKEN RISOTTO

Check out page 197 for one of the best leftover meals ever.

5 SHREDDED CHICKEN AND SPICY SAUCE

Shred 550g cold chicken or as much as you have with two forks. Peel, halve, deseed and cut ¼ of a cucumber into matchsticks. Slice 4 spring onions thinly lengthways. Finely dice a chilli. Cook, drain and cool 2 nests of thin egg noodles (following the packet instructions). Toss in a few drops of oil. SAUCE: mix 2 tbsp tahini and 2 tbsp water till smooth. Stir in 2 tsp sesame oil, 2 tsp chilli oil, 1 tsp red wine vinegar, 2 crushed garlic cloves, 2 cm finely grated ginger, 2 tsp caster sugar and a pinch of salt. Pile the chicken, onions, cucumber and chilli over the noodles and drizzle over the sauce. A great lunch box.

SAUTÉED CHICKEN THIGHS

FEEDS 2

INGREDIENTS

4 chicken thighs, bone in, skin on
5–6 medium new potatoes, washed
2 shallots
2 tbsp olive oil
a bit of butter
a small handful of fresh tarragon
*   leaves*
50ml white wine or Noilly Prat
200ml double cream/crème fraîche
1 tsp Dijon/English mustard
salt and pepper
a good squeeze of lemon juice

—— BONUS BITES ——

ROSEMARY BAKED GARLIC THIGHS
Sit the thighs in a roasting tin. Slip half a
garlic clove under each one with a bit of
fresh rosemary if available. Sprinkle with
dried oregano/thyme/rosemary. Squeeze
juice of ½ a lemon over the top. Sprinkle
with sea salt. Chuck chunks of lemon into
the tin. Bake at 220ºC/Gas 7 for 20–30
minutes until crisp and golden.

STICKY CHINESE STYLE THIGHS
Slash boneless thighs in a few places with
a sharp knife. Marinade for a few hours or
overnight in a mix of 2 tbsp hoisin sauce,
1 tbsp soy, 1 tbsp sugar/honey, 2 spring
onions, 1 crushed garlic clove and a chunk
of fresh ginger, finely grated. Bake as above
but for less time as boneless or grill for 4–5
minutes per side till cooked through.

········ TIME SAVER ········

No time for a marinade or sauce? Toss
chicken thighs in oil, salt, and paprika and
cook as per rosemary baked garlic thighs for
20–30 minutes. Sprinkle with a handful of
chopped flat-leaf parsley mixed with 1 tsp
grated lemon rind, 1 diced garlic clove and
sea salt.

Take a classic French dish, whack in some potatoes and you've got yourself a cracking meal-in-one. The chicken/tarragon partnership is a winner and this one is just beautiful…

PREP Blot the chicken thighs on kitchen paper. Leave them to return to room temperature. Using a sharp vegetable knife, cut the potatoes into 2cm chunks. Peel and dice the shallots.

COOK Heat a heavy-bottomed frying or sauté pan. Add the oil and butter. When it's hot and bubbling, place the thighs in the pan, skin-side down to brown and crisp. They should sizzle as they hit the oil. Give them 5 minutes or until good and golden.

Turn the chicken over using tongs. Add the potato chunks and half of the tarragon, tearing the leaves. Put a lid on the pan and leave to cook through on a medium/low heat for 15 minutes.

Just before the 15 minutes are up, preheat the grill. Check the chicken is white all through (give it another minute or two if needed). Remove from the pan and slap under the grill to crisp the skin for a minute or two. Remove.

Meantime, drain the majority of the fat from the pan, leaving the potatoes in there. Add the shallot and the wine and turn the heat up slightly. Cook for 2 minutes. Add the cream/crème fraîche, mustard and the rest of the torn tarragon. Let it bubble until it reduces by a third and thickens slightly. Taste it and season with salt, pepper and lemon juice. Return the chicken to the pan for a minute so it starts to soak up the gorgeous sauce.

PLATE Arrange the chicken bits on the plates with the potatoes neatly on either side. Spoon the sauce over the top. Eat with a sharply dressed green salad.

COQ AU VIN

FEEDS 4

INGREDIENTS

1 medium/large chicken
150g thick streaky bacon/pancetta
1 large onion
12 baby/2 large carrots
12 small mushrooms
1–2 tbsp oil
40g butter
8–12 shallots, peeled
salt and black pepper
1 petal from a star anise
3 fat garlic cloves, peeled and crushed
1 bay leaf
a small handful of fresh tarragon leaves
1 tbsp flour
300ml good red wine
2 tbsp brandy or a glug of balsamic
    vinegar
700ml chicken stock (p49)
2–3 tbsp water
a small pinch of sugar
a good handful of flat-leaf parsley,
    finely chopped

TIP
If you prefer oven cooking to cooking on the hob, bang this in the oven at 180°C/Gas 4 for 45 minutes after adding the chicken stock.

—— CHANGE IT UP ——
For a thicker sauce, spoon the veg and bits out of the cooked coq and into a dish. Boil the sauce, stirring until it thickens to your taste and reduces a bit. Taste and season before returning the bits to the pan.

········ TIME SAVER ········
If you don't fancy having a go at jointing your own chicken or just want to save a little time, buy a mix of breasts, thighs and drumsticks instead.

Raise your game and joint a whole bird. It's satisfying to do and saves cash. Make sure to use a nice wine for the best result in this meltingly lovely classic French chicken dish.

PREP Remove the chicken from the fridge. Cut it into joints (p48) and return to room temperature. Cut the bacon into thick strips. Peel and thickly slice the onion. Peel and chop large carrots if using (leave small ones whole). Brush the mushrooms.

COOK Heat the oil and two-thirds of the butter in a large, shallow casserole dish. Chuck in the bacon and cook for 5 minutes or so, turning, so it releases fat and browns. Remove with a slotted spoon and set aside. Add half the shallots. Fry for 5 minutes, turning or until just colouring all over. Remove and set aside. The fat in the pan will be brown and sticky.

Season the bits of chicken well. Bang them skin-side down into the hot fat in a single layer. Fry until just starting to brown (and flavour) well. Turn. Reduce the heat slightly. Cook for another 4–5 minutes. Remove.

Add the carrot, onion and star anise to the pan. Fry on a low heat, stirring, until the onion is soft, about 5–10 minutes. Discard the star anise. Add the garlic, browned shallots, chicken, bacon, bay and tarragon. Sprinkle with flour and cook for 2 minutes before adding the wine and brandy/balsamic. Increase the heat and let it bubble for a minute then add enough chicken stock to cover the chicken but not drown it. Boil for a second then reduce to a simmer and cook very slowly for 30–40 minutes, or until the meat is tender.

Meantime, melt the remaining butter with a little water and sugar on low heat. Add the remaining shallots. Simmer until soft and glazed (check they don't dry out), add the mushrooms and cook for another minute. Add the mix to the casserole for the final 10 minutes of cooking.

PLATE Sprinkle with parsley, bang the pan on the table and serve with parsley and lemon potatoes. Or spoon into big shallow pasta dishes with freshly cooked pasta (like tagliatelle) tossed in butter and seasoned.

TO GO WITH

PARSLEY AND LEMON POTATOES
Peel and halve 1.3kg floury potatoes and chuck into cold water. Add a pinch of salt, bring to the boil and cook until tender (check after 10 minutes). Drain and tip them back into the pan. Add 2 tsp butter, a squeeze of lemon juice and a handful of chopped parsley and season with salt and pepper.

CHICKEN POT PIE

FEEDS 4

INGREDIENTS

PIE BASE
900g skinless, boneless chicken
    (a mix of thighs and breasts)
a pinch of dried tarragon
2½ tbsp flour
salt and pepper
25g butter
1–2 tbsp olive oil
3 bacon rashers, cut into strips
3 good pork and apple sausages,
    roughly chopped
200g button mushrooms
4 garlic cloves, peeled and crushed
2 onions, peeled and sliced
450ml white wine
450ml chicken stock (p49)
a small handful of fresh tarragon leaves
½–1 tsp Dijon mustard
a squeeze of lemon juice
1 tsp honey (optional)
1 x quick flaky pastry (p199)
    or 1 x 500g packet puff pastry
1 egg beaten with a little water,
    for glazing
1 tbsp poppy/black onion seeds
    (optional)

✶✶✶✶ CASH SAVER ✶✶✶✶

Use sliced carrots or a few butter
beans in place of some of the chicken.

—— CHANGE IT UP ——

1. Substitute red wine for white and use
thyme or rosemary instead of tarragon.
2. Use mini-meatballs instead of sausages.
Fry 1 diced shallot in butter till soft. Mix
into 180g sausage meat with grated lemon
zest, salt, pepper and a pinch of dried or
fresh herbs. Roll and fry in butter before
adding to the pie and cooking as before.

Part of the point of a pie is that it tastes different every time you make it. Try this one from scratch topped with your own flaky pastry; or use what's left over from your coq au vin and slap a crisp, buttery lid on top.

PREP Dice the chicken into large bite-sized bits. Slap into a bowl with the dried tarragon, 1½ tablespoons of the flour and a bit of salt and pepper. Stir to coat.

COOK Heat the butter and olive oil in a wide pan or casserole. Add the bacon. Cook till crisp. Remove and set aside. Add the chicken without crowding. Fry and turn for 5 minutes or so until browned. Remove and set aside. Repeat in batches. Quickly fry the bits of sausage to brown them up. Set aside.

Add more butter if needed. Add the mushrooms and a crushed garlic clove and fry for 3–4 minutes. Set aside. Add the onions and the remaining garlic. Fry gently till soft. Add the remaining flour, stirring well for a minute. Don't let it burn. Pour in the wine and increase the heat. Stir as it bubbles and thickens.

Add half the stock, the tarragon, chicken, bacon and mushrooms. Simmer for 3 minutes. Add more stock. You want enough liquid to cover the chicken plus a bit (so your pie will have a gravy) but without drowning it. Cover and simmer on a low heat for 15 minutes. Taste the sauce. Add Dijon mustard and lemon juice to sharpen, plus a dab of honey if you like. Set aside to cool. Preheat the oven to 220°C/Gas 7. Transfer the cooled chicken mix to a 28 x 22 x 7cm ovenproof dish. Include enough of the gravy to cover the chicken well. Save any extra for pouring gravy.

Roll your chosen pastry out on a lightly floured board to a size that's larger than the top of your dish. Slip a rolling pin underneath and lift it over the pie. Sit it down. Crimp the edges to make it seal and fit. Re-roll any extra, and cut out leaves or shapes if you like. Cut a slit in the centre of the pie to release steam. Brush with egg wash. Stick on your leaves on and scatter over seeds if using. Sit on a baking tray and cook for 20 minutes. Reduce the heat to 180°C/Gas 4 and cook for another 20–30 minutes, until golden brown and bubbling.

PLATE Serve with gravy and creamy mash with shredded blanched green cabbage tossed in butter, crushed garlic and lemon juice.

SPATCHCOCK
AND SIDES

HEALTHY

FEEDS 2-3

A posh way with a squashed chicken; it tastes bloody good though. Try this with piri-piri sauce (p49) if you like it spicier...

INGREDIENTS

*1 x 1.2kg small chicken
(or 1 poussin per person)
2 tbsp olive oil
juice of 1 lemon, plus extra for serving
2 tsp paprika
a good sprinkling of dried oregano
sea salt and pepper*

TIP
Put your prepped spatchcocked bird on a baking tray. Oven-cook for 30–40 minutes or grill/BBQ for 15 minutes per side.

PREP Sit the bird on a board, breast up. Cut any string away. Turn it upside down with the legs facing you. Have a pair of kitchen scissors or poultry shears ready.

Run your fingers along the backbone of your chicken/poussin. Place the open scissors, one blade into the cavity, the other on top of the bird and cut slowly down the right of the spine – alongside it, not through it – and then down the left. Remove the spine.

Turn your bird breast up. Hold on to the legs and pull it open. Now place the heels of each hand on the top and push down slowly but forcibly. You should hear a crack as the whole thing flattens. Repeat with any remaining birds.

Brush the bird/birds with a mix of olive oil and lemon juice. Sprinkle with the paprika and dried oregano and season. Leave for 30 minutes or chill for a few hours until needed (remembering to return your bird/birds to room temperature before cooking).

COOK Heat a griddle pan. Preheat the oven to 200°C/Gas 6.

Bang the bird/birds breast side down in the pan. For chicken, cook for 10 minutes. Press down lightly with a spatula occasionally. Turn and repeat for 5 minutes. For poussin, cook for 5 minutes per side.

Transfer to a baking tray and finish in the oven for 10 minutes or till cooked through. Check and test (p49) – it's size-dependent. Don't over-cook. Leave to rest for 5 minutes.

PLATE Sit the bird/birds on a plate and pull apart with your fingers or cut with clean scissors or shears. Sprinkle with salt and squeeze over a bit more lemon juice. Enjoy with chips, mayo, ketchup and a green salad or treat yourself to spatchcock sides: sweet and sour slaw, spiced potato wedges, baked potatoes with bacon and sour cream and mango salsa.

TURN OVER
FOR SIDES

SWEET AND SOUR SLAW

Place half a head of crisp white cabbage on a board. Cut into long, thin shreds with a sharp chef's knife then tip into a bowl. Roughly grate 2 carrots and mix into the cabbage with a fork. Put 175g good mayonnaise (p153), 2½ tbsp white wine vinegar, 1 tbsp caster sugar in a small bowl, season and stir to combine. Tip into the slaw and mix well.

SPICED POTATO WEDGES

Preheat the oven to 220°C/Gas 7. Using a sharp knife, cut 900g floury spuds into quarters or sixths lengthways (size-dependent). Dry them off on kitchen paper and throw them into a freezer bag or bowl. Add 2 tbsp olive oil, 2 tsp ground paprika and a little salt and pepper and shake or turn. Arrange the wedges in a single layer on a baking sheet and bake for 30–40 minutes, until crisp and cooked through.

BAKED POTATOES WITH BACON AND SOUR CREAM

Preheat the oven to 200°C/Gas 6. Scrub and dry 4 baking potatoes, then prick them with a fork or stick metal skewers through to speed up the cooking time. For crisp skins, rub them with oil and roll in salt. For soft skins, wrap naked in foil. Bake for 1 hour or till tender. Meantime, fry or grill 4 streaky bacon rashers for 5 minutes or till crisp. Drain on kitchen paper and cut into small pieces. Punch, squeeze or cut the cooked spuds across to open. Add a little butter and seasoning and top with 150ml sour cream, the bacon pieces and a few bits of fresh dill/snipped chives/spring onion tops.

MANGO SALSA

Take a large mango: upend it on a board and, holding firmly, slice down each side of the large central flat stone, getting as close to it as you can. Sit each halved section flesh up on the board and score horizontally and vertically without cutting the bottom skin (it should look a bit like graph paper). Now turn each half inside out, cut the dice from the skin and tip into a bowl. Add 1–2 red chillies, 1 diced red onion, 1–2 tbsp lime juice and a handful of chopped coriander leaves. Mix well and season to taste.

SLOW-ROAST
CHICKEN BREAST
WITH MUSHROOM CAPPUCCINO SAUCE

FEEDS 2

INGREDIENTS

a drizzle of olive oil
a knob of butter
2 good skin-on chicken breasts
    (preferably on the bone),
    at room temperature
sea salt and pepper
a squeeze of lemon juice
MUSHROOM STOCK
25g dried mushrooms
    (mixed/porcini/shiitake)
a handful of fresh button mushrooms,
    sliced
4 garlic cloves, peeled and bashed/
    crushed
1 onion, peeled and halved
2 carrots, halved
½ tsp peppercorns
a few sprigs of fresh herbs
    (rosemary/tarragon/sage)
2 tbsp black coffee
1 litre water
SAUCE
1 litre good chicken stock (p49)
1 tbsp sherry/Madeira (optional)
1 litre double cream
a few tarragon/thyme leaves
a squeeze of lemon juice

TIP

This sauce is also great with griddled steak.

········ **TIME SAVER** ········

For a faster but still tender pan-fried
breast, bash boneless breasts until half their
thickness. Pan-fry skin-side down for 2
minutes. Turn and sear for another minute.
Bang into a preheated oven in the pan or
on a baking tray at 180°C/Gas 4 and test
after 10 minutes. Serve with the mushroom
sauce made up in advance or with hot mixed
mushrooms (p25).

*Time to get sophisticated: dress to impress. A slow roast makes for the
most tender bird and the sauce is silky rich. You'll be winning hearts
with this one. Make the sauce a day ahead and reheat if it suits you.*

PREP MUSHROOM STOCK: Tip all the ingredients into a medium pan.
Bring to the boil then simmer for 20–30 minutes. Sit a sieve over a
large bowl. Tip the mix in, pressing with a wooden spoon to get the liquid (not
solids) through. Discard the bits.

Pour the mushroom stock into a pan. Add the chicken stock and optional
sherry/Madeira. Bring it to a good boil. Keep it rolling on a high heat until the
liquid has hugely reduced. You want about 100ml of black sticky liquid (this
can take 20 minutes plus, but watch it). Transfer to a large pan. Add the cream.
Put it on the heat and bring to the boil (it will bubble up). Let it bubble for 5
minutes or until it thickens a bit to look like thin custard. Add the chopped
tarragon/thyme leaves, a squeeze of lemon juice and season with salt and
pepper. Set aside or chill till needed.

COOK Preheat the oven to 140°C/Gas 1. Put an ovenproof pan on
medium/high heat. Add the oil and butter. Put both chicken bits
in, skin-side down, for 2–3 minutes to get a good colour. Turn the breasts skin
over and spoon the oil and butter over the top to coat. Slap the pan in the oven
to slow cook till done, basting the juices over with a spoon a few times to keep
it all juicy. Test for doneness (p49) after 20 minutes (though bear in mind it
can take up to 30 and meat on the bone takes longer). Let it rest for 4 minutes.
Season with sea salt and squeeze over lemon to taste. Warm the sauce.

PLATE Place the breasts on the plate then spoon the warmed sauce over.
Serve with bread to soak up the sauce and a sharply dressed green
salad, or go for shallow-fry chips (p78) and crunchy green beans (p87).

BEEF

Beef and me go way back: steaks, roasts, cottage pies, marrow roasted up and straight from the bone, beef raw and naked as carpaccio – you name it, I've cooked and eaten it. I guess it's in the blood, coming as I do from a farming family. The cow is a magnificent beast and beef's a quintessentially British meat. Treat it with respect and nothing beats it. This big, bold ingredient is a pleasure to cook. From that moment when you catch your butcher's eye across the counter and you both know it's a case of beef love (and maybe the start of a very special retail relationship), to serving up the finished dish to family and friends. Get your skills right and it's all good.

WHICH COW FOR NOW?

For fast suppers go for steaks...

FILLET Extra tender, delicate flavour, no fat and expensive. Pan-fry/fast roast.

SIRLOIN Tender, tasty and fringed with fat – a great regular choice. Pan-fry/griddle/BBQ/skewer.

RUMP Intense flavour, great texture and cheaper. Loves rubs and marinades. Grill/griddle/stir-fry/skewer/mince.

SKIRT Cheap. Needs marinades and careful cooking but very tasty.

For Sunday roasts (or mid-week treats) go for joints...

SIRLOIN A top choice. Expensive but delicious. On the bone is sweeter.

PRIME RIB A great choice roast with a good price and a rich taste. On the bone is sweeter and cheaper.

TOPSIDE Needs cooking at a low temperature and with a good fat layer, but much cheaper.

For anyday budget pot roasts go for cheaper joints...

TOPSIDE/TOP RUMP/SILVERSIDE Tenderise lean cuts with long slow roasting in stock with vegetables.

For casseroles, braises, pies, stews and mince go for cheaper cuts...

CHUCK/BLADE/SHIN Sear then cook slowly at low temperatures with vegetables and stock.

FLANK/SKIRT/BRISKET Mince up for burgers, bolognaise, meatloaf, meatballs, kofta.

For stock, go for bones...

BOUGHT IT

TAKE OFF ANY OUTER WRAPPING AND STORE ON A PLATE, COVERED LOOSELY, **AWAY FROM COOKED STUFF.**

MEAT LASTS 3-5 DAYS IN THE FRIDGE.

COOK MINCE WITHIN 24 HOURS.

FREEZE FRESH MEAT IMMEDIATELY.

BEEF STOCK
Preheat the oven to 220°C/ Gas 7. Put 1.5kg marrow/shin bones in the sink and cover with cold water. Add 4 tsp salt and soak for 10 minutes. Drain well, blot dry and shove in a roasting tray. Drizzle with 1 tbsp oil. Bang into the oven and cook for 30 minutes. Add 1 chopped carrot, 1 quartered onion, 1 chopped stick celery and 1 halved garlic bulb to the tray and cook for another 20 minutes. Tip into a stock pan, add 5 peppercorns, 2 cloves, ½ tsp tomato purée and a bouquet garni (p19) and cover with water. Simmer very gently for 5 hours, checking and skimming off the fat as you go. Strain through a strainer or muslin-lined colander, cool and chill overnight. Remove the solidified fat on top to finish. Keep chilled in the fridge for up to 3 days or freeze in ice cube trays or freezer bags.

WHAT TO LOOK FOR

Butchers love a bit of chat and will tell you what they know, so never be intimidated – get in there. If you're not sure what you want or can't see what you need, just ask. Those big fridges at the back of the shop will be full of meat, often the more unusual cuts. Go with a plan and see what's looking good or buy to budget and ask them to recommend. When I'm buying beef here's what I'm looking for...

BREED AND SOURCE OF BEEF

Butchers (and best supermarkets) often stock locally reared beef and will label or advertise the breed. I love the rich flavour of Aberdeen Angus and Hereford but these meats are much more expensive. So treat yourself when you can or get a cheaper cut of that meat. Otherwise, use the rules and use your judgement. A meat that's local will usually have come from a happier cow, by the way. I don't fuss too much about organic but I'd rather not eat meat that's clocked up air miles.

BONES

Are essential for stocks and the butcher will often hand them out for free. It's likely he or she will only have them in on butchering/delivery days so check when that is or go in and order some specially.

MINCE

If buying mince from a butcher check that it's freshly made as it spoils quickly. Better to buy the right cut (see opposite), mince your own and even mix them up for great flavour.

COLOUR OF MEAT

Don't just point at a joint or gaze at the top. Ask to look at the side of the meat so you can judge the colour. You want a deep red with a network or marbling of creamy white fat throughout. It's an indicator of quality, a tender juiciness and flavour to come. If it looks grey, slimy or a uniform bright red colour then get out of there. The fat should be creamy white.

SUPERMARKETS

Choose one with a butchery counter if you can so you can get into conversation and see the meat properly. If you're just grabbing a steak or joint off the shelf, no problem, just use the rules, take a bit of time to weigh up the options and use your skill-set to cook it right.

AGE OF MEAT
Hanging meat over time matures the flavour. The majority is wet-hung (vac packed) to speed the process so it's cheaper. Dry-aged meat is hung naturally for a fuller flavour and tenderness but as it takes longer it's a more expensive meat. Well-hung is darker, often purple and will taste amazing – your choice.

How much?
If you don't know how much of a meat to buy, tell your butcher 'I'm cooking for so many...' and he'll tell you what you need. If the steaks on display are too big, ask for a smaller one and they'll cut it for you and you can specify size. Very small roasting joints shrink, so get a bigger one than you need and be creative with your leftovers.

BEEF ACTION - HOW TO DEAL WITH IT

BARDING tying a bit of pork fat to the top of a lean beef joint so it doesn't dry out – use string

BASTING spooning the hot oils, juices, sauces back over the meat during cooking

CUTTING ACROSS THE GRAIN slicing beef the right way to keep it tender

POUNDING using a meat hammer or improvising with a rolling pin/clean bottle to thin and tenderise

RESTING after cooking means beef relaxes and tenderises – even steaks need it

SALTING adding salt at the last minute to steaks to draw out juices and flavour

TEMPERING getting beef to room temperature before cooking so it cooks evenly

TRIMMING using a filleting, a chef's or your sharpest knife to trim exterior fat and membrane

COOKING TIMES FOR YOUR STEAK
A ROUGH GUIDE

It's dependent on type of cut, thickness and heat so this is approximate.
For a steak that's 2.5 cm thick and at room temperature:

RARE
1–2 minutes

MEDIUM
3 minutes

MEDIUM-RARE
2–2 ½ minutes

WELL-DONE
4 minutes

COW TRICK

Press your steak to judge how well cooked it is. Here's how to judge.

Hold out a relaxed hand. Press the fleshy bump under your thumb. **RARE** steak feels like this.

 Bring the tips of the thumb and first finger together. Now press the fleshy bump under your thumb again. **MEDIUM-RARE** feels like this.

Touch the thumb and middle finger for **MEDIUM.**

 Thumb and little finger is **WELL-DONE.**

MOO-TRITION
BRILLIANT FOR:

PROTEIN
BUILDS MUSCLE & BODY STRENGTH

ZINC
BOOSTS IMMUNE SYSTEM, HEALS WOUNDS, BOOSTS SKIN & HAIR

IRON
helps carry oxygen to all body cells & muscles to fight fatigue; keeps you sharp & focused; eat with vitamin c rich foods to beat anaemia

Phosphorus
STRONGER TEETH & BONES

VITAMIN B12
attacks anaemia and helps central nervous system.

OMEGA 3S
FOUND IN GRASS-FED BEEF AIDS BRAIN FUNCTION

FAT EQUALS FLAVOUR
BUT TRIM IF IT MATTERS; USE TOPSIDE, FILLET AND RUMP, MINCE-YOUR-OWN. GRIDDLE, GRILL OR ROAST ON A RACK FOR LOWER FAT.

COOKING TIMES FOR YOUR ROAST

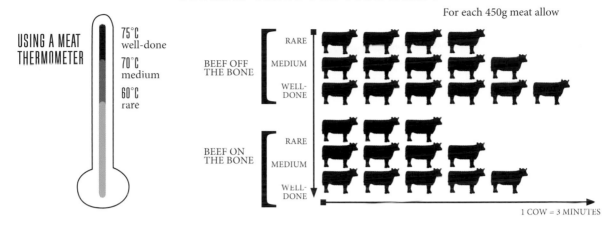

USING A MEAT THERMOMETER

75°C well-done
70°C medium
60°C rare

For each 450g meat allow

BEEF OFF THE BONE
RARE
MEDIUM
WELL-DONE

BEEF ON THE BONE
RARE
MEDIUM
WELL-DONE

1 COW = 3 MINUTES

WAYS WITH STEAK

QUICK PASTES

Blast a mix of fresh and dried herbs with spices and just enough liquid (maybe oil, lemon/orange juice, wine or vinegar, ketchup, mustard, soy or Worcester sauce) for a thick paste. A bit of crushed garlic and fresh ginger's also good. Crush with pestle and mortar or mix by hand. Spread onto your steak.

fast rubs

Bang a mix of dried herbs and spices together. Coat steaks or roasts (rub in or sprinkle). Leave for 20 minutes as the beef draws the essential oils and flavours into itself. Experiment with your choice of black pepper, chilli powder, mustard powder, ground ginger, garlic powder or crushed fresh cumin, cinnamon, smoked or hot paprika, cayenne, coriander, dried thyme, rosemary, oregano, marjoram, tarragon, a little sugar (too much burns).

SIMPLE MARINADES

Slap an easy mix of beef-loving herbs, spices and liquids together. Sit smaller steaks on a non-metallic dish, roll them in the mix. Leave for 30 minutes. To cook: blot/dry the marinade off or the beef won't sear/flavour well. Save surplus marinade to boil up fiercely for a sauce if you want to. Marinades are brilliant for griddling/bbqs.

FRIENDS

ANCHOVY ESSENCE, BALSAMIC VINEGAR, BEER, BEETROOT, CAPERS, CABBAGE, CAYENNE, CHEESE, CHILLI, CINNAMON, COFFEE, COCONUT MILK, EGGS, FISH SAUCE, GARLIC, GINGER, GOAT'S CHEESE, GUINNESS, HORSERADISH, KETCHUP, LEMON JUICE, MADERIA, MUSHROOM, MUSTARD, ONION, ONION RINGS, ORANGE ZEST, OYSTER SAUCE, PAPRIKA, PEANUTS, PORK, POTATOES, RED WINE, RED WINE VINEGAR, ROCKET, ROSEMARY, STAR ANISE, TABASCO SAUCE, TARRAGON, TERIYAKI SAUCE, THYME, TOMATO, SOY SAUCE, WALNUTS, WATERCRESS, WORCESTER SAUCE

BEEF FAJITAS
HARISSA-STYLE

HEALTHY FAST FEEDS 2

Perfect for when you're just back from work or the gym, these fajitas are packed full of lean protein, are fast to make and don't skimp on flavour. Cut the steak across the grain for a tender eat and don't hold back on the extras. Bang up the quantities if you've got loads of people coming round.

INGREDIENTS

2 x 140g rump steaks
salt
4–6 tortilla wraps, shop-bought or
    homemade (see overleaf)

MARINADE
1½ tsp red harissa paste
½ tsp hot smoked paprika
1 tsp dried oregano
2 tbsp olive oil

EXTRAS
sour cream
guacamole (see overleaf)
tomato salsa (see overleaf)
grated cheddar
shredded iceberg lettuce

TIP
If you can't get hold of sour cream, add 1 tbsp lemon juice to a 300ml tub of double cream, leave for 1 hour and use in its place (or substitute with yoghurt).

✴✴✴✴ CASH SAVER ✴✴✴✴
Use skirt steak from a good butcher. It's cheap and tasty – just marinade for longer.

── BONUS BITE ──
MARGARITA FAJITAS
Mix a marinade from the juice of 1 lemon or lime, a good splash of gin/rum/tequila, 2 tbsp torn coriander leaves, ½ tbsp brown sugar, 2 crushed garlic cloves, 4 pinches of chilli flakes and a splash of olive oil. Add to beef strips and proceed as above.

PREP 30 minutes before cooking, remove your steak from the fridge and slap it onto a board. Trim off any exterior fat using a very sharp chef's or filleting knife. Check which way the protein and fat lines run through the steak (the grain of the meat). Take your knife and make swift, clean cuts across the grain, dividing the steak into 1–2 cm wide strips.

Combine the marinade ingredients in a non-metallic bowl and mix well. Place your meat in a bowl and cover with the marinade. Organise your extras.

COOK 5 minutes before eating, put a griddle pan on to a high heat until almost smoking. To check if it's hot enough, drop a bit of cold water on the griddle pan – if it spits and evaporates, it's ready. Use a pair of tongs to drop strips of steak, well apart, down onto it.

Cook for 10 seconds then turn quickly. Cook for another 10 seconds. Shift the meat to a plate and sprinkle with a little salt. Rest for 2 minutes.

Meantime, warm the tortillas either foil-wrapped in a preheated oven, or one at a time, a few seconds a side, in a dry hot pan or a microwave, till soft and pliable.

PLATE Spoon a bit of sour cream, guacamole and tomato salsa into the centre of your tortilla. Layer in strips of beef and add the grated cheese and lettuce. Now roll up like a cigar using a bit of guacamole to hold it together. If you're making more of these to feed loads of people, bang your extras into bowls on the table and let everyone help themselves instead.

TORTILLAS Sift 200g plain white flour, ½ tsp salt and ½ tsp baking powder into a large bowl. Rub 30g lard/white vegetable fat into the flour using your fingers, then add a pinch of cumin seeds, a pinch of chilli flakes and 1 tbsp chopped coriander leaves. Pour in 125ml hot water gradually, mixing with a fork. Pull the dough into a ball, then knead it in the bowl for 3 minutes till smooth and elastic. Cover with a tea towel and leave for 15 minutes. Divide it into 6. Take 1 piece (covering the rest to stop them drying out) and knead it in the palm of your hand, pressing with your knuckles and pinching for 1–2 minutes till soft. Roll into a ball. Cover and repeat with the rest. Place a ball on a lightly floured surface and roll into an oval. Quarter turn and roll again. Keep going till you get a large, thin tortilla. Heat a large, dry frying pan, add the tortilla and cook for a minute until the underside starts to colour. Turn and repeat. Place in a tea-towel to keep soft and warm while you roll and cook the rest.

SIMPLY SMOOTH GUACAMOLE Cut around 1 ripe avocado, twist and pull to separate the two halves. Remove the stone with a large metal spoon, then scoop the flesh out. By machine: Tip into a processor with 1 garlic clove, 1 shallot, the juice of ½ a lemon, a good pinch of cayenne pepper or a finely diced fresh chilli, 2 tsp chopped coriander leaves, salt and pepper. Blitz a few seconds until smooth. Taste, and adjust the seasoning. By hand: Finely dice the shallot and mash all the ingredients together with a fork. Chill till needed, but don't make more than 4 hours ahead. Sit the stone in the bowl to stop oxidation or smear lemon juice onto cling film and lay over the mix.

FRESH AND SPICY TOMATO SALSA
Slice, deseed and chop 2 ripe vine tomatoes into rough cubes or dice. Finely dice 1 small red onion. Deseed and finely dice ½ a red chilli. Crush 1 garlic clove. Slap it all into a bowl and stir well. Add 1 tbsp chopped coriander leaves, lemon juice to taste and a good glug of olive oil. Just before eating, season with salt, pepper and a pinch of sugar. Taste. If your tomatoes aren't so good, add a pinch more sugar to balance the acidity. Spoon into a good-looking bowl if serving at the table.

ULTIMATE STEAK
AND THE WORKS

HEALTHY   FAST   FEEDS 2

INGREDIENTS

2 great sirloin/rump/rib-eye/fillet
   steaks (approx. 250g depending on
   appetite/budget)
1 garlic clove, peeled and cut across
a splash of good olive/groundnut oil
salt and black pepper
2 tsp Dijon mustard (or to taste)
2 tsp soft butter

THE WORKS (SEE OVERLEAF)

★★★★ **CASH SAVER** ★★★★

Make your steak go further by bashing
and rolling cheaper rump and skirt steaks
between layers of cling film with a rolling
pin to get them thinner. Pan-fry or griddle
for 1 minute per side. Season, rest and serve
as before but with more veg, or in a warm
panini with mustard/horseradish/ketchup/
salad or a fried egg.

—— **CHANGE IT UP** ——

Customise steaks with flavoured butters.
Beat 110g soft butter, 1 crushed garlic clove
and 1 tbsp lemon juice with herbs (2 tbsp
finely chopped tarragon/flat-leaf parsley/
coriander/rosemary) or 2 tbsp horseradish
cream/40g crumbled blue cheese and a
finely diced shallot. Roll into sausage shapes
in greaseproof paper to chill. Slice off what
you need. Or just dab some on your steaks.

TIP
If you want to grill your steak, cut all but 1cm of fat from the edge, snipping remaining fat with scissors so it stays flat when cooking. Brush with oil, garlic and herbs. Cook and turn under a high heat to suit your taste. To BBQ: sit steak over medium/ash white coals. Sit on an oiled rack for 4 minutes before sliding a spatula under to shift and turn it. Cook for another 4 minutes.

You're only allowed to cook this if you satisfy two conditions. One: get the best meat cash allows (preferably from a butcher so you can chat over options). Two: dress it properly in the instant butter and mustard sauce as it's resting, or serve with luxurious Béarnaise sauce.

PREP Get the steaks from the fridge. Leave on any of the fatty edge to maximise flavour and texture or remove after cooking. Rub the meat gently all over with the cut garlic and oil to tenderise it and prepare it for the dry pan. Add a few grinds of black pepper and leave to get to room temperature while you prep your chosen accompaniments.

Just before cooking, get a large dinner plate. On one side, put half the mustard and butter. Add a generous pinch of salt and pepper. Do the same on the other side of the plate. You'll be using this for fast saucing/seasoning once your steaks are cooked and resting. (You won't need to do this if you're making Béarnaise sauce to accompany your steak).

COOK Put a heavy-bottomed frying or griddle pan big enough to take the steaks on to high. Once it's almost smoking, slap the steaks down. If you're not sure if the heat's right, just touch the side of one steak to the pan – it should sizzle.

Cook for the required time to suit your tastes, the cut of meat, its thickness and temperature. For medium-rare, I give a 2.5cm thick steak 2 minutes on one side (don't shift it – you want that crust and colour) then turn with tongs or a spatula and cook again for 2 minutes. For a thicker steak, turn for another minute, then repeat. Really thick steaks may need finishing off in a hot oven for a minute or two, so make sure yours is preheated if you've got a big piece of cow there. Check the introduction (p70) for notes on steak doneness.

Steaks continue to cook a bit as they rest, so take them out of the pan just before they get to the perfect stage for your taste. Place each on its pile of seasonings on the dinner plate, turning once. Rest somewhere warm for 4 minutes to ensure your steak will be tender.

PLATE Transfer the steaks to clean plates with all their lovely, flavoursome juices. Serve with dauphinoise potatoes (p126) and a simple green or tomato salad. Or eat with the works – shallow-fry chips, roasted vine tomatoes, stir-fry spinach and béarnaise sauce (see overleaf) instead of the mustard/butter.

CRISP SHALLOW-FRY CHIPS

Put a pan of cold water on to a high heat, adding a pinch of salt. Peel 2–3 medium floury potatoes and cut into even-sized wedges. Add to the water, bring to the boil and parboil for 8 minutes. Drain. Quickly blot them on kitchen paper so they'll crisp up. Cool. Heat a frying pan and add enough groundnut oil to cover the bottom. Add the chips in a single layer. Fry for a couple of minutes then turn with a spatula. Repeat, cooking for 8–10 minutes or till golden on the outside, fluffy in the centre. Sit on kitchen paper to drain. Salt immediately.

ROASTED VINE TOMATOES

Preheat the oven to 200°C/Gas 6. Sit 2 medium/4 small vine tomatoes per person in a small roasting tin or on a baking tray. Leave them attached to the vine if they came with it. Scatter them with 2 finely diced cloves of garlic, a little fresh thyme/rosemary/basil and drizzle with olive oil. Season well and add a pinch of sugar. Roast larger tomatoes for 25 minutes, smaller ones for 15 minutes. Sit them next to your steak and use bread to mop up the juices.

STIR-FRY SPINACH

Heat a wok or large pan as your steak rests. Add a knob of butter and a 250g bag of washed spinach (it reduces – don't worry). Stir-fry for a minute or so to wilt. Gently press out any excess water. Season it with salt and pepper.

EASY LUXURY BÉARNAISE SAUCE

Melt 110g butter in a pan without stirring. Remove from the heat and skim off the solids floating on top. Put 5 tbsp white wine vinegar, a few chopped tarragon leaves and a chopped shallot into a small pan. Boil to reduce by a third. Strain it into an ovenproof bowl. Set the bowl over a saucepan half-full of simmering water. Whisk in two medium egg yolks and 2 tsp cold water until the mix thickens – about 5 minutes. Remove and trickle in the butter, whisking as you go. Season to taste and keep warm till needed. Don't reheat.

CRUNCHY THAI-STYLE BEEF SALAD

HEALTHY

FEEDS 2

There's a lovely fresh, zingy character to this beautiful little salad. Fresh herbs take it somewhere else and the chilli/lime/fish sauce combination is classic.

INGREDIENTS

2 steaks (sirloin/rump)
1 tbsp olive oil
2 tsp sesame oil
salt and black pepper
a small handful of dry roasted peanuts, roughly chopped

DRESSING
2½ tsp palm/caster sugar
90ml fish sauce
1 small red chilli
juice of 2 small limes

SALAD
4 ripe vine tomatoes
3 small shallots
4 spring onions
½ cucumber
a handful of mint leaves
a handful of coriander leaves
½ iceberg lettuce, washed and dried

TIP
If you're not into peanuts, top with crunchy onion rings (p82) or try a crispy shallot topping instead. Peel and thinly slice 1 large banana shallot or 4 small ones. Heat 1cm depth of groundnut oil in a frying pan. Once really hot, add the shallot for a few seconds. Turn with a slotted spoon till golden. Scoop onto kitchen paper, sprinkle with salt and toss onto salad.

—— CHANGE IT UP ——
1. Drizzle your beef with spicy sauce (p58) for a satay-style beef salad. **2.** Stuff the dressed meat salad into warmed pittas or yoghurt flatbreads (p128). **3.** For a Thai beef salad wrap, peel off and chill the iceberg leaves separately. Prep remaining salad, dressing and cook and slice meat as above. Serve in separate piles on one big plate. Spoon into the lettuce leaves, wrap and eat.

PREP Dressing: finely grate the palm sugar, if using. Mix the palm/caster sugar in a bowl with the fish sauce. Finely slice the chilli and add to the bowl with the lime juice. Set aside.

Salad: slice the tomatoes into quarters. Peel and slice the shallot. Trim the spring onions and slice lengthways with a sharp chef's knife. Peel and halve the cucumber lengthways. Deseed it with a teaspoon. Slice the flesh into half-moons. Tear the herbs. Throw the lot into a bowl. Tear or shred the lettuce with a carving knife and set aside.

Put the steaks onto a plate. Mix the oils together and pour over the steaks, turning to coat. Season with black pepper.

COOK Heat a griddle pan till almost smoking. Cook your steaks to medium rare – I give a 2.5cm thick steak 2 minutes on one side (don't shift it – you want that crust and colour) then turn with tongs or a spatula and cook again for 2 minutes. For a thicker steak, turn for another minute, then repeat. Check the introduction (p70) for notes on steak doneness.

Remove your steaks from the pan, season lightly with salt and rest for 3 minutes. Add the lettuce to the salad bowl and toss in the dressing. Sit the steaks on a board. Slice them across the grain in 1–2cm strips using a sharp chef's knife.

PLATE Pile the salad onto a plate or into bowls and arrange the steak slices neatly on top. Sprinkle over the crushed peanuts to finish.

THE ULTIMATE NEW YORK CHEESEBURGER

FEEDS 4

INGREDIENTS

4 homemade or best shop-bought
  burger buns (see overleaf)
280g chuck steak
140g skirt
140g brisket
2 smoked bacon rashers
salt and pepper
olive oil, for frying

CARAMELISED ONION
1 large onion, peeled and thinly sliced
1 tbsp olive oil
a pinch of sugar

EXTRAS
110g cheddar, grated
110g mozzarella, grated
2 smoked streaky bacon rashers
2 hamisha/large dill pickles, sliced

TIP
Chop into mince by hand. The strands
aren't distinct but it means you can still
use cheap cuts. Cut chilled meat into small
cubes on a board. Chop into coarse mince
with a sharpened chef's knife. If you've
got two, hold one in each hand and chop
rhythmically as if using drumsticks.

········· **TIME SAVER** ·········
Prep the caramelised onion up to a day
ahead, just reheat gently when needed. The
burger buns can be made days ahead and
frozen until needed.

——— **BONUS BITES** ———
EVERYDAY FAST SMOKY BURGER
Mix 1 finely chopped and gently fried
medium onion with 900g minced beef, 40g
grated cheddar, 1 tsp smoked paprika,
½ tsp mustard, a shake of Tabasco/hot sauce,
1 pinch each of dried oregano/thyme/mint,
2 tsp apple chutney or ketchup, 1 handful of
chopped fresh parsley, salt and pepper. Test
for seasoning. Shape. Chill. Fry.

Get your meat right and the technique down (mincing it yourself so the strands are separate for least resistance) and you've got yourself the ultimate burger. Don't kill it with a cheap bun– make mine or buy something nice. Skip the cheese if you don't do dairy and dice the meat up with a chef's knife if you don't have a mincer.

PREP Timings: start the burgers 40 minutes before you want to cook. They take 30 minutes to chill. If making your own buns (they transform a burger) start at least 3 hours before you need them. They're fast to prep and easy to make but need time to rise, cook and cool.

Set up your mincer. If you don't have a processor/mixer with attachment, use a hand-operated one – they're cheap, good and easy to get hold of. Fit it with a medium grinder plate. Slap your beef and bacon onto a board. Use a sharp chef's knife to cut it into chunks small enough to fit through the feeding tube. Season it lightly with salt and pepper.

Turn the mincer to top speed or get ready to turn. Cover a large baking tray with cling film and hold it underneath the mincer to catch the mince. Push the meat through the machine in a constant flow so the strands come out unbroken. Simultaneously, move the baking tray away and then back towards you a few times till the meat is used up. This makes a heaped sausage shape of ground beef with all the proteins running in the same direction; which means your burger will be beautifully tender. (N.B. This is do-able by yourself but an extra pair of hands at this stage is useful).

Without disturbing the strands, bring the sides of the cling film up to wrap the meat like a thick cracker, twisting the ends tightly to seal. Roll it in another layer of cling film and chill in the fridge for at least 30 minutes.

Meantime, caramelise the onion. Whack it in a pan with the oil and the sugar and cook very gently for about 20 minutes, or until it's soft. Set aside. Prep the rolls by slicing in two cleanly. Mix together the cheeses and spread evenly across the bottom halves of the bread. Cook the bacon on a grill preheated to high. Place on a rack for 2 minutes per side or till crisp, turning.

COOK Slice the chilled meat, through the film, into 6cm thick burgers. Put a heavy-based pan on to a high heat. Add a glug of oil. Peel the film from the burgers. Lift them carefully into the pan. Fry for 30 seconds per side, flipping with a spatula. Repeat so they cook over 2 minutes (or another minute or two for well-done). Sit on a warm plate. Season well. Leave to rest.

Grill the cheese-topped roll bottoms for 3–4 seconds till melting/gooey. Sit the tops, cut-side down, in the hot burger pan to absorb the juices.

PLATE Place each burger on a gooey, cheesy bread base. Add a bit of onion, pickle, half a strip of crispy bacon and the lids. Eat with a simple green/tomato salad, shallow-fry chips (p78) or sweet potato wedges.

HOMEMADE BURGER BUNS

Sift 575g white bread flour, ½ tsp salt and ½ tsp sugar into a bowl. Add 25g butter, 2 x 7g sachets of dried quick-action yeast and rub everything together with your fingers. Add 1 tsp black onion seeds and 50g grated cheddar and pour over 360ml of warm water. Mix well with your hands. Pull it into a ball. Knead by hand (p200) on a floured board or in a processor for 8 minutes. Bang it into a covered bowl and leave to rise for 1 hour or until doubled in size. Knead again for 2 minutes. Divide into 8 even pieces and shape each into a roll. Grease two baking trays, space the rolls evenly between each and leave to rise, covered with dampened tea towels, for a second time for 30 minutes. Preheat the oven to 220°C/Gas 7. Brush the buns with a mix of 1 beaten egg/2 tbsp milk and sprinkle over a few extra onion seeds. Cook for 25 minutes or till the domes are golden brown. Tap the base of a bun from each tray – they should sound hollow. Give them a bit of extra time if needed. Cool on a rack.

SPICED SWEET POTATO WEDGES

Preheat the oven to 220°C/Gas 7. Peel 900g sweet potatoes. Pat them dry. Slice each one into very large chips/wedges. Dry again. Drop them into a freezer bag. Add 2 tbsp olive/sunflower/groundnut oil, 1–2 tsp ground cumin or paprika, 1–2 tsp chilli flakes, a squeeze of lime if you have any and season with salt and pepper. Shake well. Tip onto a baking tray. Bake in a layer for 20–30 minutes (size-dependent) until tender and golden. Serve with sour cream or mayo, and a chunk of lime for squeezing, if you like.

CRUNCHY ONION RINGS

Slice 1 medium onion into 5mm rings. Separate the rings and cover with milk in a bowl. Scatter 3 tbsp white flour on a plate with salt, pepper and a pinch of paprika. Drop the rings in to coat. Heat groundnut oil to a depth of 8cm in a deep pan or wok until 180°C (an onion ring should sizzle at once when added). Add a few rings at a time and cook for a few seconds, turning once with a slotted spoon. Drain on kitchen paper, and salt before eating.

——— CHANGE IT UP ———

1. BOOST EVERYDAY BURGER FLAVOURS by adding:
LEMON ZEST/GRATED GINGER/SPRING ONION/ROASTED GARLIC/GRATED APPLE OR CARROT/FRESH HERBS/CUMIN/ FENNEL SEEDS/HORSERADISH SAUCE/ ONION CHUTNEY

2. PLAY WITH THE BREAD using:
BAGUETTE/GRIDDLED BUNS/TOASTED BRIOCHE/FLAT BREADS /CHILLED LETTUCE LEAVES

3. STACK with:
OTHER GOOD MELTING CHEESES/ ONION RINGS/PICKLED GINGER/ GRIDDLED BUTTERNUT SQUASH SLICES/ SLICED MANGO OR APPLE/GRIDDLED MUSHROOMS/ROCKET/WATERCRESS/ YOGHURT DRESSING/CAESAR DRESSING/ SALSAS/TAPENADE OR COLESLAWS/ FLAVOURED MAYOS

CARPACCIO

INGREDIENTS

500g beef fillet
  (in one piece and not the tail end)
a few drops of extra virgin olive oil
a good squeeze of lemon juice, to taste
sea salt and pepper

✳✳✳✳ CASH SAVER ✳✳✳✳
Use good sirloin steak or even very cheap skirt from a good butcher.

TIP
For an even easier slice, wrap the trimmed fillet tightly in foil or film and freeze for 2–4 hours. Peel the foil/film back gradually as you slice very thinly using a sawing action. Return to room temperature before serving.

BONUS BITE
FAST TOAST CRISPS
Preheat the oven to 150°C/Gas 2. Meantime, toast 6 slices of white bread lightly in a toaster. Remove the crusts with a serrated knife and slide a knife through the centre of each slice. Peel the two sides apart gently. Sit the slices, cut sides up, on a baking tray and bake for 10 minutes or till crisp and golden. Cool on a rack.

CHANGE IT UP
If you're not keen on the raw concept then sear your meat. Heat a wide frying pan/roasting tin that can fit the fillet. Add a glug of olive oil. Rub ground black pepper into the meat to sweeten it or roll in a handful of finely chopped rosemary and thyme leaves. When the pan/tin's good and hot, add the meat and sear for 30 seconds–1 minute each side. Remove. Wrap in foil/cling film and cool in the fridge for at least 30 minutes before slicing.

Here's a personal favourite. It's raw meat (or just seared) but don't let that put you off. It's bloody gorgeous. This makes a great light lunch or dinner party starter. Fillet is the finest piece of meat and this makes the most of it. Mix and match the toppings or go for a favourite.

PREP Buy a trimmed fillet or do it yourself. Sharpen a filleting or chef's knife. With the beef on a board, take hold of any white sinewy membrane or fat on the surface with one hand. Pull it away from you while sliding the knife underneath it to cut it cleanly away. Cover and chill the lean fillet for a few hours or overnight in the fridge (cold meat slices more easily).

Just before eating, remove the meat and sit it on a board. Using the sharpened knife, slice the fillet vertically very thinly. Spread a large sheet of cling film over a chopping board or clean surface. Distribute the slices neatly over the top in one layer, about 1cm apart. Cover with another piece of cling film. Very gently, run a rolling pin over the lot – don't be too vigorous or you'll break up the fibres. Hold up the cling film, it should look like a thin sheet of meaty wallpaper.

Remove the top bit of film and very carefully peel the slices off the bottom layer. Divide between individual plates as elegantly as you can, overlapping slightly.

PLATE Drizzle with olive oil, squeeze over lemon juice and season with salt and pepper. Serve with breadsticks or fast toast crisps (see left) or a simple tomato and shallot salad (p37). Alternatively add any of the following toppings.

TOPPINGS

1 MOZZARELLA, TOMATO, ROCKET & LEMON JUICE
Deseed and dice 4 good ripe tomatoes. Roughly tear a 125g ball of mozzarella. Distribute between plates of sliced naked carpaccio with a good handful of rocket leaves. Drizzle with a good glug of olive oil, a good squeeze of lemon juice, pepper and sea salt.

2 ROAST BEETROOT & GOAT'S CHEESE
Roast 500g beetroot wrapped in foil at 230°C/Gas 8. Cool. Peel. Square off the edges, cut into dice and toss in lemon juice. Leave for 20 minutes. Chop 110g hard goat's cheese or tear a soft one. Scatter the beetroot and cheese over naked carpaccio with rocket leaves, olive oil, a good squeeze of lemon juice and sea salt.

3 WARM BEANS, ROSEMARY & GARLIC
Drain a 410g can/jar of large butter beans. Tip into a pan with a glug of olive oil, 1–2 finely chopped garlic cloves, a sprig of fresh rosemary and a squeeze of lemon juice. Warm very gently on a low heat for a few minutes (add a bit of water if you want). Leave the flavours to infuse or use immediately. Divide the beans between 4 small dishes. Place centrally on plates and arrange the beef slices around them.

SPAGHETTI BOLOGNAISE

FEEDS 6

INGREDIENTS

700g best minced steak
  (or own minced chuck steak)
75g smoked streaky bacon/pancetta
50g chicken livers
  (optional, but add depth)
2 tbsp olive oil
3 tsp butter
1 large onion, peeled and finely
  chopped
½ a star anise
salt and pepper
3 garlic cloves, peeled and crushed
1 carrot, peeled and finely diced
1 small stick celery, finely chopped
300ml red/white wine
4 tbsp milk
1 bay leaf
a pinch of plain white flour
a good pinch of nutmeg
1 x 400g carton tomato passata
2–3 tbsp tomato purée
a pinch of oregano
a pinch of sugar
a dash of fish sauce/lemon juice
  (optional)
400g dried spaghetti/tagliatelle
a hunk of parmesan, for serving

This is a traditional Italian sauce (ragu) and it's delicious. The long slow cook means all the great ingredients have time to integrate. Make it ahead and let the flavours develop further: a great dish if you've got mates heading round; just get out the wine and garlic bread.

PREP Return your mince to room temperature. Dice the bacon/pancetta. Wash and dry the chicken livers if using. Remove any fat or gristle and chop into tiny pieces.

COOK Heat the oil and a teaspoon of butter in a wide frying pan/saucepan on a medium heat. Add the bacon/pancetta. Fry for 2 minutes, stirring, till brown. Reduce the heat. Add the onion, star anise and a pinch of salt. Cook for 5 minutes or until soft and translucent. Discard the star anise. Add the garlic, carrot and celery. Fry and stir on low for 5 minutes until softening. Increase the heat a bit.

Crumble the mince in with your hands, stirring as the meat caramelises. Once it's browned, add the chopped liver. Cook for 2 minutes. Increase the heat. Add the wine. Let it bubble up for 2 minutes to burn off the alcohol. Reduce the heat. Add the milk, bay leaf, flour, nutmeg, passata, tomato purée, oregano, sugar, optional lemon juice/fish sauce and lots of black pepper. Stir to mix well and let it simmer gently for 5 minutes.

To oven cook: Preheat the oven to 140°C/Gas 1. Tip the sauce into a lidded dish. Cook for 2–3 hours. Check occasionally, adding more milk if it's too thick or a bit more purée if it needs more substance. To cook on the hob: Reduce the heat to minimum and cover. Cook for 1–2 hours, checking and stirring regularly, adding more liquid if needed. Taste and adjust the seasoning with salt, pepper and lemon juice as needed.

Add the spaghetti/tagliatelle to a pan of boiling water and cook until *al dente* or as you like it (see p173 or check your packet for timings). Drain well. Return to the pan. Add the remaining butter and season. Mix the sauce and spaghetti together (or serve separately).

PLATE Tip into warmed bowls and grate over parmesan at the table. Eat with a sharply dressed green salad and crunchy garlic bread (p.178)

BONUS BITE

CLASSIC LASAGNE
Make the ragu as above, but omit the chicken livers. Make a cheese béchamel (p185). Get a 250g pack of fresh lasagne or soak dried, no-cook lasagne sheets in water for 10 mins and drain well. Grate 150g parmesan. Butter a lasagne or large ovenproof dish that's at least 5cm deep. Layer it up with béchamel, meat sauce, grated cheese, more béchamel and lasagne sheets. Repeat the layering until the meat sauce is finished. Top with lasagne sheets and cover with béchamel. Scatter over extra parmesan and dabs of garlic butter (p138). Bake at 220°C/Gas 7 for about 40 minutes. Remove from the oven and leave to settle for 10 minutes before spooning out.

SMOKING CHILLI CON CARNE

FEEDS 3-4

INGREDIENTS

3 strong red chillies, trimmed

2 x 400g cans of chopped tomatoes

3 fat garlic cloves, peeled

1 tsp ground cumin

2–3 tbsp olive oil

1 large onion, peeled and finely
    chopped

1 star anise

675g best minced steak (or mince your
    own chuck/skirt steak)

a small bunch of fresh coriander
    leaves, chopped

2 tbsp tomato purée

a pinch of sugar

a good pinch of dried oregano

1 cinnamon stick

175ml beef/chicken stock (p68/p49)

1 x 400g can of kidney/black beans,
    drained

salt and pepper

✴✴✴✴ CASH SAVER ✴✴✴✴

Make your chilli go further by turning
it into burritos. Pile the mix into wheat
tortillas with a bit of sour cream, cheddar
and spring onion. Fold into parcels and sit
them in a buttered dish. Bake, foil covered at
220°C/Gas 7 for 20 minutes. Eat as is or add
tomato sauce and grated cheese and grill till
bubbling.

TIP

Take chilli into work to microwave with a
baked potato.

This is a particularly zingy chilli. Super-charge the beef by adding chillies you've toasted on the griddle to release their oils and heat. Shower with sour cream and extras for fresh taste and contrast.

PREP Heat a griddle pan to smoking. Slice the chillies in half lengthways and add to the pan cut-side down, to toast. Press them down with a spatula for 15 seconds. Turn and repeat. Lift into a dish and cover with hot water. Set aside for 10 minutes.

Drain the chillies. Tip the tomatoes, garlic, cumin and drained chillies into a food processor or use a stick blender and blitz well. Sieve the mix into a bowl. Set aside.

COOK Heat a wide pan or a large, deep frying pan to medium-low. Add the oil, onion and star anise. Cook till soft, not coloured. Increase the heat. Crumble the minced meat in gradually, stirring. Cook for 5 minutes, or till coloured. Remove the star anise.

Stir in your sieved tomato sauce. Cook for 5 minutes. Add everything else, except the beans and half the coriander. Stir and boil for 2 minutes. Reduce to the lowest heat and cook for a further 30–40 minutes, stirring sometimes. Taste and adjust the seasoning, adding water if it looks too dry. Stir in the beans and the remaining coriander 5 minutes before serving.

PLATE Heap onto bowls of cooked rice and serve with soft tortillas (p74), sour cream, yoghurt, tortilla crisps, guacamole (p75), diced red pepper, chopped spring/red onion, grated cheddar, diced red chilli and lime wedges. It's also good in warmed tortillas with fried eggs.

BONUS BITE

FAVOURITE COTTAGE PIE

Heat 1 tbsp olive oil in a large casserole or pan. Cook 450g best minced steak, turning, for 3–4 minutes until browned. Add 1 very finely chopped large onion, 1 large grated/finely diced carrot, 1 finely diced stick celery and 3 crushed garlic cloves and cook for 3 minutes. Add 2 tbsp Worcester sauce/mushroom ketchup, 2 tbsp tomato purée and a pinch of dried thyme. Cook for 2 minutes. Increase the heat. Add 1 small glass of red wine and 275g chicken/beef stock. Boil for 2 minutes. Reduce the heat. Simmer for 15 minutes on low heat. Meanwhile, boil 900g floury potatoes until soft. Drain and mash with 50g butter, 110g grated cheddar, 2 egg yolks, salt and pepper. Tip the cooled meat mix into a dish and top with mash. Dab with garlic butter (p138) and bake at 200°C/Gas 6 for 30–40 minutes, until browned and bubbling.

ROUGH BEEF AND VEGETABLE STEW WITH HERB DUMPLINGS

FEEDS 4

INGREDIENTS

2 large onions
4 carrots
2 parsnips
250g butternut squash
1 leek, washed
2 garlic cloves, peeled
900g good stewing/chuck steak
2 tbsp plain flour
salt and pepper
1 tbsp oil
25g butter
500ml chicken stock (p49)
1–2 tbsp Worcester sauce
1 tbsp tomato purée
1 tsp sugar
1 bay leaf
a few pinches of dried/fresh thyme
a splash of balsamic vinegar/lemon juice
6 small button/chestnut mushrooms, chopped (optional)
1 x 5cm strip of orange zest (optional)
a small handful of parsley, chopped

HERB DUMPLINGS
110g self-raising flour
50g butter
2 tsp dried marjoram
1 small egg

**** CASH SAVER ****
Substitute a drained 400g can of butter
beans for half the meat.

—— CHANGE IT UP ——

1. Enhance the flavour with a sprinkle of
gremolata (p88). **2.** Add dried prunes or
apricots for a bit of fruity comfort food.
3. For goulash, stir 400g chopped tomatoes,
4 tsp paprika and a few caraway seeds into
the stew. Omit the stock – use ale instead.
Stir in a dollop of sour cream to finish.
4. For hotpot, cook the stew as above,
then cover with thin slices of overlapping
potatoes. Dot with butter, cover in foil and
bake for 2–3 hours as above. Remove the foil
to brown for the last 30 minutes.

*Here's a really good basic stew with loads of vegetables to balance out
the meat and get your cash going further. I'd make this for a weekend
and then enjoy it through the week or freeze some for later.*

PREP Preheat the oven to 180°C/Gas 4. Peel and chop the onions, carrots,
parsnips and butternut squash. Slice the leek. Crush the garlic. Cut
the meat into 5cm cubes. Shake it in a bag with the flour, salt and pepper.

COOK Heat a large casserole dish or pan. Add the oil, butter and a pinch
of salt. Fry the vegetables and garlic in batches gently till slightly
softened, not coloured. Remove from the pan and set aside.

If the pan is dry, add a bit more oil. In small batches, add the meat and sear
quickly on all sides, turning with tongs, until nice and brown. Remove to the
plate as it's done. Repeat until all the meat is seared.

Tip the meat and vegetables back into the pan. Add the stock, Worcester sauce,
puree, sugar, herbs, balsamic vinegar/lemon juice, mushrooms and orange
rind. Boil for a minute. Reduce the heat. Oven-cook for 2–3 hours or simmer
on the hob on very low heat for ½–2 hours. Check that it doesn't dry out.

Make the herb dumplings. Sift the flour into a bowl. Rub in the butter, add
the dried marjoram and the egg and mix together with a fork to form a sticky
dough. Shape into dumplings, add to the casserole, cover and cook for a
further 20–30 minutes. Taste and adjust the seasoning.

PLATE Spoon into big bowls, sprinkle with parsley and eat with crunchy
green beans and mash (see below); crushed lemon and parsley
potatoes (p60), or just scooped up with slices of good thick bread and butter.

•••••••••••••••••• TO GO WITH ••••••••••••••

CRUNCHY GREEN BEANS

Wash 60g of fine green beans per person. Cut the tops off with a paring
knife and add to a pan of boiling salted water. Boil for 4–5 minutes or
till softening but with a bit of bite still. Drain and season.

CREAMY FRENCH MASH

Put 900g floury potatoes (unpeeled) and 2 garlic cloves into a pan of
cold salted water. Boil for 20 minutes or till tender. Drain. Put them
through a ricer or strip the skins off as soon as you can handle them.
Put the potato back into the warm pan. Mash with 50g butter and 4
tbsp milk. Beat in 110g gruyére cheese and add 2 finely chopped spring
onions. Taste and season.

BOEUF BOURGUIGNON WITH GARLIC CROUTONS

FEEDS 4

INGREDIENTS

110g streaky bacon
1.1kg chuck steak, in a piece or cubed
1 tbsp olive oil
25g butter, plus extra for frying
1 large onion, peeled and sliced across
1 medium carrot, sliced across
4 garlic cloves, peeled and crushed
1 star anise
2 tbsp plain flour
salt and pepper
600ml red wine
400ml beef/chicken stock (p68/p49)
1 tbsp tomato purée
1 bay leaf
a pinch of dried thyme
12 shallots, peeled
a pinch of sugar
12 baby mushrooms
GARLIC CROUTONS
3 tbsp oil
1 garlic clove, peeled and crushed
6 slices of coarse bread

—— CHANGE IT UP ——

1. For a taste blast, spread the garlic croutons with strong mustard (serving mustard-side down). **2.** Replace the garlic croutons with gremolata. Sprinkle with a mix of 1 finely chopped garlic clove, 3 tbsp chopped parsley, grated zest of ½ a lemon, and scatter over the bourguignon before serving.

········ TIME SAVER ········

1. Make the day before to let the flavours develop and take the pressure off. **2.** To skin shallots or baby onions easily, cover with boiling water for 60 seconds. Drain. Run under cold water. Slice the tips and stems. Peel the skins off.

A brilliant traditional French dish packing layers of flavour. Unlike most casseroles where the textures melt together, these stay distinct. Add the mushrooms and onions towards the end of cooking. Top the finished dish with crunchy croutons and other bits and pieces for even more contrast. Enjoy with French mash and crunchy green beans (p87) for a perfect marriage.

PREP Blanch your bacon to de-salt it: put a pan of water on to boil. Cut the bacon into 2cm strips. Add to the pan. Simmer for 5 minutes. Drain and leave to cool. Trim any excess fat from your beef. Cut it into regular 5cm cubes so that it cooks evenly. Dry them really well on kitchen paper.

COOK Put a large, wide casserole dish onto medium heat. Add the oil and a knob of butter. Preheat the oven to 220°C/Gas 7. Sit a plate near the hob. Add the bacon to the hot fat and cook for 5 minutes till crispy, turning using a wooden or slotted spoon. Spoon onto a plate. Increase the heat. Add a few cubes of meat to the bacon fat to brown. Don't overcrowd the pan or it'll stew (you want a good dry brown crust without overcooking). As each edge browns, turn it quickly with tongs. Once browned, remove from the pan and place on the plate. Repeat till all the meat is seared.

Decrease the heat. Add the onion, carrot, 3 of the crushed garlic cloves and star anise. Cook gently for 5–10 minutes until softening, not coloured. Remove the star anise.

Sprinkle the beef and bacon with the flour and some pepper. Stir to coat it well. Tip it all back in with the vegetables. Stick it in the oven for 5 minutes or until the flour browns up. Reduce the temperature to 150°C/Gas 2.

Remove the casserole dish from the oven and place it on a medium heat. Add the wine and just enough stock to cover the ingredients – don't swamp them. Add the purée and herbs. Boil for 1 minute, then cover. Return to the oven and cook for 3 hours (check after 2 to see it's not drying out) until deliciously tender.

Meantime, put the shallots in a pan with just enough water to cover. Add the sugar and butter. Simmer on a very low heat for 10–15 minutes till tender but still holding their shape. Fry the whole mushrooms in a little butter with the remaining garlic, shaking to turn brown. Season lightly. Add to the bourguignon with the onions to heat through. Taste and adjust the seasoning.

Make the garlic croutons. Mix the oil with the garlic and rub over the bread slices. Place on a baking tray, add to the oven and bake for 10 minutes or until very crisp.

PLATE Spoon the bourguignon into bowls. Top with garlic croutons. Serve with green beans and creamy French mash or slices of good thick bread and butter for mopping up the gravy.

ROAST BEEF WITH ALL THE TRIMMINGS

FEEDS 4-6

INGREDIENTS

1.8 kg well-hung beef rib on the bone
sea salt and pepper
a little finely chopped rosemary/dry
    mustard
2 tbsp olive oil/beef dripping
TRIMMINGS (see overleaf)

········ TIME SAVERS ········

1. Prep the potatoes the night before and
chill in the fridge in cold water until needed.
2. Make the Yorkshire batter the night
before. Get to room temperature and whisk
again before using.

TIP

Make the most of your leftovers. For a hot
roast beef sandwich, carve cold meat thinly.
Add to 2 thick slices of white bread with a
slathering of hot mustard or horseradish
sauce. Heat any leftover gravy. Pour it over.
Sandwich it (it's messy – enjoy it!). If you've
got Yorkshires left over, reheat in a warm
oven or microwave and fill with thinly sliced
meat and piping hot gravy.

—— CHANGE IT UP ——

1. To give your beef a crisp crust, rub
1 tbsp flour and 1 tbsp mustard powder
into the fat.
2. For fat-free joints ask a butcher for a bit
of pork fat (it's free). Sit it on top of the meat
and tie with bits of string. The fat will melt,
protecting the meat while cooking.

Recipes for roast beef are one of those things that get passed down through the generations and I'm not about to change that, so this is my mum's version. Once again, the key is buying a great piece of meat as no amount of skill can transform a scraggy piece of beast. Get a joint with a decent covering of fat which will baste the meat naturally as it cooks, and go for a joint with bones. It makes any Sunday.

PREP
Start early – maybe the night before so the beef can take up flavours. Check its weight and calculate and record cooking times (p71). Using a sharp knife, slash the top of the fat lightly across into a criss-cross pattern. This will release fat as the meat cooks to keep it tender. Mix salt, pepper and a little chopped rosemary/mustard powder together and rub into the fat only. Bang the meat in the fridge. Remove 2 hours ahead to get it to room temperature.

COOK
Preheat the oven to 230°C/Gas 8. Sit the beef, fat-side up, in a roasting tin (preferably one big enough to take some potatoes). Rub half the oil/dripping into the meat and season lightly all over. Add the remaining oil/dripping to the tin. Put it into the oven. After 15 minutes, reduce the temperature to 180°C/Gas 4. Spoon juices over the meat a few times. Prep your trimmings, adding your roasties to the pan when the time is right.

10 minutes before the cooking time is up, stick a metal skewer into the joint for 30 seconds. Remove then lay it on your wrist. If the beef is rare, it'll feel cool. For medium-rare it's just warm (my choice). For medium, it's warm. For well-done, it's hot. Juices run red for rare, pink for medium, clear for well-done. Put it back to cook for longer if you need (though it cooks on a bit as it rests, so don't overdo it). Move to a warm plate. Cover loosely with foil. Rest for 20–30 minutes in a warm place – don't worry, it'll stay hot.

PLATE
Sit the meat on a board, fat-side up. Using a freshly sharpened carving knife, cut through the string and follow the contour of the meat down between the bones (hold onto the bones to steady the operation with your free hand). The bones will come away as one. Hold the deboned meat with a fork and, using an easy sawing action, slice the joint vertically across the grain in slices as thick or thin as you like. Serve with loads of gravy and your trimmings of choice.

BONUS BITE

ROAST TOPSIDE (FOR 2–3)
Preheat the oven to 180°C/Gas 4. Heat a frying pan large enough to take a 900g beef topside joint. Rub the joint all over with 1 tbsp olive/groundnut oil. Add the meat, fat-side down first to sizzle and brown. Turn and sear for another 2 minutes, until all the sides are sealed. Transfer to a roasting tin, adding some parboiled potatoes if you like or throw in a mix of halved red onions, beetroot, carrots and potatoes with a bit of oil or a splash of wine. Season the beef with salt and pepper. Reduce the heat to 160°C/Gas 3. Roast for 40–50 minutes for rare/medium. Test with a skewer or meat thermometer. Leave to rest for 15 minutes before carving.

ROASTIES ━━━━━━

Peel, cut and boil 12 medium floury potatoes for 10 minutes. Drain well. Shuffle them in the colander to roughen their edges. Bang them in with the beef 45 minutes before it's cooked, adding a bit more oil or fat to the tin if you think it's needed. As you take the meat out to rest, increase the temperature to 220°C/ Gas 7 and crisp the potatoes. Sprinkle with sea salt.

YORKIES ━━━━━━

Make up a Yorkshire batter:
By machine: mix 4 large eggs, 300ml milk and a pinch of salt in a processor or with a stick blender. 10 minutes before the meat is done, blitz in 250g plain white flour until smooth. By hand: beat the eggs, milk and salt with a whisk. Sift the flour into a bowl. Whisk the liquid bit by bit into a hollow in the centre.

Before cooking, put 2 x 4-hole Yorkshire pudding trays or muffin tins into the very hot oven while the meat is resting to preheat for 5 minutes. Add a dash of dripping or oil to each hole and heat for another 5 minutes (the hotter they are, the higher the puds rise). Pour the batter into the smoking tins until two-thirds full and cook for 20 minutes.

GRAVY

Once the meat and potatoes have been removed from the tin, spoon out any excess oil, leaving 1–2 tbsp. Sit the tin on the hob over a medium heat and add 300ml water/stock. Using a wooden spoon, scrape the tasty bits off the bottom to incorporate. Simmer gently to reduce for a thin, tasty jus. Add any juices that seep from the meat as it rests. Season. Pour into a jug, skimming off any fat.

CARROTS IN FOIL

Cut 4 large peeled carrots into sticks with a paring knife. Cut out a large piece of foil. Turn the edges up slightly. Distribute the carrots. Add a squeeze of lemon/orange juice, the grated rind of ½ a lemon/orange and a star anise. Season. Add a knob of butter and a sprinkle of dried thyme. Bake with the beef for 30 minutes.

NO-FUSS TASTY BAKED ONIONS

Cut 6 medium red onions (skin on) in half lengthways. Drizzle a glug of olive oil on a plate sprinkled with sea salt and dried thyme. Rub the onions into it cut-side down. Sit on a baking tray and rub the tops with a cut garlic clove. Add black pepper. Roast for 20–30 minutes as the potatoes are crisping up.

PORK

Oh isn't the pig a beautiful beast? Not only lovely in life, it serves up a rich bounty of amazing meat in its passing. From nose to tail there's barely a bit I wouldn't consider cooking and eating. Ok we'll quickly pass over the deep-fried tail and slow braised trotter just for now anyway (they're both delicious by the way) but who'd not go for a classic bacon sandwich or a great hunk of deliciously roasted meat with a cheeky bit of crackling. Pork's the only meat that features large in our national breakfast – and that has to mean something. But it doesn't stop there. This meat's a globetrotter. Try gorgeous melt-in-the mouth Chinese style belly pork or a finger-licking scorching southern rack of ribs. It's an international star in my book. Now when it comes to buying it – get yourself to a proper butcher or the meat counter in your local supermarket. See what they've got. If in doubt ask for Gloucester Old Spot or other rare breed pork which will have been properly cared for, have a much richer flavour and is far less likely to dry out in the cooking. Get piggy…

STASH IT

BANG pork into the fridge as soon as you get it back.

KEEP it in its original cling filmed trays.

REMOVE butcher's paper. Plate it and cover with foil/greaseproof.

WRAP bacon once the pack has been opened or store in a container.

KEEP pork, bacon and sausages away from cooked and fresh foods.

Use **mince** within a day of purchase.

Smoked bacon lasts for 10 days. Unsmoked bacon keeps for 7.

Pork will keep in the freezer for up to 6 months.

Fresh **pork** lasts for 2–3 days in the fridge.

Cooked pork lasts for 4 days.

Bacon freezes for a short time in vacuum packs.

PORK
Buyer's Guide

LOOK FOR:

SKIN THAT'S DRY AND SMOOTH

MEAT THAT'S PINK AND FIRM WITHOUT A DAMP OR OILY SHEEN

FAT THAT'S WHITE AND THICK

JOINTS WITH A GOOD LAYERING OF FAT (IT CONDUCTS HEAT TO THE SKIN WHICH HELPS MAKE GREAT CRACKLING)

AVOID:

MEAT THAT LOOKS SLIPPERY

YELLOW FAT

THIS LITTLE PIGGY WENT TO MARKET.... TO BUY

1 SHOULDER
A versatile cut and not too expensive. A shoulder joint makes a great cheaper **slow roast** *for loads of people. Get* **SHOULDER CHOPS** *for* **slow braising**. **DICE IT** *up for* **stews and casseroles** *made with cider and apples and friends.* **MINCE IT** *up for* **burgers** *and create your own* **sausages and sausage rolls**. *Shoulder is* **CURED** *to make* **bacon joints**.

2 LOIN
Your everyday pork purchase could well come from this cut and be a loin chop or loin steak. Easy to cook (but don't dry them out). Healthy (cut any fat off after cooking if you want but remember fat is flavour). Loin is cured for making back and short back bacon.

FILLET Very lean and versatile, it absorbs flavours. Thin it for saltimbocca. Roast with care (it can dry out fast). Stuff it. Wrap it. Slice into medallions. It's great for stir-fry.

LOIN EYE STEAK Equivalent to beef sirloin. A premium cut.

RIB CHOP Fry, griddle or roast it fast. This is a lovely, tender bit of pork.

RACK A proper joint on the bone, this looks great on the table.

LOIN JOINT A very nice roasting joint.

3 PORK BELLY
One of the cheaper sweeter cuts and packed with juicy flavour. Belly is cured for making streaky bacon and pancetta.

SPARE RIBS Get them in a rack or ask the butcher to separate. Marinate then roast, deep-fry or BBQ to keep everyone happy.

FLAT BELLY A really beautiful cheaper joint that's perfect for long, slow cooking so the fat disappears as the skin crisps and crackles.

BELLY JOINT Rolled flat belly is ideal for stuffing and long slow cooking.

BELLY SLICES Try marinating then braising until tender.

4 PORK LEG
Home of the classic roast and leg steaks but less fat so cook carefully. Gammon joints are cured from pork leg.

LEG STEAK A cheap lean cut which you can griddle, fry, grill, stew or braise.

LEG JOINT Ask your butcher to score it for crisp crackling or buy a Stanley knife. Roast, braise or pot-roast.

ESCALOPE Thin it out and fry for an easy fast meal.

PIG NUTRITION

PORK IS A RICH SOURCE OF

VITAMIN B1 (THIAMIN)

METABOLISES CARBS essential for growth and repair of nerve and muscle tissue.

RIBOFLAVIN facilitates the release of energy from food and promotes HEALTHY SKIN AND EYES.

NIACIN

SUPPORTS THE NERVOUS SYSTEM and digestion and energy release from carbs, proteins and fats.

Phosphorus

BUILDS BONES AND TEETH

PORK CONTAINS **B6 + B12** WHICH WORK ALONGSIDE → **IRON** AND **PANTOTHENATE** to promote blood health and keep you mentally alert.

PORK'S RICH IN

ZINC

a deficit of which undermines THE NERVOUS SYSTEM. LEAN PORK CONTAINS

29G OF **PROTEIN** PER **100G**

MAKING IT GREAT FOR BODY BUILDING AND MAINTENANCE.

OK IT CONTAINS **FAT** but it's generally a lean meat and we need some fat to stay healthy.

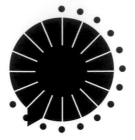

Start your joint at **230°C/ Gas 8** for 10 minutes.

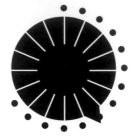

Reduce to **180°C/Gas 4** for the rest of your cooking time.

JOINTS ON THE BONE

30 MINUTES PER 450G

plus an extra 30

JOINTS OFF THE BONE

35 MINUTES PER 450G

plus an extra 30

COOK IT

Pork should be cooked through until the juice runs clear and it's no longer pink. But don't overcompensate or you'll create leather… Test and use your judgement.

IS IT DONE YET?

SKEWER IT

Thrust into the joint of meat at the thickest point, avoiding the bone. Count to 10. Place it on your wrist. If it's very hot (and the juices are clear) it's done.

Science

Insert a meat thermometer, avoiding the bone. It should read 80°C.

VISION

Cut into it with your knife. The meat should be moist and just white.

Pork Secrets
A CRACKLING LOVER'S GUIDE

Buy pork with the rind still intact. Ask the butcher to score it. To do it yourself, get your sharpest knife or a Stanley knife. Sit the meat on a board. Cut in the direction of carving to make life easier. Stab down into the rind and the top of the skin then bring your knife down a bit and score your line. Do this at 5mm intervals. Pat the meat dry with kitchen paper (purists use a hairdryer). Leave uncovered in the fridge for up to 24 hours if possible. Heat your oven to its highest temperature. Once it's there, rub the rind generously with Maldon sea salt (too soon and it draws out the moisture). Don't put any fats/oils on it. Blast with heat for 15 minutes before dropping the temperature to 180°C/Gas 4 (or much lower for belly pork/long slow cooks). Don't baste it. If it doesn't crackle to your taste, cut it away from the cooked joint and while that rests, crank up the oven and blast it with extra heat.

BRINGING HOME THE BACON

WET CURE Often oozes water as it cooks, so not so good.

DRY CURE Cooks up nicely and good value, also lower in nitrates so healthier.

SINGLE PIECE Chop or slice as an ingredient.

RASHERS Neat and convenient for instant cooking.

SMOKED Distinctive flavour (bear this in mind if including in a recipe).

UNSMOKED A blander taste.

BACK BACON Leaner but more expensive.

STREAKY Very tasty because it's fattier.

MIDDLE BACK Contains a bit of back and streaky.

BACON/HAM JOINTS

COLLAR Good for boiling as a cheap, tasty joint.

HOCK Great cheap cut, really tasty.

GAMMON Boil or roast, or boil then roast. Lovely, lean and versatile.

GAMMON & BACON

Perfect if you're working crazy hours; these guys have a long shelf life uncooked and cooked. And they're cash-stretchers, so perfect for feeding yourself for days or a load of people. Cook: remove packaging. Immerse in cold water. Chill for hours. Change the water. Chill again. This reduces the saltiness and moistens the meat.

BOIL AND GLAZE

1. Put the *joint* (string intact to keep it whole) into a pan of cold water or mix of *water and cider*. **2.** Leave plain or add an *onion/carrot/bay leaf*. **3.** Cover and boil (if scummy replace the water). **4.** Reduce to simmer for 20 minutes per 450g. **5.** Remove. **6.** Score diamond shapes into the fat. **7.** Stud with *cloves* and slap a glaze of *honey/mustard* on top. **8.** Finish for 10 minutes in a hot oven.

FRIENDS APPLE, APRICOT, BLUE CHEESE, CARAWAY SEEDS, CHESTNUT, CHILLI, CIDER, CINNAMON, COCONUT, CORIANDER, CREAM, CUMIN, FENNEL, FIG, GARLIC, GINGER, GRUYÈRE, HONEY, LEMON, MARMALADE, MUSHROOMS, MUSTARD, ONION, ORANGE, PAPRIKA, PEAR, PEAR CIDER, PLUM, POMEGRANATE MOLASSES, POTATO, RHUBARB, ROSEMARY, SAGE, SOY, STAR ANISE, THYME, WATERCRESS

SPANISH MEATBALLS

FEEDS 4

INGREDIENTS

250g good-quality minced pork
250g good-quality minced beef
50g fresh white breadcrumbs (p201)
50g parmesan, grated
2 spring onions, finely sliced
3 garlic cloves, peeled and crushed
½ tsp turmeric
grated zest of ½ lemon
½–1 tsp smoked paprika
2–3 tbsp finely chopped parsley,
    plus extra for serving
salt and pepper
a glug of olive oil, for frying
TOMATO SAUCE
olive oil, for frying
3 garlic cloves, peeled and sliced
a pinch of chilli flakes
2 x 400g cans good-quality chopped
    tomatoes
1 tbsp tomato purée
a pinch of sugar

········· TIME SAVER ·········

Stir crushed garlic and a squeeze of lemon
into shop-bought mayo for a quick aioli.

TIP

If you're having trouble getting the meatball
mixture to hold together, add a little beaten
egg to it.

One of the stars on a table of tapas, these tasty little meatballs tick all the boxes and make a cracking meal anytime. Treat them lightly as you're shaping and cooking so they stay nice and soft and sweet. Team with garlicky aioli and paprika potatoes.

PREP Make the meatballs: Tip all the ingredients except the oil into a bowl and mix together lightly with a fork. Dampen your hands. Divide the mix and roll it very lightly into large, walnut-sized balls. Place on a plate and leave to chill in the fridge until needed.

COOK Make the sauce: Heat a little oil in a pan over a low heat. Add the garlic and chilli and cook for 1 minute without colouring before adding the tomatoes, tomato purée and sugar. Season lightly. Whack up the heat to high and bring to the boil, then reduce and leave to simmer for at least 10 minutes. Taste and season again. Set aside.

Heat the oil in your biggest frying pan. Add the meatballs (in batches if necessary) and fry gently for a couple of minutes or until browned all over, rolling to turn with tongs or a spatula. Shift each one to a plate once done. Return the balls to the pan. Pour the sauce around them (you may not need it all). Simmer very gently. Turn them with care after 2 minutes for even cooking. Cook for 10 minutes or till done, but don't overdo it or they dry out. Add a splash of water to the sauce if needed. Taste and season.

PLATE Spoon the meatballs and sauce into earthenware tapas dishes (or equivalent) and sprinkle with parsley. Drizzle with aioli and serve with paprika potatoes or any of the tapas suggestions overleaf. These are also great with mussels baked in garlic butter (p138), paprika chicken wings (p53) a good red wine and some nice bread.

BONUS BITES

ITALIAN BAKED MEATBALLS
Preheat the oven to 190°C/Gas 5. Cook the meatballs as above until browned all over. Spread three-quarters of the tomato sauce over the base of a large heatproof dish and arrange the meatballs on top. Add the remaining sauce, a handful of torn basil and a handful of grated parmesan or mozzarella cheese. Drizzle over a little oil and bake at 190°C/Gas 5 for 20–30 minutes, or until the cheese is melted and golden.
MEATBALLS AND PASTA
Cook up a big pot of ribbon noodles or spaghetti following the packet instructions. Drain and toss in a little oil. Sit the meatballs and sauce on top. Sprinkle with a little parmesan. Eat with garlic bread (p178).

TAPAS EXTRAS

PAPRIKA POTATOES

Preheat the oven to 200°C/Gas 6. Peel and cut 4 large floury potatoes into 5cm cubes with a sharp knife. Roll them in kitchen paper or on a tea towel to dry before throwing them onto a baking tray. Add 1 tsp oregano, 1 tsp smoked paprika, salt and olive oil to coat. Toss to combine. Bang into the oven and cook for 30–40 minutes, turning once, until crisp.

AIOLI

Measure 200ml light olive oil and 50ml groundnut/ vegetable oil into a jug. Put 2 egg yolks, 3 crushed garlic cloves and 1½ tbsp of lemon juice/white wine vinegar in a bowl. Beat vigorously with a wooden spoon or a balloon whisk. Whisking steadily all the time, add the oil, drop by drop at first, then in a thin, steady stream once the mayo starts to form. Taste and adjust the seasoning, Add a drop more lemon juice/vinegar if it lacks acidity, or water if too thick. Chill in the fridge until ready to use.

CATALAN TOASTS

Toast or griddle thick slices of French stick/coarse white loaf. Rub with a cut garlic clove and halved ripe tomatoes (discarding the squashed shells). Drizzle with olive oil and sea salt. For tapenade toasts: Rub the crisp toasted bread with tapenade (black olive paste).

CHORIZO AND SHERRY

Preheat the oven to 180°C/Gas 4. Slice a length of chorizo cooking sausage into 2 cm pieces. Share between individual ovenproof dishes in a single layer. Add enough dry sherry to cover. Bake for 10 minutes or until sizzling hot. Mop up with good bread.

HOT DATES AND BACON

Run the back of a chef's knife along the back of rashers of streaky bacon to thin them. Halve them across. Wrap each half round a whole fresh pitted date. Spear on mini-skewers. Grill 4 minutes per side or until hot and crispy.

SALTIMBOCCA

FAST

FEEDS 2

Saltimbocca is Italian for 'jump in the mouth'. Squeeze a little lemon juice over these thinned pork fillet and sage leaf beauties and they'll do just that. This dish delivers a complex set of flavours for very little effort and makes an impressive supper.

INGREDIENTS

1 x 300g pork fillet
salt and pepper
3 slices of serrano/Parma ham, cut in half
6 large sage leaves
75g plain white flour
1 tbsp olive oil
30g butter
150ml pear cider (perry)
150ml double cream
1½ tsp English mustard
1 lemon, cut into wedges

PREP Pat the pork fillet dry with kitchen paper. Sit it on a board and, using a sharp filleting or chef's knife, cut it into 6 equal pieces with clean, smooth movements. Place the first slice, cut surface facing up, between two pieces of cling film. Roll and bash it with a rolling pin (without tearing it) until it's 5mm thick. Repeat with the remaining slices.

Season the slices with pepper and cover each with a piece of ham. Sit a sage leaf in the centre of each ham slice. Fix all three together securely with a toothpick or cocktail stick threaded from one edge through to the other and back again. Tip the flour onto a plate. Season it with salt and pepper. Dip the *saltimbocca* pieces in to cover completely.

COOK Heat the oil and butter in a pan. When foaming, add the pork slices, sage-side down, without crowding the pan (you may need to cook in batches). Fry for 1½ minutes, until the underside is golden and crispy. Check with a spatula. Flip and cook for 45 seconds, or until just cooked through. Lift them onto a warm plate. Sprinkle with sea salt.

Increase the heat under the pan and add the pear cider. Let it bubble to reduce by two-thirds. Add the cream and mustard, stirring. Reduce by a third again. Taste the sauce and season. Return the pork to the pan to warm for a few seconds or serve separately.

PLATE Sit the saltimbocca on your plates with lemon wedges for squeezing to jazz it up. Drizzle the sauce artfully, if serving separately. Eat with a twist of buttered ribbon pasta and a watercress salad with chicory and caramelised walnuts (p194).

—— BONUS BITES ——

LEMON SALTIMBOCCA

Cook the meat as before, but skip the sauce. Deglaze the pan with a glug of white wine to bubble (stir to pick up the meaty bits/ flavours) then add a squeeze of lemon juice and a knob of butter. Season to taste. Drizzle over the saltimbocca to finish.

MOZZARELLA SALTIMBOCCA

Place a thin slice of mozzarella in the centre of each thinned fillet slice before adding the ham and sage. Cook as above but without the sauce. Deglaze the pan with white wine, pour over the meat and serve with lemon, easy tomato sauce (p176), mashed potato or pasta.

SOUTHERN
RIBS
FEEDS 6

INGREDIENTS

2 pork spare rib racks
(approx. 1.2kg each)

THE RUB
3 tbsp smoked paprika
1½ tbsp sea salt
1½ tbsp cracked black pepper
1½ tbsp ground cumin
1½ tbsp chilli powder
1½ tbsp dark brown sugar
1 tbsp cayenne pepper
½ tbsp ground ginger

THE BBQ SAUCE
2 tbsp runny honey
2 tbsp maple syrup
1 tbsp Worcester sauce
3 tbsp low-salt soy sauce
4 tbsp tomato ketchup
4 tbsp cider vinegar
2 garlic cloves, crushed
1 tsp grated fresh ginger
2 tsp English mustard
4 tbsp orange juice
a pinch of paprika

BONUS BITE

SWEET BBQ RIBS
Finely chop a small onion and fry until soft. Add 200g chopped tomatoes. Simmer for 5 minutes. Add to the BBQ sauce ingredients and blitz till smooth. Pour over separated spare ribs. Marinade for at least 30 mins. Preheat the oven to 200°C/Gas 6. Cook on a rack, turning once, or in a foil parcel in a tin for 1 hour (open and brown for 10 mins).

TIP
If you don't have cracked pepper handy, bash regular black peppercorns in a pestle and mortar.

These slow-oven-cook ribs come with a heat warning. The spice mix is scorching but deliciously addictive: tone it down (just a bit) with sweet BBQ sauce. Mightily impressive – enjoy all year round. Team with wings, burgers, sweet and sour slaw (p65) and a lager loaf (p205) for a big event.

PREP
Preheat the oven to 130°C/Gas ½.

Take the ribs out of any vacuum packaging. Dry them on kitchen paper. Sit them on a board and leave to return to room temperature. Meantime, mix the ingredients for the rub in a bowl. Spoon half of it over the racks to coat them well. Rub it in thoroughly. Store the excess in a jar (it keeps for months). Sit the racks on a baking tray.

Mix all the ingredients for the BBQ sauce in a jug. Chill till needed.

COOK
Roast the racks for 3 hours, or until the meat is so tender they pull apart easily. Rest for 10 minutes. If you're having a BBQ, sit the roasted racks on the grill in a high position over very low coals. Let them smoke for 10 minutes to finish.

PLATE
Brush the ribs with a little of the BBQ sauce to glaze before separating (carve or pull them apart). Pile onto a big plate. Serve with the remainder of the sauce in a bowl for dipping.

CASSOULET

FEEDS 6

INGREDIENTS

2–3 duck legs
sea salt and pepper
2 large onions, peeled and sliced
5 garlic cloves, peeled and crushed
3 carrots, peeled and sliced
300g butternut squash, peeled and cut
    into chunks
2 tomatoes, roughly chopped
1 bouquet garni (p19)
1 x 110g belly pork
    (from a joint or rashers)
200g lardons/streaky bacon rashers
50g chorizo sausage
3 tbsp olive oil
1 x 400g can of butter beans, drained
1 x 400g can of haricot bean, drained
300ml cider
500ml chicken stock (p49)
75g fresh breadcrumbs (p201)
12 Toulouse sausages
a handful of parsley, chopped

TIP
If you feel the flavours here need lifting, add
a squeeze of lemon juice with the seasoning.

Get a load of people round to share this version of a French classic. Strictly speaking you should soak dried beans overnight before cooking them for hours, but I've cheated and used canned beans. The roasted duck legs here add flavour and texture and make a great meal in their own right.

PREP A day ahead: Preheat the oven to 200°C/Gas 6. Put the duck legs on a baking tray, prick all over with a fork and sprinkle with sea salt. Roast for 30–40 minutes, until crisp. Remove. Cool, then cover and leave to chill in the fridge. Save the fat by tipping it into a bowl, cooling, covering and chilling (use for this recipe or for frying crispy potatoes).

On the day: Prep the veg and bouquet garni and set aside. Sit the belly pork on a board. Slice the skin away, then cut the meat into 4 cm pieces. Cut the bacon into 2.5cm squares if not using ready-prepped lardons. Slice the chorizo.

COOK Heat the olive oil and a tablespoon of the reserved duck fat in a large, wide casserole. Fry the belly pork for 2–3 minutes, turning with tongs. Transfer to a plate. Add the bacon and fry, turning, until crisp and golden. Transfer to the plate. Add the onions to the pan and cook, stirring, for 8–10 minutes until softened. Stir in the garlic, carrot and butternut squash. Cook for a further 2–3 minutes. Add the chorizo and drained beans. Increase the heat. Add the cider. Boil for 2 minutes then add the chicken stock. Boil for another 2 minutes. Add the tomato, bacon, bouquet garni and black pepper. Reduce the heat. Simmer gently for 15 minutes.

Preheat the oven to 180°C/Gas 4. Spread the breadcrumbs on a tray to dry out as it heats up. Remove when they're golden. Heat a little oil in a frying pan. Add the sausages and fry gently, turning, for a few minutes to brown them up.

Take the casserole off the hob. Tuck the sausages and pork belly into the mix to cover well. Push the duck legs in round the edges. Add a bit more liquid if it's looking dry. Taste and adjust the seasoning. Scatter the dried breadcrumbs evenly over the lot. Put it in the oven and cook for an hour. Remove and leave to settle for 10 minutes before serving.

PLATE Scatter over the parsley and bang on the table with a bowl of aioli (p100), mustard, apple chutney and warm bread. Get everyone to spoon it into warm wide bowls. Enjoy with a good red wine or chilled cider.

A BOX OF HOT SAUSAGE ROLLS AND RHUBARB CHUTNEY

MAKES 6 ROLLS

INGREDIENTS

9 good-quality sausages (or 600g
    sausage meat)
salt and pepper
1 x 375g pack all-butter puff pastry
1 egg, beaten with 1 tsp water
poppy seeds for topping (optional)

PORK AND BLACK PUDDING

15g black pudding, roughly crumbled
2 fresh sage leaves, chopped

PORK AND LEMON

25g fresh white breadcrumbs
grated zest of ½ lemon
a pinch of dried sage
¼ of an onion, grated
1–2 tsp beaten egg

PORK AND BEAN

grated zest of ¼ lemon rind
2 sage leaves
4 tbsp baked beans

RHUBARB CHUTNEY

4 sticks of rhubarb
1 eating apple
40ml water
1 small onion, peeled and sliced
2cm piece of fresh ginger, grated
50ml cider vinegar
100g caster sugar
10g brown sugar

—— CHANGE IT UP ——

1. Make your own sausages: mince up 450g
pork belly slices. Mix with 110g fresh white
breadcrumbs, 1 beaten egg, 1–2 tsp dried
sage, salt and pepper and additional flavours
such as crushed garlic/paprika/lemon
zest. Shape and fry a small piece to test the
seasoning. Adjust if you need to. Divide the
rest equally and shape into sausages.
2. Replace puff pastry with quick flaky
pastry (p199).

Who doesn't love a sausage roll? Do a huge batch for a party and watch them go missing. Get creative with your own sausage mix variations. The chutney gives these babies a different dimension.

PREP Make the chutney: Slice the rhubarb and chop the apple. Put them into a pan with the water. Cook over a low heat for a few minutes, stirring, until they start to soften. Add the onion and ginger to the pan and cook down for a minute or so. Stir in the vinegar and sugars. Boil for 1 minute then cover. Simmer on a very low heat for 25 minutes, stirring occasionally.

Make the sausage roll mixes: if using sausages, split them lengthways to release the meat and divide it equally between three bowls. If using sausage meat; split as before and season it lightly with salt and pepper.

Break the meat up with a fork. Now add each of the 3 flavourings to the bowls so you have 3 fillings (don't add the beans to number 3 yet! Mix lightly with a fork and then your hands.

Preheat the oven to 220°C/Gas 7. Grease a large baking tray.

On a large lightly floured board or clean surface, roll the pastry into a 30 x 25cm rectangle. Neaten the sides with a sharp knife and divide into 6.

Divide each of your fillings in two and roll into thick, even sausages. Sit each sausage in the middle of a pastry rectangle. For the sausage and bean roll, spoon 1–2 teaspoons of beans on top of the meat.

Brush the surrounding pastry lightly with beaten egg. Fold the pastry over the roll and join the edges securely. Neaten the ends if you need to. Turn and sit them seam-side down on the baking tray. Make 4 light diagonal slashes across the top of each one. Brush with beaten egg and sprinkle with poppy seeds, if using.

COOK Bake for 20 minutes, or until cooked and golden. Place on a rack.

PLATE Serve warm or cold with the rhubarb and ginger chutney and ketchup. They also make a great snack to go or a good lunch with cheese, fruit, bread and pickles.

BEER BATTERED
TOAD IN THE HOLE

FEEDS 4

INGREDIENTS

25g beef/pork dripping
 (or 2 tbsp olive/groundnut oil)
6–8 pork/pork and apple sausages
110g butternut squash, cubed
 (optional)

BATTER
150ml cold milk
75ml cold water
130g plain white flour
a pinch of salt
½ teaspoon mustard powder
2 large free-range eggs
75ml chilled light beer/lager/dry cider
(or more cold water)

——— BONUS BITES ———
BACON TOADS
Slit the sausages down one side. Peel off the
skins. Twist a strip of pancetta or a rasher of
thinned and stretched streaky bacon round
each one. Add to the sizzling fat 8 minutes
before you add the batter. Turn once.
VEGGIE TOADS
Add good vegetarian sausages to sizzling oil
2 minutes before you add the batter. Throw
in quartered onions with the oil if you like.
BAKED BANGERS
Roll sausages (skins intact) in very thin
bacon. Brown and bake with chunks of
potato, butternut squash, onion quarters,
lemon, garlic, herbs and oil in a roasting tin
at 200°C/Gas 6 for 30–40 minutes.

········ TIME SAVER ········
For fast gravy: mix and heat 3 tbsp water
and a squeeze of lemon juice/3 tbsp red wine
with 3 tbsp onion marmalade (p144).

Banging beer in your batter lightens it and boosts the flavour.
Dripping gives it an extra dimension. Get the tin and the fat good and
hot to guarantee a good rise. Buy a quality sausage for this classic.

PREP Make the batter 30 minutes before you cook the toad (chilling
improves it). By hand: Measure the milk and water into a jug (if
using beer, add that at a later stage). Sift the flour, salt and mustard into a bowl.
Make a well in the centre. Crack the eggs into it. Add 2 tablespoons of liquid.
Beat with a wooden spoon or balloon whisk, gradually incorporating the flour
as you pour the rest of the milk and water in very slowly for a smooth batter.
By machine: Blitz everything (except beer/lager/cider if using).

Make the gravy (see below) at this stage so the onions have time to caramelise.

COOK Preheat the oven to 230°C/Gas 8. Put the dripping or oil into a
roasting/enamel tin (I use a 30 x 12 x 7cm tin as it gives the batter
room to rise, but a small one works too). Heat it up for a good 10 minutes.
Remove the tin. Close the oven door to retain heat. Add the sausages and
return the tin to the oven immediately. Cook for 5 minutes. Remove the tin
again, add the squash and turn the sausages. Brush fat up the sides of the tin
with a pastry brush. Return to the oven for 5 minutes.

If using beer/lager/cider, beat it into the batter for 1 minute. Take the tin from
the oven and pour your batter straight in. Return to the oven immediately.
Cook for 25 minutes without opening the oven door, until the toad is puffed
and golden.

PLATE Get your toad to the table before it sinks. Spoon or cut it out (it's
not elegant). Spoon over the gravy and serve up with mustard mash
(opposite) and shredded Savoy cabbage, blanched then tossed in a little butter
and garlic.

TO GO WITH
ONION GRAVY
Finely slice 2 large onions. Heat a little butter and 2 tbsp oil in a pan
over a medium heat. Add the onion slices, 1 crushed garlic clove and a
pinch of sugar. Cook very gently, stirring, for 10–15 minutes until the
onions are softened and slightly browned. Stir in 1 tbsp flour, before
slowly pouring in 200ml chicken stock and 250ml beer or dry cider,
stirring all the time. Add 1 tsp each of Worcester sauce and balsamic
vinegar. Season to taste. Simmer for 10–15 minutes.

A PROPER PORK CHOP
WITH MAPLE SYRUP APPLES

 FAST

FEEDS 2

INGREDIENTS

2 x 150–200g good pork chops
   (bone in or out)
2 sharp eating apples
a squeeze of lemon juice
salt and pepper
1 tbsp olive oil
a knob of butter
a glug of maple syrup

A proper chop is a great test of some key skills: track down the best meat and judge exactly how far to push it with the heat so your pork isn't overcooked. You want it to hang on to its juices and yet develop the best flavour it can from the pan before slapping on those sweet apples…

PREP Remove the chops from the fridge and allow to return to room temperature. 5 minutes before cooking, core your apples and slice lengthways into centimetre-thick half moons. Toss in lemon juice. Season the chops with salt and pepper.

COOK Add the oil and butter to a heavy-bottomed pan over a medium-high heat. When it's good and hot, slap the chops down. Leave the undersides to brown for 2–3 minutes as you spoon the juices over the top of the chops. Turn, spooning still, and fry till the pork is white all through but soft and juicy still (6–8 minutes altogether but test it). Remove to a plate to rest in a warm place. Add a sprinkle more salt.

Spoon off some of the fat from the pan if you think you need to. Return it to the heat. Add the apple pieces and fry for a minute or two, turning with a spatula, till they're just softening but holding their shape. Add a glug of maple syrup and stir to coat the apple in the hot toffee, turning the heat off under the pan so it doesn't burn.

PLATE Sit the chops on a plate. Spoon the apple pieces neatly on top with the lovely sweet sauce. Enjoy with mustard mash and steamed broccoli or cabbage.

BONUS BITES

GRIDDLED HERB CHOPS

Bash a garlic clove and a little snipped rosemary/sage/thyme in a pestle and mortar with 2 pinches of sea salt, zest of ½ lemon, 2 tbsp lemon juice and olive oil. Rub into your chops. Get a griddle pan searing hot. Cook for 2–3 minutes per side until golden, rest and plate up with a fresh and spicy tomato salsa (p75) and baked baby potatoes.

CRISPY BUTTERFLY CHOPS

Butterfly 2 large, thick, bone-in pork chops, open them up and thin out. Dip in seasoned flour, then beaten egg, then a mix of panko breadcrumbs (p201) and parmesan. Fry for 3 minutes per side till white and juicy inside, crispy outside. These are brilliant hot with salad or cold to go for a lunch or picnic.

FREESTYLE GRILLED/BBQ CHOPS WITH FRUIT SALSA

Trim the fat off the chops with scissors, making a few snips in the remaining fat on the edges to stop them curling in the heat. Rub them with a mix of chilli, paprika, ground coriander and oil. Cook over a high heat, grill or BBQ till done. Eat with a mix of chopped mango/peach, lime, coriander, diced fresh red chilli and sea salt.

TO GO WITH

MUSTARD MASH

Put 600g peeled potatoes on to boil in a pan of cold water and with a pinch of salt. Cook for 15–20 minutes or until tender. Drain. Return to the pan adding a splash of hot milk, 50g butter, 1 tsp mustard, a squeeze of lemon juice and seasoning. Mash and beat till creamy, adding a bit of chopped basil/parsley if you have some handy.

SIMPLE ROAST PORK
AND BAKED APPLES

FEEDS 4

INGREDIENTS

1 x 1.35kg pork loin joint (bone in)
1–2 tsp fennel seeds
½ tbsp dried thyme/sage
a few sprigs of rosemary/sage
a few garlic cloves, peeled
sea salt and pepper
4 eating apples, halved
200ml cider
300ml chicken stock/water
1 star anise
juice of ½ a lemon (optional)

TIP
If you'd rather use a boneless rolled joint just adjust the cooking times (p96).

—— CHANGE IT UP ——
1. Replace the apples with plum halves drizzled with honey and cinnamon. **2.** Add potato, red onion and beetroot wedges to the tin for the last hour. **3.** Fry walnut-sized balls of my sausage meat, sage and black pudding mix (p106) till brown before finishing in the tin for 20 minutes.

Autumn on a plate and unashamedly traditional. Check out page 97 for notes on crackling and look forward to sweet meat, crunchy skin and apple gravy. Totally delicious.

PREP Weigh the joint and calculate the cooking time (p96). Before it returns to room temperature, score the fat on the pork using a sharp paring or Stanley knife. Don't add any oil. Squeeze the fennel seeds and dried herbs into the scored lines. Sit fat-side up in a roasting tin. Tuck the fresh herbs and the garlic cloves underneath. Preheat the oven to 230°C/Gas 8. Rub the skin all over with sea salt at the last minute and bang in the oven.

COOK Roast for 15 minutes. Reduce the heat to 180°C/Gas 4. Cook for a further 1 hour 40 minutes. Add the halved apples, cut-side down. Start to check the meat for doneness with a skewer or meat thermometer – it should be white with clear juices (it may need a further 20 minutes). Remove when done. Leave to rest in a warm place for 10–15 minutes.

Meantime, remove the apples, garlic and herbs from the tin and arrange on a plate. Put the tin on the hob. Add the cider, stock/water and star anise. Stir well, scraping up all the caramelised bits. Bring to the boil and simmer, whisking, until reduced by a third. Remove the star anise and season to taste. Add lemon if it needs a little acidity.

PLATE Using a sharpened carving knife, cut the crackling neatly away from the meat and remove it in once piece. Cut the meat away from the bone and carve into slices. Arrange on a plate with the roasted apples and serve with the gravy, onion sauce, red cabbage, cauliflower cheese, roast potatoes or mustard mash (p109).

SIDES

RASPBERRY VINEGAR
RED CABBAGE

Preheat the oven to 180°C/Gas 4. Remove the core and strip the outer leaves from 1 red cabbage and slice into thin strips (½cm thick). Core, peel and slice 2 apples. Peel and slice 1 onion, and crush two garlic cloves. Layer the cabbage, garlic, onion and apple in an ovenproof dish, sprinkling with a little mixed spice and 1 tbsp brown sugar as you do so. Dot with butter and pour over 2 tbsp raspberry vinegar. Put in the preheated oven and cook for 20 minutes. Stir and season to taste before returning to the oven for a further 20 minutes.

ONION SAUCE

Peel and finely chop 1 large mild onion. Melt a knob of butter in a heavy pan. Add the onion, cover with greaseproof paper and leave over a very low heat for a few minutes until soft and translucent without a hint of colour. Whip the paper off and stir in 150ml whipping cream. Let it bubble gently to reduce by half. Season with salt and white pepper. Blend with a stick blender or in a food processor. Add 1 tsp of finely chopped sage, cover and keep warm until serving.

CAULIFLOWER CHEESE

Preheat the oven to 230°C/Gas 8. Peel an onion and place in a pan with a bay leaf and 600ml milk. Bring it to the point of boiling and turn it off immediately. Leave for at least 30 minutes for the flavours to infuse. Meantime, cut the leaves and base from a cauliflower and break into florets. Bring a pan of water to the boil. Add the cauliflower and cook for 10 minutes or till just turning tender. Drain into a colander.

Melt 50g butter gently in a heavy-bottomed pan. Add 50g plain flour and stir with a wooden spoon on a low heat for 2 minutes as the mix cooks into a paste (or roux). Remove from the heat, take the onion and bay leaf out of the milk and add it to the roux a bit at a time, whisking to incorporate it smoothly. Return the pan to a low heat. Whisk or stir for 8 minutes until thickened. Throw in 150g strong cheddar, 1 tsp mustard, the juice of ½ a lemon and a dash of Worcestershire sauce/mushroom ketchup. Season to taste. Throw the cauliflower into one big dish or small ones, pour the sauce over and top with 25g more cheese. Bake for 20–30 minutes until golden.

CRISP CHINESE PORK BELLY

FEEDS 4-6

INGREDIENTS

1 x 1.5kg piece of boneless pork belly
MARINADE
3 garlic cloves, peeled and crushed
a pinch of sugar
1 tbsp groundnut oil
½ tsp sesame oil
2 tsp fine salt
1½ tsp Chinese five spice
RUB
1 tsp fennel seeds
1 tsp Chinese five spice
1 tsp sea salt

—— BONUS BITE ——

ROAST PORK BELLY AND WALNUT SALAD
Preheat the oven to 220°C/Gas 7. Score and
stab your pork belly all over. Press 2–3 tsp
fennel/cumin seeds, some dried rosemary/
sage/thyme and sea salt into the cracks. Bang
it into the oven and blast for 20 minutes.
Reduce the heat to 150°C/Gas 2. Roast for
3–4 hours until the meat's meltingly tender
and the crackling crisp (slip under the grill
for a quick final crisp if needed).

To make the dressing: put 2 tsp Dijon
mustard into a bowl. Whisk in 2 tbsp white
wine vinegar, drop by drop. Add 125ml
walnut oil, whisking drop by drop till creamy.
Season. Set aside. Boil 300g baby potatoes for
10 minutes till tender. Assemble: Arrange a
mix of lettuce/watercress/chicory in a bowl.
Add the drained potatoes. Toss in dressing.
Carve the meat into ribs (if boned) or
lengths. Scatter over the salad pieces of crisp
streaky bacon or caramelised walnuts (p194).

Pork belly absorbs Chinese flavours beautifully. Follow the ritual to get the skin good and crisp. It's delicious eaten warm, though I also like it cold, dipped in soy or hoisin sauce.

PREP Score the skin for crackling (p97). Stab it all over with a sharp knife. Pour a bit of boiling water into a large dish. Invert the meat and stick a fork into either side. Hold the top of the joint (the fat and skin only) in the water for 5 minutes. Remove and pat dry.

Mix the marinade ingredients in a large dish. Sit the pork in it, skin-side up. Leave to chill, uncovered, for 3 hours or overnight. Remove and return to room temperature before cooking.

COOK Preheat the oven to 220°C/Gas 7. Rub the fennel seeds, five spice and salt into the cracks. Put the meat in a tin and cook, skin-side up, for 20 minutes. Lower the oven to 200°C/Gas 6 and cook for another 50 minutes till crisp and tender. Remove.

Preheat the grill to high. Sit the meat under it for 2–3 minutes to crisp. Leave to rest for 15 minutes.

PLATE Carve or break into chunks with a cleaver. Eat on bowls of rice drizzled with hoisin sauce.

LAMB

Sheep have everything going for them. They're cute and tasty. Joking aside, lamb's a wonderful meat full of unique, powerful flavour. Yet again it's all about breed and sourcing if you want to avoid the tough old rubbish that can hit the market. Start by getting your hands on young spring lamb. It's the most tender. Check out salt marsh lamb too – it's got a unique salty tang that, as with all lamb, reflects the taste of the environment it's lived in. Rare breed lamb is actually on the increase. If in doubt about where to start, have a chat to your local butcher and hopefully he/she will hook you up with some fantastic produce. Let's also not forget the older ladies and gents. Hogget, a sheep of 9–18 months old, has a beautiful, deeper flavour. It needs a longer cook but is well worth the wait. Mutton, older than 18 months, has an even richer, gutsy flavour and is great when cooked nice and slow. From the humble stew to exotic curries, the sheep really gives you its all while retaining its own robust identity. Get stuck in (and don't make any baaaaa-d jokes – sorry).

WHICH LAMB IN THE PAN?

NECK/SCRAG END A bargain cut to mince up for **BURGERS, MEATBALLS** etc. or slow **BRAISE** in stock with vegetables to bring out its flavour.

NECK FILLET A great little cut, best diced and slow cooked in a **CASSEROLE** or flavoured in a nice marinade for **SKEWERS**.

SHOULDER Richly sweet flavoured meat, good for **ROLLING, STUFFING** and **ROASTING**.

DICED SHOULDER The obvious choice for **STEWS** and **CURRIES**, nice and juicy, don't rush it.

RACK OF LAMB A rack of small cutlets in a single sweet piece makes a really fast **ROAST**. Lean, so needs well oiling or protecting with a crust.

CUTLETS Sweet and tender chops which are great for fast suppers. Versatile and lovely – **GRIDDLE, PAN-FRY** or **OVEN ROAST**.

LOIN Like beef fillet, it's tender, expensive and likes a fast **ROAST**. Eat it pink.

NOISETTE A cut from the loin and a neat eat. **GRILL** or **PAN-FRY**. It loves a good sauce.

LOIN CHOP A leaner chop, **GRIDDLE, GRILL, PAN-FRY, BRAISE**. Eat pink.

CHUMP A great fast cook cut. Cube for **KEBABS** or eat as **STEAKS**.

CHUMP CHOP Bigger than loin chop and sweet as it's on the bone. **GRILL** or **FRY**.

BREAST Cheap and sweet, but fatty. Cook **WHOLE ON THE BONE** or get it boned, roll it up, **STUFF** it and slap in the oven. Or chop and use as a **STEWING** meat.

LEG OF LAMB Perfect for **ROASTING**, bone in or out. Stuff it if you like. Open it up, spice it up and butterfly it for a **BARBECUE**. Whole or half-leg works for a medium-fast roast to eat pink, or a long slow roast to get it falling off the bone.

DICED LEG Good for faster **STEWS** and **CURRIES**.

LEG STEAKS Versatile. **GRIDDLE, GRILL**, quick cook in the **OVEN, SKEWER, BBQ** or **STIR-FRY**.

SHANKS The tip of the leg. Great sweet meat when given a very long **BRAISE** with wine or stock.

CHILL pre-packaged lamb in vacuum packs etc. in original sealed containers.

LOOSELY WRAPPED or bagged meat needs to be taken out of its packaging.

PLACE it on a dish/plate that's large enough to contain any drips/liquids.

COVER it loosely in foil or greaseproof paper. Store away from cooked and raw foods.

FREEZE individual portions by tightly wrapping them in cling film before putting into freezer bags, so you can grab them easily as you want them.

REFRIGERATE roasts, steaks and chops for 3–5 days; diced meat for 2 days; mince for 1 day.

If you want to **MARINATE** lamb; store roasts, steaks and chops in the mix for up to 4 days. Diced and stewing meat can be marinated for 2 days.

Lamb roasts, steaks and chops can be **FROZEN** for 9 months; mince for 3 months.

WHAT TO LOOK FOR
in your LAMB

LOOK FOR:

GOOD MARBLING

FIRM-TEXTURED MEAT WITH A PINKISH HUE

WHITE AND FIRM FAT

AVOID:

DARK AND WET MEAT

YELLOW AND SOFT FAT

TOO MUCH FAT

LAMB ACTION

BUTTERFLYING

This is a nice, relaxed way with a leg of lamb. Get it boned out (ask the butcher to 'tunnel bone it') then marinate, barbecue, oven-cook or grill it.

1. Lay the leg on a board.

2. Stick your filleting or sharp chef's knife into the cavity left from the bone.

3. Cut it open from top to bottom

4. Open the joint out (it looks like a butterfly). Turn upside down.

5. Make a slight cut through the centre, like the hinge in a book, to keep it flat.

6. Turn it over. Make some light criss-cross cuts to take any rubs, spices etc.

7. Cook as per your chosen recipe.

SUPERMARKET SHEEP SHOPPING

Supermarkets keep the most common cuts - easy roasts and lots of useful quick-cook chops and steaks. Their butcher counters can tell you about provenance (good ones are hot on this) and will cut joints etc. to the size you want. Plus, they save their best meat for the counter. The best lamb is aged for 8 days for flavour. If you're in a hurry and can't go through the detective work, use your eye and judgement. Lamb freezes better than other meats. So, save yourself cash and pick up bargains from the freezers. Better, buy spring lamb in season and freeze your own. If you're after rare breed lamb, check out what's available on the internet.

SHEEP DOCTOR

LAMB PROVIDES...

AMINO ACIDS

WHICH YOUR BODY NEEDS TO BUILD AND KEEP STRONG

PROTEIN

JUST 90g PROVIDES 43%

OF YOUR DAILY RECOMMENDED DOSE

That's support for healthy hair, skin, eyes, bones, muscles

B VITAMINS

to help fight depression, maintain a healthy nervous system and SUPPORT GOOD MENTAL AND PHYSICAL HEALTH

IRON

necessary to get you performing at peak, physically and mentally.

ZINC HELPS PREVENT INFECTIONS, AID

healing and knock off colds.

Omega 3s

found in grass-fed lamb help with mental agility.

VITAMIN D

A KEY VITAMIN WHICH HELPS STRENGTHEN BONES, BATTLE

S.A.D *(seasonal affective disorder)*

and is now thought to be a useful tool to help battle cancers

---

COOKING TIMES FOR LAMB

I like my lamb just pink, not raw and never overcooked.
Times depend on heat and size so are approximate.
Always test it. Rest cuts for 5 minutes. Roasts for 15.

FAST CUTS

PER SIDE [CUTLETS / CHOPS / STEAKS

1 LAMB = 1 MINUTE

KEBABS

RACK OF LAMB

1 LAMB = 1 MINUTE

BIG ROASTS

Cook your roasts at 220°C/Gas 7 for 10 minutes. Reduce to 180°C/Gas 4.

RARE
18 minutes per 450g

MEDIUM
25 minutes per 450g plus 20

WELL-DONE
30 minutes per 450g plus 25

TESTING, TESTING
Is it done yet?

SKEWER TRICK – poke it into the thickest bit of meat. Avoid the bone. Count to 5.

 HOLD IT ON YOUR WRIST.
COLD (rare)
WARM (medium)
SCALDING (well-done).

80°C
well-done

70°C
medium

60°C
rare

MEAT THERMOMETER NEEDS TO READ...

FLAVOUR IT UP

Lamb can take really strong flavours, so treat your chops, roasts and cutlets to some creative herb and spice mixes. Leg and shoulder joints can be changed completely by stuffing. Spread the mix over your unrolled shoulder or into your boned leg, then tie it up to flavour from the inside out.

Marinate with...

1. Olive oil, lemon juice or white wine vinegar, Dijon mustard, garlic and thyme
2. Yoghurt, cumin, garlic, coriander, turmeric, cinnamon and lemon
3. Smoked paprika, lime, chilli powder and yoghurt
4. Chinese wine/vinegar, soy sauce, garlic, oyster sauce and coriander

RUB WITH...

1. Pesto and oil and lemon
2. Harissa paste, garlic and lemon
3. A bit of your favourite curry paste, oil and apricot jam
4. Tapenade, oil and lemon

STUFF WITH...

1 Salsa verde or tapenade mixed with breadcrumbs
2 Softened onion, chopped mint, pine nuts and cooked couscous
3 Cubed dried apricots, breadcrumbs, garlic, softened shallot, lemon juice and rosemary

COVER WITH...

1. HERB CRUST Blitz up 175g white bread with 2 garlic cloves, 2–3 tbsp finely chopped herbs, 50g soft butter and season with salt and pepper. Mix it up. Spread Dijon mustard over your lamb and press the crust into it.
2. MUSTARD AND GARLIC BREAD CRUST Blitz bread with garlic, dried mint, lemon zest and mustard powder. Brush melted redcurrant jelly over lamb. Add the crumb.

A SHEEP *(carving)* TRICK

Instead of faffing about here's a quick carving trick. Sit the joint on a board, fat end down. Hold the shank. Cut straight down one side as close to the bone as you can. Do the same with the other side. Cut the meat across into thick slices. Done...

FRIENDS ALMOND, ANCHOVY, APRICOT, AUBERGINE, BEANS, BULGUR WHEAT, BALSAMIC VINEGAR, BUTTERNUT SQUASH, BLACK PUDDING, CARDAMOM, CHESTNUT, CHICKPEAS, CHILLI, CINNAMON, CORIANDER, COURGETTES, CUCUMBER, CUMIN, COUSCOUS, DRIED FRUITS, FETA, GARLIC, HARISSA PASTE, HUMMUS, LEMON, MINT, NUTMEG, ONION, OREGANO, PARSLEY, PEAS, POTATO, RED WINE, RHUBARB, ROSEMARY, STAR ANISE, SWEDE, THYME, TOMATO, YOGHURT

GRIDDLED CUTLETS
WITH HOT BREAD AND FRESH HERB SALSA

HEALTHY · FAST · FEEDS 2-3

No fancy tricks: it's simply sweet meat teamed up with a saucy herby concoction. To mix it up a bit, slap on a marinade (p117). Eat your salsa rough or blitz it into a smooth sauce.

INGREDIENTS

3–4 cutlets per person, whatever size you want (at room temperature)
a little olive oil
sea salt and pepper
4–6 slices of bread (coarse-textured white or sourdough)
FRESH HERB SALSA
15g mint (leaves only)
15g fresh coriander
½ tbsp small capers, drained and roughly chopped
5 anchovy fillets, finely chopped
juice of ½ a lemon
4 tbsp olive oil
1 tsp Dijon mustard

TIP
Team the salsa with lamb steaks/roasts/griddled chicken. The smooth version's good with cheese soufflé (for dipping) or spread in an omelette.

········ TIME SAVER ········
Make up the salsa ahead and chill in a covered bowl until ready to use. The smooth one stores for up to 2 weeks.

——— CHANGE IT UP ———
1. Rub a bit of mint sauce and balsamic vinegar into the meat to flavour before oiling the pan and griddling.
2. For sweet griddled cutlets, brush a mix of honey, mint and lemon juice onto plain cutlets 2 minutes before they're done.
3. Try baking your cutlets: marinate for at least 30 minutes, then bake at 180°C/Gas 4 for 10 minutes per side.

PREP Make the salsa: Wash and dry the mint leaves and coriander. For a rough salsa, chop the herbs pretty finely on a board with a sharp chef's knife. Place in a bowl with the chopped capers, anchovies, lemon juice, oil and mustard. For a smooth salsa, blitz everything in a food processor or hand-held blender until smooth.

Prep the cutlets: Trim off any excess fat if necessary, and rub a few drops of oil into the meat with your fingers (or use a pastry brush, if squeamish). Season lightly with pepper and a tiny bit of salt.

COOK Heat a griddle pan till it's almost smoking hot. Slap the meat down and cook for 2 minutes without shifting. Flip. Repeat for 2 minutes to colour well and flavour up. Turn each cutlet onto its fatty back with tongs and hold for a few seconds to brown up. For well-done, give the meat another minute per side. Test to see it's done as you like it (p116). Rest it on a plate and sprinkle with sea salt.

Griddle the bread in the hot pan for 30 seconds per side, or until crisp and marked by the lamb juices.

PLATE Pile the cutlets and bread on a plate and let people grab. Serve the salsa in a bowl for dipping. Enjoy with tabbouleh (p128) or couscous salad, any griddled vegetables and mezze dips such as hummus (p38), cucumber tzatziki (p40) and yoghurt mixed with crushed garlic.

BONUS BITES

A RACK OF CUTLETS
Preheat your oven to 220°C/Gas 7. Sear the rack on both sides in a very hot pan with a bit of oil. When cool, spread the fat side with 1 tbsp smooth salsa/pesto/Dijon mustard. Blitz up 2 handfuls of fresh herbs, 2 handfuls of crustless white bread, 1 garlic clove and press on top of the lamb to form a crust. Roast for 15–20 minutes. Combine a little redcurrant jelly and red wine in a pan and simmer for a minute. Drizzle over the cutlets to finish.

STICKY SPICED CUTLETS
Rub the cutlets in a mix of 1 tsp grated ginger, 1 tsp cumin, ½ tsp coriander, ½ tsp turmeric, 2 crushed garlic cloves and 3 tsp groundnut/vegetable oil. Griddle as before. Eat with rice and raita (p130).

CUTLETS AND BEANS
Rub the cutlets with a bit of olive oil, lemon juice, crushed garlic and dried oregano. In a pan warm a glug of olive oil, 1–2 diced garlic cloves, a sprig of rosemary and 400g drained canned cannellini beans for 5 minutes. Griddle the cutlets as before and serve on the beans with crunchy bread.

GREEK LAMB PIE

FEEDS 4

INGREDIENTS

1–2 aubergines (roughly 450g)
salt and pepper
olive oil
1 tsp dried oregano/thyme
2–3 floury white potatoes
2 medium onions, peeled and chopped
2–3 garlic cloves, peeled and crushed
grated zest of 1 lemon
a handful of fresh oregano/thyme/
    parsley
700g best minced lamb
¼ tsp ground cinnamon
50ml red wine
1 x 400g can chopped tomatoes or
    squashed plum tomatoes
2 tbsp tomato purée
1 tsp sugar
125g feta cheese, cut into cubes
a handful of freshly grated parmesan

—— CHANGE IT UP ——

For all-Greek moussaka, use two-thirds
aubergine, one-third potato. Finish with
a layer of aubergine and cover with a
béchamel sauce (p185) made with
feta cheese instead of cheddar.

—— BONUS BITE ——

ALL-LANCASHIRE HOTPOT

Coat 700g cubed stewing lamb (or 2 lamb
shoulder chops, bone in and excess fat
removed, per person) in flour, seasoning and
dried rosemary. Brown it off in a pan. Sweat
3 thickly sliced large onions in oil and butter
for 10 minutes. Peel and thinly slice 900g
floury potatoes. Layer up the lamb, onion
and potato, finishing with a final layer of
potato. Add 200ml chicken stock, but don't
submerge it. Dot with butter, cover with foil
and bake at 200°C/Gas 6 for 1½–2 hours,
uncovering to brown for the last 10 minutes.

*Lancashire goes to Greece in this great concoction: you've got layers
of gorgeous aubergine in a tasty lamb moussaka sauce topped with
crunchy, succulent golden potatoes.*

PREP
Preheat the oven to 220°C/Gas 7.

AUBERGINES: Slice into 1cm rounds. Sprinkle with a little salt and leave to sweat
(de-gorge) on a board in a single layer for 15 minutes. Pat the salt off and blot
dry using kitchen paper. Sit on a non-stick baking sheet, brush with oil and
sprinkle with the dried oregano/thyme. POTATOES: Peel and slice into 3mm
rounds. Pat dry. Sit in a single layer on another baking sheet. Brush with oil. Put
the 2 baking sheets into the oven. Bake for 10 minutes or until the aubergine is
softening and the potato is starting to turn golden. Remove and set aside.

Meantime, make the sauce. Heat a glug of oil in a large sauté pan or casserole
dish. Add the onion, garlic, lemon zest and fresh herbs. Fry the mix gently
without colouring for 5 minutes or so, or until the onion is translucent. Keep
stirring so it doesn't catch. Increase the heat a bit. Crumble the meat in. Stir to
colour for a minute or two. Add the cinnamon. Increase the heat, add the wine
and let it bubble. Add the tomatoes, purée and sugar. Reduce to a low heat and
simmer for 10 minutes, stirring occasionally, until the sauce is reasonably
thick but not at all dry. Taste and add seasoning.

Spoon a little sauce into the base of one large or 4 small ovenproof dishes.
Cover with a single layer of aubergine. Scatter over a few feta cubes. Add more
sauce. Add a layer of potato. Scatter over some parmesan. Add more sauce,
aubergine and feta, finishing with potato arranged in slightly overlapping
circles on top.

COOK
Cover with foil and bake in the oven for 20 minutes. Remove the foil
and cook for another 5–10 minutes, or until the potatoes are golden
and the insides are bubbling away. Remove and let it settle for 5 minutes.

PLATE
Bang individual pies onto small plates. Sit a large pie on the table
and spoon it out. This is perfect with spoonfuls of cool tzatziki
(p40) and dressed tomato salad.

MINTED SHEPHERD'S PIE

FEEDS 4

INGREDIENTS

5g porcini or other dried mushrooms
100ml boiling water
1 medium onion, peeled and finely
    chopped
3 garlic cloves, peeled and crushed
2 medium carrots, diced
1 tbsp olive oil
a knob of butter
salt and pepper
4 streaky bacon rashers, sliced
    and diced
700g best minced lamb
100ml red wine
50ml chicken stock (p49)
2 tbsp tomato purée
½ tsp dried thyme
½ tsp dried oregano
a handful of fresh parsley
1–2 tbsp mushroom ketchup (optional)
a squeeze of lemon (optional)
1–2 tsp good mint sauce/jelly
TOPPING
1.1kg floury potatoes, peeled
salt and pepper
25g butter
2 tsp mustard
juice of ½ a lemon
a splash of milk (optional)
a handful of freshly grated parmesan

*A shepherd's pie can be predictable; this on the other hand is not.
Adding just a few extras makes all the difference. Beautiful…*

PREP Pour the boiling water over the dried mushrooms and leave for 10 minutes. Prep the veg. Heat a large sauté pan, wide shallow pan or casserole dish. Add the oil, butter and a pinch of salt. Slap in the onion and garlic and cook gently for 5 minutes, or until transparent. Add the carrot. Cook for 3–4 minutes. Add the bacon and cook until the fat starts to run.

Drain the porcini over a bowl (saving the water). Chop them and add to the pan. Raise the heat a bit. Crumble the mince into the pan, breaking it up with your fingers. Stir it round to brown for a few minutes. Add the wine, mushroom soaking water and stock. Increase the heat and boil for a few seconds. Reduce to a very low simmer.

Add the tomato puree, thyme, oregano, parsley and mushroom ketchup, if using, and season with salt and pepper. Cook till you get a thick, rich sauce. Add more stock if it's too dry. Taste and adjust the seasoning, adding a squeeze of lemon, if you want.

Meantime, add the potatoes and a pinch of salt to a pan of cold water. Boil for 10–15 minutes until done (test with a knife). Drain, return to the pan and shuffle on the heat for a few seconds to dry. Put the dried potatoes into a potato ricer, or use a masher/fork to break them down. Add the butter, mustard and lemon juice and season with salt and pepper. Beat till smooth (don't use a processor). Add a drop of milk if stiff, but it mustn't be a sloppy mash. Taste, season and set aside.

COOK Preheat the oven to 200°C/Gas 6. Spoon the sauce into 1 large dish or 4 small ovenproof dishes till three-quarters full. Dribble a subtle amount of mint sauce/jelly over the top. Add the mash. Use a fork and spoon to blob it over then bring it to the edges and ensure the meat is fully covered. Make ridges/peaks for a crunchy finish. Sprinkle over the parmesan and sit the dish on a baking tray. Cook for 30 minutes, or till crusty and bubbling.

PLATE Spoon from the large dish or eat straight from your own. Serve with ketchup and brown sauce.

TIP

Boil whole unpeeled potatoes if you have
time, for a drier, finer result. Put them
through a ricer or peel to mash once cooked.

A LAMB IN A PAN

FAST

FEEDS 2

Sometimes you want to save on the washing up. So, slap some beautiful lamb steaks on top of soft potatoes to share their juices and eat straight from the pan. Why not?

INGREDIENTS

2 medium potatoes, peeled
1 shallot/small onion, peeled
2 good-sized lamb steaks (leg or other lean cut), at room temperature
olive oil, for frying
salt and pepper
a bit of chopped fresh rosemary (or a pinch of dried rosemary/thyme/sage)
2 garlic cloves, peeled and crushed
75ml white wine
1½ tsp Dijon mustard

PREP Preheat the oven to 180°C/Gas 4. Cube the potatoes: Using a sharp vegetable knife, slice off their ends to square them up, then cut into 2cm wide slices. Cut the slices into 2cm batons. Cut those into 2cm cubes. Dry them on kitchen paper. Dice the shallot/onion.

Prep the lamb: If fat's an issue, trim the edges with a sharp knife (though you'll lose flavour). Rub or brush your steaks with a little oil on both sides. Season with pepper.

COOK Heat an ovenproof frying pan over medium/high heat. Slap the steaks down. Sizzle and sear for a minute per side or till golden brown. Lift with tongs and hold any fatty edges of the meat down on the pan to brown up. Remove and set aside.

Add a splash more oil to the pan. Add the potato cubes and fry off for a few minutes, turning, until lightly golden. Add the herbs, shallot/onion and garlic. Fry a few minutes more. Increase the heat. Add the wine and stir in the mustard. Sit the lamb steaks on top.

Transfer the pan to the oven. Roast the lamb in the pan for 5 minutes, or until the potatoes are soft. (Be careful not to overcook the meat: test it with a knife and lift it off early if need be.) Remove. Sprinkle with sea salt. Rest the pan in a warm place for 3 minutes before serving.

PLATE Go rustic. Slap the pan (on a mat) in the middle of the table and help yourselves: eat with salad, fresh greens, a good dollop of mustard and bread for mopping up the juices.

——— BONUS BITES ———

LAMB IN A DISH

Preheat the oven to 180°C/Gas 4. Boil a handful of new potatoes for 10 minutes till just soft. Drain, crush them a bit and throw into a roasting tin with quartered onions, cherry tomatoes and chunks of courgettes and aubergine. Fry the steaks in hot oil for 2 minutes till browned. Sit them on the veg. Add a bit of oil, dried herbs, salt, garlic, lemon juice, and pesto/smooth fresh herb salsa (p118). Roast for 20–30 minutes. Remove the lamb early if the veg needs longer.

BATTERED LAMB

Bash your lamb steaks to thin them out. Coat in seasoned flour then dip into an egg beaten with 1 tsp mustard and 1 tbsp chopped basil. Coat in 2 handfuls of fresh breadcrumbs (p201) mixed with a little grated parmesan. Fry for 1–2 minutes per side till golden and cooked to your taste. Sprinkle with salt. Serve with lemon chunks.

THREE LAMB SKEWERS
WITH BEETROOT TZATZIKI

FEEDS 3-4

INGREDIENTS

TURKISH KEBABS
450g good lamb (leg or steak)
1 small onion, peeled and grated
a glug of olive oil
milk
KOFTA
750g good minced lamb
4 garlic cloves, peeled and crushed
100g white onion, peeled and grated
grated zest and juice of 1 lemon
1 tsp ground cumin
1 tsp ground coriander
a small bunch of coriander, chopped
KIBBE
1 x kofta mix (above)
125g bulgur wheat
1 tsp dried chilli flakes

✳✳✳✳ CASH SAVER ✳✳✳✳
Alternate the cubes of lamb kebab with
oil-brushed quartered onions, chunks of
courgette, mushrooms and cherry tomatoes.

········· TIME SAVER ·········
Prep skewers ahead for your BBQ, but give
them time to return to room temperature.

———— BONUS BITES ————
LAMB BURGER
Divide the kofta mix into 4 and shape into
burgers. Fry in oil or grill for 4 minutes a
side or till cooked. Stack in pitta/buns/wraps
with dollops of hummus and yoghurt mixed
with crushed garlic, a few rocket leaves, a bit
of crumbled feta and some slices of tomato.
FETA MEATBALLS
Divide the kofta mix into 8 balls. Flatten
each in your hand. Put a cube of feta in the
centre of each and pinch the meat into a
ball around it. Fry in oil for 3 minutes till
browned. Poach for 10 minutes in a pan of
easy tomato sauce (p176). Crack an egg in
per person and cover till cooked. Pile onto
pasta and enjoy.

*Forget your late-night van kebab: you can serve these up to the most
discerning customers. Cook all three on the BBQ to celebrate summer days
with mates or have your favourite skewer inside anytime; enjoy with healthy
beetroot tzatziki.*

PREP KEBABS: Chop the meat into bite-sized pieces with a chef's knife.
Add it to a bowl with the onion, olive oil and cover the lot with milk.
Chill and leave to marinate for at least 1 hour. Remove from the marinade. Blot
dry. Thread onto metal or pre-soaked wooden skewers.

KOFTA: Mix all the ingredients in a bowl using a fork. Break off and fry a nut-
sized piece in hot oil. Taste to check the seasoning's right. Adjust if you need
to. Use damp hands to scoop up a quarter of the mix and gently shape it into a
long sausage around the skewer. Repeat with the remainder. Chill the mix for
10 minutes.

KIBBE: Tip 125g bulgur wheat into a pan with 600ml cold water. Bring to the
boil. Reduce. Simmer on low for 15 minutes or till tender. Drain in a sieve.
Spread to dry or twist it in a tea towel. Fluff with a fork. Leave to cool. Make up
a batch of kofta mix. Lightly mix the two with a fork, adding the chilli flakes.
Test for seasoning and shape it onto skewers as for kofta.

Get your skewers to room temperature. Brush them lightly with oil. Season
lightly with salt and pepper.

COOK KEBABS: Heat up a griddle pan. Lay the skewers down and cook
quickly for 1–2 minutes, turning, until browned on the outside, a bit
pink and tender on the inside. Alternatively, cook on a medium BBQ. KOFTA/
KIBBE: Preheat a grill. Grill the skewers for a few minutes, turning regularly,
until cooked right through. Don't overcook or they'll toughen up.

PLATE Stack your skewers up on a plate. Eat with beetroot tzatziki, couscous
and griddled vegetables, or as part of a mezze platter (p38–40).

········· TO GO WITH **·········**

BEETROOT TZATZIKI
Peel 2 small (uncooked) beetroot and grate them thickly into a bowl.
Stir in 4 tbsp Greek yoghurt, the juice of ½ a lemon, a small bunch
of finely chopped mint, 1 tsp horseradish sauce and season to taste.
Leave for 30 minutes to infuse.

SLOW ROAST
LEG OF LAMB WITH BAKED AUBERGINES AND DAUPHINOISE POTATOES

FEEDS 6

INGREDIENTS

1 large leg of lamb on the bone
  (2kg plus)
6 fat garlic cloves
a small bunch of fresh rosemary
8–10 anchovy fillets
1 lemon
1 tbsp olive oil
salt and pepper
a few sprigs of fresh thyme/
  2 pinches of dried oregano
250ml red wine
250ml water/chicken stock (p49)
a bit of lemon juice (optional)
1 tsp redcurrant jelly (optional)

—— BONUS BITE ——
FASTER ROAST SPRING LAMB WITH LEMON

Preheat the oven to 220°C/Gas 7. Stab a piece of spring lamb (on or off the bone) and insert sprigs of rosemary and 6 sliced garlic cloves into the cuts. Rub with oil and seasoning. Roast in a tin without any liquid for 20 minutes. Pour the juice of 1 lemon over the lamb and reduce the heat to 180°C/Gas 4. Cook till done to your taste (p116). Rest it. Carve it traditionally and serve with gravy made from white wine.

Here's one for a Sunday dinner in autumn or winter. Don't fuss about the anchovies. They add a sweet, salty richness but your lamb won't taste of them. Team with gloriously rich dauphinoise potatoes and silky aubergines baked with cheese.

PREP
Start the night before or first thing. Dry the lamb with kitchen paper. Sit it on a board. Slice the garlic cloves into sticks. Pull the leaves off the rosemary stalks. Cut two-thirds of the anchovy fillets into halves. Thinly peel a third of your lemon and slice the zest into thin strips.

Stab the meat randomly with a sharp chef's knife to make defined cuts of about 2.5cm depth. Slot bits of garlic, anchovy, lemon and rosemary into them with bits of herb showing. Chill until needed (remembering to return to room temperature before cooking), or cook now.

Preheat the oven to 200°C/Gas 6. Rub the oil into the lamb, working round the herbs. Season lightly and sprinkle with the thyme/oregano. Sit the meat on top of the remaining anchovies in a roasting tin or dish. Pour the wine and water/stock into the tin. Put it into the oven.

COOK
After 20 minutes, reduce the temperature to 130°C/Gas 1. Roast for 4 hours or more, basting every 20 minutes, until you can see the meat is done – it should look soft and be practically coming away from the bone. Do the skewer test (p116). The meat won't be pink like young, faster-cooking spring lamb but it will be very sweet and tender. Remove from the oven and rest the meat, foil covered, for at least 20 minutes.

Make the gravy: Spoon off any excess oil from the meat juices. Put the tin on the hob. Add water/stock or a bit more wine. Boil it up and stir with a wooden spoon to reduce the mix a bit. Taste and adjust the seasoning. Add a bit of lemon juice if it needs it or a teaspoon of redcurrant jelly for sweetness.

PLATE
Carve the lamb the easy way (p117) by cutting into lovely thick slices. Serve with dauphinoise potatoes and baked aubergines for a real event or with peas, mint sauce and parsley and lemon potatoes.

TO GO WITH
BAKED AUBERGINES

Slice and de-gorge 3 large aubergines (p16) and fry in olive oil until just softening. Make up 1 quantity of easy tomato sauce (p176) or mix a jar of good passata with 3 crushed garlic cloves. Slice 2 balls of mozzarella and grate 150g parmesan. Spread a little tomato sauce over the base of an ovenproof dish. Add a layer of aubergines and a bit of the sliced mozzarella and parmesan, seasoning. Layer it up and finish with aubergines on top. Add what's left of the mozzarella and parmesan. Cover with a domed bit of foil. Bake with the lamb for an hour then remove the foil and stick the heat up to finish or cook under the grill. Alternatively, bake for 30 minutes at 200°C/Gas 6, removing the foil for the last 5 minutes.

TO GO WITH 🐑

DAUPHINOISE POTATOES

Preheat the oven to 180°C/Gas 4. Mix 300ml double cream, 100ml semi-skimmed milk, 6 crushed garlic cloves, seasoning and a pinch of dried thyme and nutmeg in a jug. Butter an ovenproof dish. Peel and slice 900g floury potatoes very thinly, using a sharp knife or mandolin. Layer half into the dish and pour over half the cream mix. Layer up the rest and pour over the rest of the cream. Cover with foil. Bake for an hour. Uncover and dot with 25g butter. Bake for a further 30 minutes or until tender (test with a knife).

MINT SAUCE

Drop 4 tbsp finely chopped fresh mint leaves into a bowl with 2 tbsp boiling water. Add 1½ tsp caster sugar, 1½ tbsp white wine vinegar and 2 pinches of salt. Leave for at least 30 minutes. Taste and adjust seasoning.

SLASHED ROAST LAMB AND YOGHURT FLATBREADS

FEEDS 3-4

INGREDIENTS

1 x 900g half leg of lamb (on the bone)
100ml yoghurt
4 garlic cloves, peeled and crushed
1 tbsp harissa paste
juice of ½ a lemon
salt and pepper
FLATBREADS
275g plain white flour
1 tsp cumin or fennel seeds
225ml natural yoghurt
a pinch of salt

✲✲✲✲ CASH SAVER ✲✲✲✲

Slash a lamb shoulder all over and sprinkle
with salt and paprika only. Rub with olive oil
and roast at 160°C/Gas 3 for 3 hours plus.

.... TIME SAVER ....

Substitute warm tortilla wraps or pitta
breads for the flatbreads.

——— BONUS BITE———

**FAST BUTTERFLY LAMB FOR THE OVEN
OR BARBECUE**
Get your butcher to butterfly a boned
lamb leg or do it yourself (p115). Slash the
underside and rub with a mix of 1 tbsp
paprika, juice of 1 lemon, olive oil and
6 crushed garlic cloves. Leave to marinate
for a few hours or overnight in a large sealed
plastic bag. Preheat the oven to 200°C/Gas
6. Cook in a tin till done and still pink inside
(p116). To barbecue, sit over a medium heat
on a rack that's 25cm from the coals. Baste
regularly and turn once.

A Moroccan take on lamb: this meat takes to yoghurt and spices.

PREP Sit your lamb on a board. Use a sharp chef's knife to slash 2.5 cm
deep cuts into the top of the joint in a criss-cross diamond pattern.
Mix the yoghurt, garlic, harissa and lemon juice together to form a paste and
season with salt and pepper. Rub into the top of lamb. Put it in a tin/dish and
leave to come to room temperature. Preheat the oven to 180°C/Gas 4.

COOK Put the lamb in the oven to cook. Test after 30 minutes. Once done
to your taste (p116), leave the meat to rest for at least 10 minutes.

Meantime, make the flatbreads. Sift the flour into a bowl. Add the rest of the
ingredients. Mix with a fork or your hand to form a dough and bring together
into a ball. Transfer to a lightly floured board. Divide into 8 pieces. Roll each
one out into a thin circle, quarter turning the dough with each roll as you go to
get it even. Heat a large flat frying/crêpe pan. Cook the flatbreads individually
for a minute or so till browning, then turn over to cook for another few
seconds. (Don't over-do it as you want them soft.) Keep the cooked wraps in a
tea towel to stay warm/soft as you repeat.

PLATE Carve the meat by cutting down each side of the bone (p117).
Slap it straight onto the fresh, warm flatbreads and wrap with
rocket, tomato, red onion, hummus and yoghurt mixed with crushed garlic or
lay it on top of a big pile of couscous salad or tabbouleh.

> **• • • • • • • • • • • TO GO WITH • • • • • • • • • •**
>
> # TABBOULEH
>
> Tip 125g bulgur wheat and 600ml water into a pan. Bring to the boil,
> reduce the heat and simmer for 15 minutes. Drain through a sieve
> and spread it out on a large plate to dry, or tip into a sieve/colander
> lined with a tea towel, bringing the ends of the towel together and
> twisting to squeeze moisture from the bulgur. Drop it into a bowl and
> fluff it with a fork. Mix in a pinch or two of salt, 2 tbsp each of finely
> chopped mint and flat-leaf parsley, 2 deseeded diced tomatoes, ½ a
> cucumber, deseeded and diced, ½ diced red onion, 2–3 tbsp good
> fruity olive oil and 3 tbsp lemon juice. Mix lightly with a fork. Top
> with a handful of pomegranate seeds and your choice of extras: a few
> crumbled walnuts/pistachios; a handful of lightly toasted pine nuts;
> crumbled feta; griddled slices of halloumi cheese; chopped dried/fresh
> apricot or cubes of beetroot.

AROMATIC LAMB MADRAS WITH NAAN AND SIDES

FEEDS 4

INGREDIENTS

700g lamb leg/shoulder
2–3 green chillies
2 large onions, peeled
4–5 tbsp vegetable/sunflower/
    groundnut oil
4 cloves
6 cardamom pods
salt and pepper
4 fat garlic cloves, peeled
    and crushed
a thumb-sized piece of fresh ginger,
    peeled and grated
1 tsp red chilli powder
½ tsp ground cumin
½ tsp ground coriander
1 tsp turmeric
50ml water
½ x 400g can of chopped tomatoes
1–2 tbsp tomato purée
2 tsp tamarind paste
½ x 400ml can of coconut milk
a handful of fresh coriander leaves,
    chopped

—— CHANGE IT UP ——

1. Blanch a handful of green beans in a pan
of boiling water for a few minutes. Drain.
Add to the pan with a handful of spinach
leaves for the last few minutes of cooking
before serving.
2. Chop up 2 large tomatoes and add to the
mix before serving. 3. Use mutton in place
of the lamb. It will take longer to cook but
has a lovely rich flavour.

········ TIME SAVER ········

1. Make this a day or even two days ahead –
the flavours will continue to develop.
2. If you don't have time to make the spice
mix yourself, use 2–3 tbsp of a good curry
paste instead.

Nothing like a take-away: here's a gorgeously soft, aromatic lamb curry. Fresh spices tenderise the meat and give it a subtle range of flavourings. Try this mix out on beef and chicken too.

PREP If in one piece, cut the lamb (across the grain) into 4cm cubes. Organise your spices so you can throw them into the pan as soon as you need. Finely chop the chillies. You can deseed or leave them in for extra heat. Finely dice the onions.

Put a large heavy-bottomed frying pan/casserole dish on to heat. Add the oil. Toss in the cloves and cardamom and cook for a minute, so the spices release their fragrance.

Add the onions and a bit of salt. Cook over medium/high heat, stirring, for 10 minutes or so. Let them brown up to create a rich curry base (without burning). When good and coloured, add the garlic, ginger and chillies. Cook and stir. Add the chilli powder, cumin, ground coriander and turmeric. Cook and stir for 2 minutes.

Add the lamb. Stir and mix well to coat. Add the water, tomatoes, purée and tamarind paste. The mix will look quite dry but it will loosen up as the meat releases its juices.

COOK Cover the pan and simmer on a very low heat. Bang it into the oven at 180°C/Gas 5 if the heat on your hob is too fierce. Check to see it's not too dry and stir every so often.

After 45 minutes, add the coconut milk and a bit of fresh coriander. Stir well. Return to simmer for another 45 minutes, or for as long as your cut of lamb needs. Taste the sauce and adjust the seasoning.

PLATE Serve this up in a good-looking dish topped with lots of fresh coriander. You'll want a bowl of raita to sooth the chilli effect. Eat with naan bread or wraps, spinach dhal and bombay crush potatoes.

TURN OVER
FOR SIDES

HONEY MINT RAITA

Mix together 240ml Greek yoghurt, 1 tsp good-quality mint sauce, ½ tsp salt, ½ tsp sugar, 3 tsp runny honey and a small handful of finely chopped coriander. Serve.

MADRAS SIDES

SIMPLE SPINACH DHAL

Wash 110g split red lentils in a sieve. Tip 400ml water into a pan. Add the lentils and bring to the boil. Cook for about 10 minutes, or until soft. Drain well. Put 110g spinach leaves into a pan with 1–2 tbsp water and heat until the leaves wilt. Drain immediately and squeeze a bit of the water from the leaves. Heat 1 tbsp sunflower oil in a clean pan. Add 1 tsp each of turmeric and chilli powder and 1 crushed garlic clove. Add the lentils, spinach, 3 tsp lemon juice/2 tsp tamarind paste, 2 tsp tomato purée and salt. Simmer for 15 minutes. Taste and adjust seasoning. To serve: Fry 3 sliced garlic cloves, a pinch of mustard seeds and a few whole coriander leaves. Bang them onto your dhal.

BOMBAY CRUSH

Scrub 450g waxy new potatoes to remove most of the peel. Cut into smallish pieces. Add to a pan of cold salted water with a few pinches of turmeric. Boil until a knife passes into them easily, 10–15 minutes. Drain. Spread on a plate and crush them a bit with a fork. Add a pinch of salt. Heat 3 tbsp oil in a pan or wok. When hot, add 2 dried curry leaves, ½ tsp dried chilli flakes and 2 pinches each of cumin seeds, onion seeds and black mustard seeds. Cook for a minute. Add 2 finely chopped onions, 2 crushed garlic cloves, 1 tsp tamarind paste, 2 finely chopped fresh green chillies and a handful of chopped coriander. Cook until the onions are soft and everything's melting together. Add the potatoes and 1 tbsp water, stir well and heat through. Season with salt and the juice of ½ a lemon. Top with torn coriander.

NAAN BREAD

Put 150ml semi-skimmed milk and 2 tsp caster sugar into a pan. Heat very gently till lukewarm, stirring to dissolve the sugar. Pour into a bowl. Add a 7g sachet of fast-action dried yeast, stir once, cover and leave to froth for 5–10 minutes, until it has developed a good head. Meanwhile, sift 450g plain flour into a bowl. Add a pinch of salt, 1 tsp baking powder and 1–2 tsp onion seeds. Add the yeast mix, 2 tbsp vegetable oil, 1 beaten egg and 150ml yoghurt and, using your hands, mix together into a dough. Shape into a ball, sit on a lightly floured board and knead well for 10 minutes or knead in a machine for 8 minutes.

Sprinkle with flour, cover and leave to rise in a warm place for an hour or so until doubled in size. Put a large baking tray in your oven and preheat to its highest setting. Put your grill on to high. Slap your dough back onto the board. Knead for a minute then divide into 8 bits. Roll each into a long, tear-drop shape. Brush with a little melted butter and scatter with a few more onion seeds. Remove the hot tray from the oven, cover with half your naan and bang back into the oven for 3–4 minutes until they've puffed up. Finish under the grill for a few seconds till golden. Remove. Cover with a tea towel while you finish the rest.

Fish and Shellfish

My tasty relationship with fish began with my grandad. A keen fisherman, he taught me how to value it for what it is – versatile eating and brilliantly nutritious. If you're not catching your own, get to a good fishmonger (or even the fish counter in a supermarket) and treat yourself to some fishy banter. These guys will tell you what's freshest and in season, will do all the tricky descaling, butterflying and gutting as well as advising you on how to cook your chosen fish. Most importantly though they can tell you what's sustainable, as many fish and shellfish stocks are seriously depleted these days. Sourcing sorted, it's down to your skill set. Don't overload your delicate fish with heavy sauces, try and keep it simple so the fresh fish flavours shine through. Doneness is all: fish is at its very best when it's only just cooked. Don't rely on cooking guides – trust your eye.

Is it fresh?
WHAT TO LOOK (AND SNIFF) FOR...

WHOLE FISH:

EYES Fish eyes should sparkle brightly and look lively.

GILLS The undersides should be bright red (oxygenated) and clean.

SKIN Should be glistening, with shiny scales intact and undiminished natural patterning .

GENERAL The whole fish should look stiff, firm and moist, with a stiff tail as though it's just posing before swimming off. If it looks sad, soft, dull, don't buy it.

SMELL IT Sea-fish should have a faint but refreshing and pleasant tang of the sea. If fish smells unpleasant it will taste that way – don't be ripped off. Don't buy it.

FILLETS/STEAKS Harder to tell, but white fish should be white and translucent.

SMOKED FISH Choose glossy-looking fish.

PRAWNS Raw prawns should be firm and glistening with no black age spots.

MUSSELS go for cleaner, undamaged shells (not shells caked in mud/ covered in barnacles).

── ONCE HOOKED ── – BEST STORAGE

Fish spoils fast (oily fish faster than white) so **EAT** fresh fish within 24 hours of buying.

Get it home **FAST** and into the fridge. Store it at 0–5°C.

RINSE whole fish, pat dry, sit on a plate and seal with cling film before storing at the bottom of the fridge.

LEAVE pre-packed fish in its packaging until you cook it.

KEEP smoked fish well-sealed, so it doesn't flavour other foods.

ALLOW fish to return to room temperature for 30 minutes before cooking.

DEFROST frozen fish in the fridge, then drain and pat dry before using.

OILY FISH

SALMON A hugely nutritious, affordable, versatile pink fleshed fish. Get steaks, fillets or whole. Avoid Atlantic (over-fished). Organic farmed is best. Pan-fry, griddle, grill, BBQ, roast, bake, poach, steam or stir-fry. Cook in foil or paper packets. Good in fishcakes and pies. Bake or poach whole. Smoked salmon is convenient but can be expensive. Get cheaper off-cuts to throw into pasta dishes, salads, sandwiches or bagels with cream cheese.

TROUT Brown or rainbow, whole or filleted. Go for organic farmed. Cook as salmon.

MACKEREL Super-food on a budget with a distinctive taste and fast cook. Buy whole or fillets. Pan-fry, grill or BBQ. Smoked mackerel is vacuum-packed and its long shelf life makes it a good buy.

SARDINES Abundant, richly nutritious, cheap, chic and sleek. Grill and BBQ over high heat for a crispy skin. Tinned sardines are great on toast.

ANCHOVIES Get marinated from delis for salads and baking into casseroles/pasta dishes/fish pies. Canned/bottled are salty and need soaking in milk for an hour before using. Sophisticated, cheap and nutritious – a brilliant ingredient for beefing up your cooking.

HERRING Kipper (the smoked version) is very cheap, highly nutritious and easy to cook. Bang one or two, head down in a deep jug. Cover with boiling water. Leave for 2–3 minutes. Remove. Eat with bread and butter.

TUNA Expensive and threatened. Best left alone for now.

WHITE FISH

COD* An over-fished delicious full-flaked fish. It comes as loin, fillets or whole. Buy sustainable line-caught and try substitutes. Pan-fry, griddle, grill, poach, batter, breadcrumb, or bake. Makes perfect fishcakes/pie/fish and chips/fish fingers.

HADDOCK* Sweeter than cod but good flakes. Get fillets, steaks, or whole and use as cod. Smoked haddock is great added to pies, fishcakes, kedgeree or omelettes for character.

HAKE* A cod cousin with a more subtle, but meaty, flavour.

POLLACK A good cod-substitute. Grill, fry, pie or deep fry.

PLAICE* Fine-textured and delicate. Get it whole or filleted. Fast pan-fry this flat fish or coat it in breadcrumbs or batter.

SEA BASS Popular fish with a fine texture, and really good flavour, which can be baked whole or stuffed. Fillets are great for fast cooking.

LEMON SOLE Thin and delicate. Fry the fillets simply.

GURNARD A cheap, meaty white fish to use in stews/curries/soups.

TILAPIA A firm white fish which takes strong marinades. Grill/fry/bake/BBQ.

BREAM A sweet firm fish. Good baked whole and barbecued with garlic/lemon.

MONKFISH Sold as steaks from the tail and cheeks. It's lean, expensive, bone-free and works with strong flavours. Marinate raw (ceviche), wrap, bake or BBQ.

DOVER SOLE* Expensive and delicate. A fishmonger will skin the dark side for you. Fry or grill whole with the white skin on.

SHELLFISH

MUSSELS Sweet, cheap and nutritious. Buy live part-cleaned rope-grown mussels by weight or in neat nets.

PRAWNS Nutritious, delicate and highly versatile shellfish. If buying ready-cooked (pink) prawns, get the right size for your needs. Buy fresh or frozen and twice as many if their shells are on. Check for a sustainable label. Raw can be frozen on the boat to maximise freshness or fresh (the fishmonger may have just defrosted them so ask). They will be grey/black/blue and of varying sizes. Uncooked prawns need to be de-veined. Pan-fry/griddle/stir-fry/BBQ/grill/poach/steam/bake or add to curries/pies/bakes/tapas/salads/sandwiches/prawn cocktails.

OYSTERS A sensual treat and best eaten raw. Shells need to be closed tight and undamaged. Get native/rock/pacific. Farmed native are available all year.

CRAB Filled with delicate white and rich brown meat. Get freshly boiled crabs or ready-dressed to eat with mayo etc.

LOBSTER Hugely expensive. Freeze then boil or steam in the shell, or split and grill/BBQ.

SCALLOPS Sold in the shell or ready-shucked (look for plump, sweet smelling specimens with a pink coral). They're expensive, versatile and good pan-fried or steamed.

FISH SKILLS

DESCALE A good crisp bit of fish skin is delicious but it usually needs de-scaling. Ask your fishmonger or do it yourself. Fish like plaice or mackerel have fine scales so leave them on, but larger fish like salmon, cod, haddock and bass need attention. Do so before gutting (if necessary). Snip off the gills with scissors and hold the fish by the tail in a large plastic bag (or scales cover everything). Working from the tail towards the head, scrape down smoothly but firmly with the back of a chef's knife. The scales will pop off.

GUT Most fish is sold gutted. If it hasn't been, ask the fishmonger to do it for you, or do it yourself (it's easy). Set up next to the sink. Snip the gills off with scissors. Use the scissors or a sharp knife to snip or slash along the belly line from the tail towards the head, stopping short of the gills. Pull the inner bits out with your fingers and discard. Rinse the cavity of your fish under running water, using fingers or a teaspoon to scrape out any stubborn bits. Drain and pat dry.

FILLET Ask your fishmonger. Or…

FLAT FISH

1. Sit it on a board.

2. Feel for the central bone. Insert the blade and cut the fish from head to tail just to the left of the bone, cutting down to it.

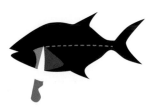

3. With the knife almost flat and working from the bone to the edge, use big long smooth strokes to cut the first fish fillet away from the bones, separating them cleanly. Keep it neat with as little wastage as possible.

4. Turn the fish and separate the second fillet.
5. Turn over and repeat. Trim the fillets.

ROUND FISH

1. Sit it on a board

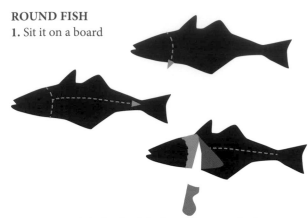

2. Cut around the back of the head down to the bone. Cut the skin from the head to the tail along one side of the backbone. Using the knife flat as above, cut long even strokes to separate the flesh and bone, pulling the fillet away as you cut. Turn and repeat.

SKIN Sit your fish fillet, skin-side down, on a board. Using your flexible knife, tuck the sharp blade edge between the skin and the flesh. Hold the skin in one hand (salt your fingers) and, holding the knife at a 45 degree angle, use a sawing action to separate the two.

DEBONE Check every bit of fish you cook for pin bones. Run your fingers over the flesh and nip out any offenders with tweezers.

CLEANING MUSSELS Start by discarding any that don't close when tapped sharply and any cracked/damaged mussels. Scrape away any barnacles using the back of a knife. Scrub and scrape them under running water. Rinse several times. Pull out the beards (threads) just before cooking.

Shelling and de-veining prawns

Pull the heads off. Peel the shells off smoothly. Use a sharp knife to cut along the black vein running along the back. Remove it with your fingers or the top of the knife. Rinse and pat dry. To butterfly, cut through the back and splay open without cutting all the way through. Rinse again and pat dry.

DOCTORS FISH & SHELLFISH

Fish and shellfish are stacked with **SUPER-NUTRIENTS** eat at least twice a week and keep it varied. They're high in

PROTEINS

for essential growth and development and are very low in fat, so suit weight watchers. PRAWNS, MUSSELS AND SARDINES CONTAIN →**IRON** which protect against anaemia,

ZINC WHICH STRENGTHENS THE IMMUNE SYSTEM AND *Selenium* WHICH SUPPORTS THE LIVER. Crab, oysters, lobster are hot on

COPPER

which is great for the skin, hair, vision, teeth, bones and heart, while mackerel is packed with

VITAMIN D essential for healthy teeth and bones.

LINOLEIC ACID

in salmon helps with nerve repair and is good for hair and skin. OILY FISH IS UNIQUELY RICH IN FATTY ACIDS

OMEGA-3 & OMEGA-6

balancing good/bad cholesterol, boosting heart health, memory and protecting against blood clots, soothing arthritis and helping with chronic skin and nerve problems.

FRIENDS

WHITE FISH
BACON, BUTTER, CABBAGE, CHEESE SAUCE, CORIANDER, DILL, GARLIC, HUMMUS, KETCHUP, LEMON, LIME, OLIVES, ONIONS, PARSLEY, PEAS, POTATOES, SPRING ONIONS, TAPENADE, TOMATO SAUCE, VINEGAR, WINE

SMOKED FISH
BACON, CHEDDAR CHEESE, CREAM, MILK, MUSTARD, POACHED AND BOILED EGGS, ONIONS, PARSLEY, POTATOES

FISH IS HIGH IN KEY *B vitamins* INCLUDING

B12 B6 ESSENTIAL for growth and blood health and WHICH AIDS insulin production, boosts blood health and helps to counter PMT, diabetes, asthma and depression. BONE-BUILDING

CALCIUM

can be found in fish bones of sardines, whitebait, anchovies.

OILY FISH
BEETROOT, CUCUMBER, CHILLI, CUMIN, CURRY PASTE, GARLIC, GINGER, HARISSA PASTE, LEMON, LIME, MUSTARD, OLIVES, ONION, POTATOES, RHUBARB, WASABI

SHELLFISH
BACON, BREADCRUMBS, CAPERS, CHEESE SAUCE, CHICKEN, CHILLIES, CIDER, COCONUT MILK, CORIANDER, CUCUMBER, DILL, EGGS, GARLIC, GRUYERE AND CHEDDAR CHEESE, LEMON, LIME, MAYONNAISE, NOODLES, OLIVES, PARSLEY, THYME, WHITE WINE

IS IT DONE YET?

Raw fish is translucent. It becomes **OPAQUE** as it cooks (or sets) and starts to look obviously **FLAKY**.

So, **POKE IT** in the thickest part with a sharp knife to check. You'll quickly learn the right feel and look. Fish will continue to cook when you take it off the heat, so factor that in. If it's not done, bang it back.

POACHED PRAWNS WITH MAYO AND SHALLOT VINEGAR

 HEALTHY FAST FEEDS 2

INGREDIENTS

1 x essential mayonnaise (p153) or
   6–8 tbsp good shop-bought mayo
3 litres cold water
3 tbsp salt
8 peppercorns
2–3 sticks celery (optional)
¼ of a lemon (optional)
8–16 raw North Atlantic/king/tiger
   prawns, shells on

SHALLOT VINEGAR
2 shallots, peeled
4–6 tbsp malt vinegar
2 tsp caster sugar

—— CHANGE IT UP ——
1. Switch the mayo for aioli (p100).

Speedy preparation for a lovely, lazy lunch: enjoy yourself with the cracking and dipping ritual. If you're feeling flush, switch the prawns for langoustines. The mayo/vinegar combo here is great with stacks of crab, mussels and other shellfish. Prawns aren't just delicious – they're brilliantly good for you.

PREP Start with the dips. If you are making your own mayo, do so at least an hour ahead and chill. Make the shallot vinegar: dice the peeled shallots. Mix with the vinegar and sugar in a bowl.

Make up a court bouillon (poaching liquid): Measure the cold water and pour into a large pan. Add the salt, peppercorns and optional celery/lemon and bring to the boil on a high heat.

COOK Add the prawns to the boiling water. Cook for 1 minute or a little longer for larger prawns. Test. They should rise as they're done, feel firm and turn pink. Remove, drain and cool in a single layer.

PLATE Spoon mayo onto the side of your plates. Serve the vinegar in two small bowls for spooning onto the prawns. Pile the prawns onto the plates and serve with slices of buttered brown bread/soda bread muffins (p205) and lemon wedges. To eat: pull the heads off the prawns and peel and crack the outer shells and legs off with your fingers. De-vein (p134), if necessary. Alternatively, peel the cooked prawns before plating.

BONUS BITES

GRILLED FRESH PRAWNS
Heat the grill to high. Thread as many raw prawns as you fancy (shells on) lengthways head through to tail onto small metal skewers. Grill them for 3 minutes per side, or until firm and pink. Sprinkle with salt. Dip into mayo or garlic butter (p138).

BBQ PRAWNS
Defrost as many frozen peeled tiger prawns as you like and marinate in a mix of chopped garlic, grated lemon zest and olive oil for 2 hours. Skewer them lengthways. Season and cook on a lightly oiled rack for 1–2 minutes per side, or until firm but still juicy.

SALT AND PEPPER PRAWNS IN CRISPY BREADCRUMBS
Shell, de-vein and butterfly 8 large raw tiger prawns (p134). Toss them in a mix of 50g white flour, 1 tsp fine salt, 1 tsp crushed Sichuan/black peppercorns and ¼ tsp Chinese five spice powder. Dip in beaten egg then roll on a plate of panko/homemade dried breadcrumbs (p201). Deep-fry in a pan one-third full of groundnut oil (hot enough to cook a cube of bread in 30 seconds) and cook for 1–2 minutes, or until golden-crisp but pink inside. Drain on kitchen paper. Dip in a mix of 2 tbsp caster sugar, juice of ½ a lime, 2 tbsp soy sauce, 2 tbsp rice wine and 1 tbsp black rice/malt vinegar.

MUSSELS IN CIDER AND BACON WITH A MUSTARD CREAM SAUCE

 HEALTHY FAST

FEEDS 2

Seafood, cider and smoky bacon (or use real ale for a darker sauce); team these nutritious fast-food beauties with crisp frites for a luxurious classic on a budget.

INGREDIENTS

1kg mussels
75g smoked bacon
4 shallots/1 onion, peeled
2 garlic cloves, peeled
a few tarragon leaves/thyme sprigs
1 tbsp olive oil
200ml cider/real ale
1 tbsp lemon juice (only if using cider)
50ml double cream
3/4 tsp Dijon mustard
a handful of flat-leaf parsley, chopped

—— CHANGE IT UP ——

1. Switch the frites for shallow-fry chips (p78) or sweet potato wedges (p82)
2. For simple mussels, chuck a small wineglass of water/white wine/beer/cider to the pan, add the mussels and cook until opened.

—— BONUS BITE ——

MUSSELS BAKED IN GARLIC BUTTER
Cook the mussels (see above) until all opened. Drain. Separate the shells and discard the tops. Sit the remaining halves on an ovenproof dish. Preheat the oven to 190°C/Gas 5. Cream 175g soft butter with 3 crushed garlic cloves, 1 tbsp finely chopped onion/shallot and 1 tbsp finely chopped parsley/tarragon and spoon evenly over the mussels. Sprinkle with 2 tbsp dried breadcrumbs (p201) and grated parmesan/cheddar/gruyère cheese. Bake for 10 minutes. Eat straight from the oven with bread to soak up the garlicky juices.

········ TIME SAVER ········

The frites can be prepared and given their first fry up to 24 hours in advance of eating. Cover and chill until needed.

PREP

MUSSELS: Select, scrub and clean the mussels as per the detailed process on p134, discarding any that are cracked, damaged or refuse to close when tapped. Scrub them several times and tug out any black fibrous beards. SAUCE: slice the bacon into strips. Finely chop the shallots/onion. Crush the garlic. Finely slice the tarragon or strip the thyme.

COOK

Heat a wide sauté pan/casserole dish large enough to take all the mussels. Add the oil. Throw in the bacon and fry gently for 5 minutes. Remove with a slotted spoon. Add the shallots and garlic. Stir and fry very gently in the bacon oil for 5 minutes, or until soft and translucent. Increase the heat. Add the cider and lemon juice or the real ale and bring the mix to the boil. At that moment, whack the mussels in. Cover the pan immediately and cook for 3–4 minutes, shuffling the pan a few times to keep it even. Turn the mussels once and check progress. Once they're opened, drain the pot into a colander over a bowl. Keep the mussels warm. Return the liquid to the pan. Add the tarragon/thyme and boil for a minute to reduce and intensify the flavour. Add the cream and mustard. Stir, boil taste and season it. Add the bacon. Pile the mussels into bowls. Pour over the sauce and scatter over parsley.

PLATE

Serve with warm bread to soak up the juices and frites (below) or chips to dip into mayo.

TO GO WITH

FRITES

First fry (an hour before needed): Peel 2 large floury potatoes (600g). Cut across into 5mm slices. Stack and slice into 5mm sticks. Soak in cold water for 30 minutes. Drain. Dry thoroughly. Heat groundnut oil to 160°C in a deep fryer or flat-based wok or saucepan no more than one-third full until a cube of bread will brown in 60 seconds. Add the frites gradually, in batches if you have to – don't overfill and don't leave the pan at any time – and cook for 6 minutes or until soft but still pale. Drain in the fryer basket or use a slotted spoon to lift onto kitchen paper. Set aside. Final fry: reheat the oil in the fryer to 180°C. A cube of bread browns in 30 seconds. Fry frites for 1–2 minutes until golden. Lift onto kitchen paper. Keep warm in a preheated oven at 180°C/Gas 5 until needed.

THAI-STEAMED MUSSELS

FEEDS 2

INGREDIENTS

a thumb-sized piece of fresh ginger
1 lemongrass stalk
4 spring onions
1 large red chilli
1 large handful of coriander
1 lime
1 tbsp groundnut oil
400ml coconut milk
600g mussels, cleaned and de-bearded
*   (p134)*
salt or a shake or two of fish sauce
*   (optional)*

PREP Peel the ginger and cut into thin matchsticks. Crush the thin end of the lemongrass to bruise it. Cut off a 3cm piece. Chop it very finely. Slice the spring onions thinly. Deseed and chop the chilli (p16). Chop the coriander roughly. Halve the lime.

COOK Heat the oil in a wok or large, wide frying pan. Add the ginger, lemongrass, spring onions and chilli. Stir continuously over a medium heat for 2 minutes, or until soft and fragrant. Add the coconut milk and the juice of half of your lime. Stir and let it bubble for 2–3 minutes to integrate the flavours. Add the mussels. Raise the heat a bit and cover. Cook for 3–4 minutes, stirring once or twice, till the mussels have opened.

Scoop the mussels into bowls using a slotted spoon. Taste the sauce. Season with a little salt or fish sauce if you think it needs it and add half the coriander. If you'd rather have the sauce a little thicker, cook it for a few minutes longer.

PLATE Pour the sauce over the mussels and top with the remaining coriander. Cut the remaining lime half into wedges and serve on the side. Eat with good bread for soaking up the juices.

MUSSEL AND TOMATO LINGUINE

FEEDS 2

INGREDIENTS

4 tbsp olive oil
4 shallots/1 onion, finely chopped
½ red chilli, deseeded and diced
4 garlic cloves, 3 of which chopped
150ml dry white wine
1 x 450g can of chopped tomatoes
1 tbsp tomato purée
a pinch of caster sugar
1 tsp capers, drained
salt and pepper
175g linguine
2–3 tbsp torn flat-leaf parsley/basil
450g fresh mussels, cleaned
*   and de-bearded (p134)*
a knob of butter

PREP Make the sauce. Heat 2 tablespoons of the oil in a deep, wide frying pan, add the shallot/onion and chilli and fry on low heat for 5 minutes. Add the chopped garlic and cook for a few minutes until soft but not coloured. Increase the heat and pour in half the wine. Let it bubble for a few seconds, then add the tomatoes, tomato purée, sugar and capers and season. Reduce the heat after 30 seconds. Simmer on low for 20 minutes, stirring occasionally and checking that the sauce doesn't dry out. Set aside.

COOK Boil a large pan of salted water. Add the linguine and cook for 7–8 minutes from when the water re-boils or as the pack directs. Meantime, put the tomato sauce on to reheat. As it begins to simmer, add the herbs, the rest of the oil and the remaining wine. Let it bubble for 1 minute. Taste and adjust the seasoning. Bang the mussels into the pan. Slam the lid on. Cook on medium/high heat for 3 minutes, covered, turning once or twice. Taste and adjust the seasoning.

Drain the pasta. Return it to the pan. Crush the remaining garlic clove and stir through the pasta with the butter. Season with salt and pepper.

PLATE Divide the pasta between 2 large plates or wide shallow bowls and spoon the mussels and sauce on top, or mix everything together in one big bowl if you prefer it that way.

FAST SHALLOW-FRY FISH WITH DRESSED PEAS
AND HERB AND GARLIC POTATOES

HEALTHY

FEEDS 2

Beautifully simple: enjoy it for what it is. Use whatever type of white fish fillet you like – plaice, lemon sole, pollack, sea bass, cod, haddock or hake – it's up to you.

INGREDIENTS

2 x 110–175g good fresh/defrosted white fish fillets, skins on
2–3 tbsp plain white flour
salt and pepper
olive/groundnut oil and butter, or clarified butter
1 lemon

DRESSED PEAS
110g frozen/fresh peas
2 tsp white wine vinegar
½ tsp Dijon mustard
1 tsp caster sugar/honey
4 tsp olive oil

HERB AND GARLIC POTATOES
2 large potatoes
1 tbsp olive oil
1–2 tbsp fresh rosemary needles (or a good sprinkle of dried)
2 garlic cloves, peeled and crushed
a knob of butter

—— CHANGE IT UP ——

Make a maître d'hôtel butter by mixing 50g soft butter with 1 tbsp chopped parsley/dill/ tarragon/basil, 2 tsp lemon juice, salt and pepper. Add to your fried fish for an instant sauce.

PREP Organise your fish: If your fishmonger hasn't done so already, de-scale it (p134). Then feel it all over to check for large or smaller pin bones (they're often not visible) and remove them with tweezers. Pat the fish dry and set aside until needed.

Potatoes: peel and cut the potatoes into 1–2cm cubes Put a heavy-bottomed frying pan on a medium heat. Add a good coating of oil. When hot, add the potatoes, rosemary and garlic. Fry them gently for 15–20 minutes, checking and turning for even cooking, until the potatoes are crispy and golden.

Mix the dressing for the peas: Beat the vinegar, mustard, sugar/honey and a pinch of salt in a bowl till amalgamated. Beat the oil in very slowly. Taste and adjust for balance and seasoning. Boil the peas in a little salted water for 3 minutes. Drain and add to the bowl.

Fetch the fish. Spread the flour on a plate and season with salt and pepper. Turn the fish in the flour to coat.

COOK Heat a frying pan that's large enough to take both bits of fish (or fry them in turn). Add a bit of oil and butter or use clarified butter. When it's pretty hot, add the fish fillets, skin-side down. Cook for 2 minutes, until the skin is very crispy and the upper edges look opaque. Press down with a spatula if it arches up. Turn and cook for another 1-2 minutes or till done. It's best moist, not dry. Don't overcook it.

PLATE Lay your magnificent fish on a warm plate, skin-side up so it stays crisp. Add the peas in dressing. Serve the spuds in bowls with mayo and ketchup or tartare sauce.

—— HOW TO ——
CLARIFY BUTTER

Butter burns at low temperatures; clarify it (lose the salt/milk solids/impurities) and it manages much greater heat, adds gloss to a sauce and keeps for much longer. Use it to pan-fry fish, shellfish, omelettes and sauté meats without browning/burning.

Sit **250G BUTTER** (or the amount you need) in a heavy-bottomed pan. Leave to **MELT VERY GENTLY** on a very low heat. **DON'T STIR/TOUCH/DISTURB IT**. Remove from the heat. It will have split into **3 LAYERS. SKIM THE FOAM** from the top using a large metal spoon; discard it. **POUR OFF** the middle layer to keep – store it in the fridge or freeze. **DISCARD** the bottom **MILKY LAYER**; or stir it into a sauce or soup if there's one going.

GRIDDLED MACKEREL WITH PICKLED CUCUMBER AND BEETROOT AND POTATO SALAD

FEEDS 2

INGREDIENTS

4 small mackerel fillets
   (see p134 if prepping your own)
100g plain flour
salt and pepper
a knob of softened butter
a handful of lamb's lettuce or
   watercress
1 tbsp lemon juice
½ tsp sugar
3 tbsp olive oil

BEETROOT AND POTATO SALAD

300g waxy potatoes (e.g. Charlotte)
150g cooked beetroot
4 tbsp crème fraîche
2–3 tsp horseradish sauce
a squeeze of lemon juice
4 tbsp chopped chives

CUCUMBER PICKLE

1 tbsp cider vinegar
1 tbsp caster sugar
2 shallots, peeled and finely sliced
½ cucumber

How to magic a piece of regular oily fish into something pretty special? It's all about the contrasts, as ever. Beetroot and mackerel's a classic combination. The pickle adds a bright note.

PREP Start with the potato salad: Boil the potatoes in salted water until tender. Peel and cut them into 2cm cubes. Cube the beetroot similarly. Mix the crème fraîche, horseradish, lemon juice and some seasoning together, tasting and adjusting until it's got a bit of a kick to it. Add the cubed veg and chives and turn them through. Set aside.

Mix the pickle: Stir the vinegar, sugar, shallots and a pinch of salt together. Slice the cucumber very thinly. Add to the liquid and set aside.

Check the fish for pin bones, removing any you find with tweezers. Spread the flour on a plate and season with salt and pepper. Turn the fish to coat it, patting gently between your hands to remove any excess flour. Spread softened butter evenly over the fleshy top of each fillet.

Wash the salad leaves. Put the lemon juice and sugar in a bowl with a good pinch of salt and a bit of pepper. Whisk/beat the oil in drop by drop until combined. Set aside.

COOK Put a griddle pan on to a high heat. Sit the fish, buttered-side down, onto the pan to sear. Cook for 2–3 minutes until the skin is crisp. Turn and cook for 1 minute more or until done. Remove immediately.

PLATE Sit the cooked mackerel on plates and season with salt and pepper. Dress the leaves in lemon dressing and heap those on. Add a pile of drained, pickled cucumber and the potato salad. Enjoy with soda bread (p205) and butter.

BONUS BITES

GRIDDLED HARISSA MACKEREL (OR TROUT)
Stuff 2 gutted, descaled mackerel/trout with a bit of fresh coriander, 2 sliced garlic cloves, the juice of 1 lemon/lime, a little salt and 1 small, deseeded sliced chilli. Slash the outer skin 3 times diagonally so they won't burst. Push a little extra sliced garlic into the slits then rub the fish all over with a mix of 2 tbsp harissa paste and 1 tbsp olive oil. Chill for 30 minutes. Cook on a searing hot griddle pan for 3 minutes per side, or until cooked through. Serve with a pile of well seasoned couscous tossed with fresh coriander, lemon juice and olive oil.

A BIG PIECE OF PAN-ROASTED WHITE FISH WITH CHAMP

FEEDS 2

Let the fish shine through: never rely on timing guides with this delicate ingredient. It's all about eye, touch and building up your judgement. Here's a truly glorious taste-fest.

INGREDIENTS

2 x 250g good fresh firm thick white
*   fish fillets (sustainable haddock/cod/*
*   pollack etc.), skin on*
salt and pepper
2 tbsp olive oil
CHAMP
3 garlic cloves
2 spring onions
450g floury potatoes
75g butter
3–4 tbsp double cream/milk

PREP Make the champ: Peel the garlic and slice the spring onions. Boil the potatoes and garlic in a pan of lightly salted water for 20 minutes, or until tender when tested. Peel and press through a potato ricer into the warm pan or mash it in there. Add two-thirds of the butter, the cream or milk and season with salt and pepper. Beat until smooth. Stir in the spring onion. Add the remaining butter, cover with foil and keep warm.

Meantime, prep the fish: If your fishmonger hasn't already done so, de-scale and debone your fillets, removing large bones and pin bones with tweezers. Pat the fish dry. Season with salt and pepper. Set aside until needed. Preheat the oven to 220°C/Gas 7.

COOK Heat the oil in a large ovenproof pan on a high heat. Add the fish, skin-side down. Fry for 2 minutes, or until very crisp, then transfer to the oven. Roast for 6 minutes or until the fish is opaque but moist (check frequently as this is size-dependent).

PLATE Spoon champ onto plates. Sit the fish on top. Eat with onion marmalade (below) and lemon wedges. Or fresh herb salsa (p118). Or a mixture of diced cherry tomatoes and black olives in balsamic dressing.

TIP

If you don't have an ovenproof pan, just slide the fish onto a metal baking tray before transferring to the oven.

·········· TIME SAVER ··········

Frozen white fish fillets come ready-skinned and deboned. Defrost a few hours ahead to cut your prep time down. Pour off any excess water and pat dry before flouring.

—— BONUS BITE——

TASTY FISH KEBABS

Chop 4 x 110g pieces of white fish/mackerel into bite-sized chunks. Marinate in a mix of the juice of 1 lemon/lime, 2 crushed garlic cloves, 2 tbsp olive oil, 2 tbsp chopped coriander and a bit of salt and pepper, for 30 minutes. Thread onto metal skewers. Grill under a preheated grill for 3–4 minutes, turning, until the fish is cooked through. Eat with paprika mayo (150ml mayo mixed with 1 tsp smoked paprika) and shallow-fry chips (p78).

TO GO WITH

ONION MARMALADE

Thinly slice 700g red and 700g white onions. Heat 20ml olive oil and 10g butter in a large thick-based pan. Add the onions, ¼ tsp black pepper, 200g dark brown sugar, 50g white sugar and an (optional) muslin-wrapped stem of rosemary. Simmer on a low heat for 40 minutes to reduce, checking and stirring regularly. When soft and amalgamated, remove the rosemary, if using, and add 450ml red wine, 50ml water, 50ml balsamic vinegar, 150ml red wine vinegar, 4 crushed garlic cloves, 2 tsp lemon juice and 2 pinches of sea salt. Boil fiercely. Reduce and fast cook (checking it doesn't burn) for 20–30 minutes, or until the mix is sticky. Taste and adjust seasoning. Remove and spoon into a clean sterilised jar. Seal till air-tight.

CLASSIC SEASIDE
FISHCAKES

HEALTHY   FEEDS 3-4

Simple but delicious: a bit of very lightly poached white fish with just a taste of smoked fish folded into the driest of mash with some flat-leaf parsley, then fried off. A luxury budget meal.

INGREDIENTS

450g floury potatoes
salt and pepper
1 x 350g fillet of fresh/defrosted white fish (sustainable haddock/ cod/pollack etc.), skin on
110g smoked haddock (un-dyed if you can get it)
1 plump shallot, peeled and grated
milk, to cover
4 tbsp torn flat-leaf parsley
2–3 tbsp plain white flour
olive/groundnut oil and a bit of butter, for frying (or use clarified butter p141)

PREP Boil the whole, unpeeled potatoes in salted water for 20 minutes, or until tender. Drain well. Strip the skins away. Press through a ricer for the smoothest mash or use a fork/masher to bash out the lumps. Season lightly with salt and pepper.

Poach the fish: bang it into a large frying pan/saucepan in a single layer with the shallot and season. Cover with the milk. Bring to the point of boiling, then reduce the heat and simmer for 3 minutes, till the fish is barely cooked (white outside, still a bit gelatinous inside). Remove with a slotted spoon. Remove any skin and tweeze out stray bones without breaking the fish pieces up too much. Cool before mixing carefully into the potato with the torn parsley, trying to keep the chunks of fish nice and large. Chill for 1 hour or till firm.

Sprinkle the flour on a plate and season with salt and pepper. Shape the fish and potato mixture into 4–6 cakes with damp hands. Turn the fish cakes in the flour to coat and protect them well. Chill till needed or cook now.

COOK Preheat the oven to 200°C/Gas 6. Heat the oil and butter in an ovenproof pan. Fry the cakes on medium heat for 2 minutes per side until golden, then finish in the oven for 10 minutes. Or fry, turning once, until crisply golden outside and piping hot all through.

PLATE Enjoy these crisp, fishy beauties with a heap of peas or a bit of steamed broccoli drizzled with Caesar dressing (p29); or eat with shallow-fry chips (p78) and tartare sauce (p150).

BONUS BITES

CRUNCHY SALMON AND BLACK OLIVE FISHCAKES
Make up 225g mashed potato as above, adding 110g finely chopped onion fried in 1 tbsp olive oil until soft. Mix in 2 tbsp torn fresh coriander and 8 chopped black olives and season. Poach 2 x 110g pieces salmon for 3 minutes as above but using water, not milk. Remove from the water, strip off the skin and break up into rough chunks. Cool before mixing into the mash and chilling as above. Shape into 4 cakes and turn in seasoned white flour. Dip into beaten egg then roll in a few good handfuls of panko or homemade dried breadcrumbs (p201) to coat. Fry for 5 minutes per side (or fry/bake as above) till hot and golden.

CHILLI AND LEMONGRASS BABY CAKES
Chop and drop 350g deboned, skin-free white fish into a processor. Add 50g fresh white breadcrumbs, 2 tsp very finely chopped lemongrass, 3 fat chopped garlic cloves, the sliced whites of 5 spring onions, 1–2 deseeded red chillies, the juice of 1–2 limes, 2 tsp fish sauce, 2–3 tbsp chopped fresh coriander and a little salt. Pulse for a few seconds until processed but not too finely. Shape into 6–8 little cakes. Turn in seasoned flour to coat and dip in beaten egg. Fry in groundnut oil for 2–3 minutes per side or till cooked through. Dip into chilli or other sauce or serve on top of noodle salad.

A VERY PROPER
FISH PIE

FEEDS 4

INGREDIENTS

500g thick fresh white fish fillets,
   skin on
150g smoked haddock
110g hot-smoked salmon
1 onion, peeled and halved
a few black peppercorns
2 garlic cloves, peeled
400ml milk
salt and pepper
150g cooked prawns
2 hard-boiled eggs
a squeeze of lemon juice
SAUCE
30g butter
30g plain white flour
100ml dry white wine
100ml double cream
1 tbsp chopped fresh dill
   (or parsley/tarragon)
TOPPING
1.3kg floury potatoes
2 tbsp butter
a good squeeze of lemon juice
a handful of grated gruyère cheese
2–4 tbsp milk
salt and pepper

——— CHANGE IT UP ———

1. Add mussels to the pie. Add a dozen
or so cleaned mussels to a pan with 2 tbsp
white wine or water and cook as per
p138. Extract the mussels from their shells
and add to the fish when assembling.
Sieve the juices and add to the sauce to
boost the flavour.
2. Replace the mashed potato with a puff
pastry topping. Assemble the pie as far as
the topping, putting a pie funnel in the
centre of the dish if you have one. Thinly roll
out a piece of bought all-butter puff pastry
to fit your pie dish, cover and crimp the
edges. Brush with a mix of beaten egg and
milk and bake for 30 minutes, until crispy
and golden.

*This is fish pie done properly. No short cuts, and building layers of
texture and flavour. If you're not into prawns use extra white fish. For
real depth of flavour, add the mussels (below).*

PREP Make the topping: Peel the potatoes and bring them to the boil in a
large pan of cold, lightly salted water. Lower the heat and simmer for
15–20 minutes, or until tender when pierced with a knife or skewer. Drain then
bang them back into the pan and shuffle over a low heat for a minute or so to
dry them. Put them through a ricer if you have one or mash them. Add the
butter, lemon juice, gruyère and half the milk and beat well. Add the remaining
milk only if needed (don't let it get too wet – you'll want it to hold texture and
crisp up) and season to taste.

Sit the white and smoked fish in a large frying pan/roasting tin. Add the onion,
peppercorns and garlic. Cover with the milk and add a pinch of salt. Simmer
over a very low heat until the fish is just cooked. This may take as little as
3 minutes depending on thickness. Scoop each piece out as it's done and put
it on a plate. Set the milk aside for later. Peel any skin off the fish, trying not
to break it up. Feel for any bones and remove. Set aside. Preheat the oven to
200°C/Gas 6.

Make the sauce. Strain the reserved milk through a sieve. Put it into a jug and
add any juices from the fish plate. Melt the butter in a large heavy-based pan.
Add the flour. Stir over a low heat for 2 minutes to form a thick paste (roux).
Remove from the heat and beat in the wine to form a smooth sauce. Return to
the heat and cook, stirring, for another 5 minutes or so. Pour the milk into the
sauce very gradually off the heat, beating as you go, return to the heat and cook
for 2 minutes. Add the cream, dill or other herb, season to taste and set aside.

Assemble the pie: Spread a bit of the sauce into a baking dish (an oval 28 x 5cm
is perfect) or 4 small ones. Break the fish into big bits. Scatter over the base,
mixing the types up. Add the prawns. Squeeze lemon juice over them. Season.
Peel, slice and lay the eggs evenly over the top. Cover the lot with white sauce.
Use a fork and spoon to arrange the mash over the sauce in peaks. Sit the dish
on a baking tray.

COOK Bake the pie in the oven for 20–30 minutes, or until browned and
crisp on top and piping hot inside (pierce the centre with a skewer
to test for heat). Remove from the oven and leave to settle for 5 minutes.

PLATE Serve at the table with a choice of fresh herb salsa (p118), aioli
(p100) or a chicory and green leaf salad in honey mustard dressing
(p26). Or go traditional and eat with peas.

SALMON NIÇOISE

FEEDS 2

INGREDIENTS

2 eggs
salt and black pepper
2 tbsp soy sauce
1 tsp caster sugar
1 tbsp rice vinegar
1 star anise
2 x 150–175g salmon fillets

SALAD
75g fine green beans
4 handfuls of green salad leaves
6 spring onions
¼ of a cucumber
4 radishes
6 cherry tomatoes
2 bundles of somen noodles
8 black olives

MARINADE
½ red chilli, deseeded and diced
a small handful of torn coriander
a thumb-sized piece of fresh ginger
1 tbsp soy sauce
1 garlic clove, peeled and crushed
1 tbsp lemon/lime juice
2–3 tbsp homemade (p153) or shop-
    bought mayonnaise

ORIENTAL DRESSING
4½ tsp white wine vinegar
a pinch of caster sugar
1 tbsp soy sauce
1 shallot, peeled and sliced
1 garlic clove, peeled and crushed
75ml sunflower/groundnut oil
1 tsp sesame oil

TIME SAVER

Use teriyaki sauce to marinate the salmon in
place of the suggested marinade

An Asian restyling of a French classic: it's unusual but bloody good.

PREP Fill a small pan with enough water to cover the eggs. Bring it to the boil. Add a pinch of salt and reduce to a simmer. Lower in the eggs and cook for 9 minutes until hard-boiled. Sit the eggs under cold running water until cool. Roll on a board to crack and peel neatly, starting from the air pocket at the rounder end. Mix the soy, sugar, vinegar and star anise together in a bowl, add the eggs and set aside for 3 hours to flavour and colour. Turn once.

Mix the marinade ingredients together in a dish. Turn the salmon pieces in it and chill for at least 30 minutes, fish skin-side up. Mix the dressing ingredients together in a bowl and set aside.

Prep the salad: trim the beans then boil in lightly salted water for 4 minutes or until tender. Drain and refresh in cold water. Drain again. Wash and dry the leaves. Finely slice the spring onion at an angle into long diagonal strips. Peel, halve and deseed the cucumber, then slice widthways. Slice the radishes and halve the tomatoes. Cook the noodles in lightly salted boiling water for 5 minutes or until just soft. Drain and rinse in cold water, then toss in 1 tablespoon of the dressing.

COOK Pat the salmon dry then brush lightly with oil. Put a griddle pan on to a high heat until almost smoking. Transfer the fish to the pan and cook skin-side down for 3 minutes or until it's good and crispy. Lower the heat a bit, turn and cook for a further 2 minutes or until the salmon is firm, opaque and juicy with just a trace of pink in the centre. Remove immediately.

PLATE Toss the noodles in the remaining dressing, reserving a little for finishing. Toss the salad ingredients separately. Sling the noodles onto plates. Arrange the salad and olives on top. Cut the eggs in half. Perch a piece of salmon on each plate (or break them up into pieces if you prefer) and give the whole thing a final drizzle of dressing before serving.

BONUS BITES

FAST EGG, BACON AND SALMON SALAD
Hard-boil 2 eggs as above. Cool in cold water and peel. Fry 3 rashers of bacon in a pan until crisp, reserving the fat in the pan. Cut 2 skinless salmon fillets into bite-sized chunks and roll in the juice of ½ a lemon, 1 tbsp olive oil, 1 crushed garlic clove, 1 tbsp finely chopped dill/tarragon/coriander and season with salt and pepper. Add the salmon to the pan and fry in the bacon fat, turning with tongs, for 3 minutes or until cooked through. Throw a handful each of green leaves, cherry tomatoes and croutons into a bowl and toss with a honey mustard dressing (p26). Crumble over the crispy bacon and top with the salmon pieces and halved eggs.

SALMON SASHIMI
Using a sharp knife, slice a chilled 250g top-grade fresh salmon fillet across the grain at a 45 degree angle into pieces 5mm thick. Wipe the blade between cuts. Arrange in slightly overlapping single lines on 2 plates and serve with a small bowl of soy sauce, a heap of wasabi paste/strong English mustard and a few bits of pickled ginger. Eat with chopsticks.

FISH AND CHIPS WITH HOMEMADE TARTARE SAUCE

FEEDS 2

INGREDIENTS

2 large floury potatoes
groundnut/sunflower oil/beef dripping
    for frying
350g white fish fillet
4 tbsp plain white flour
salt and pepper
BATTER
175g self-raising flour
1½ tsp baking powder
2 egg yolks
300ml lager or soda/mineral water
TARTARE SAUCE
1 tbsp tarragon
1½ tbsp flat-leaf parsley
25g gherkin or cornichons
3 tbsp homemade (p153) or shop-
    bought mayonnaise
3 tbsp sour cream or natural yoghurt
1½ tbsp capers, drained
2 tbsp lemon/lime juice

—— CHANGE IT UP ——

1. If you don't want to deep-fry, fill a
deep frying pan with 2–3cm oil and cook
the fish over a medium/high heat for
3 minutes per side. **2.** Shallow-fry chips
(p78) and sweet potato wedges (p82) also
work well with this fish and don't need deep-
frying

—— BONUS BITE ——

FISH IN GOLDEN CRUMBS
Prep the fish as before. Coat in flour, dip
into beaten egg then panko/homemade
dried breadcrumbs (p201). Shallow-fry for 3
minutes per side, or until crisp and golden.

DIY FISH FINGERS
Cut a couple of skinned white fish fillets
into fingers. Dip in flour, beaten egg
and panko/dried breadcrumbs as above.
Shallow-fry, then eat on a plate with ketchup
or in a sandwich.

*Succulent white fish sealed in crisp golden batter with delicious chips
and herby tartare sauce: a few smart skills and it's yours on a plate.
Go for smaller bits of fish here as they make for easier deep-frying.*

PREP
Start by making the chips and giving them their first fry: Peel the
potatoes and cut into 1cm slices. Stack these up and slice into 1cm
sticks. Soak in cold water for 30 minutes. Drain, then dry thoroughly on
kitchen paper or a tea towel.

Fill a deep-fat fryer with your chosen oil or use it to one-third fill a deep
saucepan or wok. If you have a cooking thermometer, heat it to 130°C.
Otherwise, drop a breadcrumb in – if it's golden after 1 minute, the oil is ready.
Add the chips gradually and fry for 5–6 minutes until tender but pale. Drain
on kitchen paper and set aside.

Sort the tartare sauce: Chop the tarragon, parsley and gherkin finely. Mix
everything together and divide between two small ramekins. Chill.

Prepare the fish: Check for bones by feeling for them with your fingers. Remove
any skin using a sharp, flexible knife (p134). Cut larger fish into smaller
portions (approximately 10 x 5cm is good but it depends on thickness). Dry it.

Sprinkle the white flour on a plate with a little salt and pepper. Roll the fish in
it to coat thoroughly. Set aside. Preheat the oven to 180°C/Gas 4.

Finish the chips: Reheat the chip oil, raising the temperature to 190°C/Gas 5 (a
cube of bread will crisp up in 30 seconds). Slip the chips gently into the hot oil.
Cook for 1–2 minutes or until golden and crispy. Scoop out onto a tray covered
with kitchen paper using a slotted spoon. Sit them in the oven while you cook
your fish. Don't salt them.

Make the batter just before you fry: Sift the flour, baking powder and a pinch of
salt into a bowl. Make a well in the centre and drop in the egg yolks with a glug
of the beer, if using. Break the yolks up with your balloon whisk or wooden
spoon then start to incorporate the flour, pouring the beer or water in as you
do until you get a totally smooth batter the thickness of single cream.

COOK
Reheat the oil to 190°C/Gas 5. Dunk two floured fish pieces into the
batter and coat well, letting any excess drip off. Lower each piece
into the hot fat very gently. Let it fry for 4 minutes (or 5–6 for thicker pieces)
until golden, crispy and puffed up. Remove to kitchen paper. (I like to sit it on a
rack in a preheated oven so it retains its crunch). Repeat with remaining fish.

PLATE
Bang the fish bits onto plates with the chips and tartare sauce.
Serve with lemon wedges for squeezing, malt vinegar and ketchup,
salting at the table so chips and fish stay crisp.

EGGS AND DAIRY

I don't know about you but my shopping list always includes 'eggs' 'cheese' 'other dairy bits' written in automatic scribble. Maybe I'm guilty of taking them for granted: something I'm not proud of given how much my cooking and diet depends on them. Just imagine a world without the perfectly poached egg; the same goes for a chunk of cheddar or a slice of mellow stilton or a cool slick of butter on a good bit of bread. Of course these guys aren't just great in their own right, we're talking here about some of the most useful ingredients on the planet. Without them, so many dishes just wouldn't be possible – think soufflés, tarts, sauces, ice-creams, cakes, crêpes and meringues – and then there's the excitement and skill-set involved in cooking them. It's easy enough to bang a home-roasted chicken on the table but a perfect eggs benedict and impeccable omelette, a butter that doesn't burn as soon as you turn your back on it, or a custard that doesn't curdle – now that's confident cooking.

LAYING IT OUT
EGG OPTIONS

HEN'S EGGS: at their freshest these are unbeatable. Boil, scramble, poach, fry, and bake: use in omelettes, batters, sauces, custards, mayonnaise, ice-cream, pasta, pastry, baking, coatings, soufflés, meringues and mousses. They come in four sizes: small, medium, large, XL. Always get large for baking. Consider free-range/organic or omega-3 enriched eggs (great but more expensive).

DUCK'S EGGS: richer and creamier, these super-size statement eggs are now widely available. Excellent soft- and hard-boiled, poached, bread crumbed/deep-fried or scrambled. They make richer yet lighter cakes and puddings. The whites take longer to whisk but hold air brilliantly.

QUAIL'S EGGS: delicious mini-eggs with a sweet, delicate taste and a larger proportion of yolk to white. Hard boil to eat with salt. Add to fish pies. Bang onto salads (soft- or hard-boiled). Poach, fry or deep-fry wrapped in sausage meat for Scotch eggs. They have a very long shelf-life (tough shells), look cute and are increasingly available.

CRACKING EGGS:
What to look for

Eggs vary wildly in quality and welfare: shop around for the best you can get. Deli, corner shop, farm gate, supermarket, street market, here's what to look for.

SHELLS: colour: white, brown, pastel, speckled, it's cosmetic – they'll taste the same.

CONDITION: must be undamaged/crack-free. Lift each egg to check before you buy.

STATE: shells are porous so go for clean shells.

FRESHNESS: the fresher the better. Check the box (or egg – they're often date stamped) for the 'best before' date and stick to it. If the egg isn't stamped or you're in doubt test them. Sit the whole egg in its shell in a bowl or glass full of cold water. Fresh eggs will sink and settle horizontally. Slightly older eggs will rise up at the round end – they're still good for baking. Old stale eggs float to the top – don't use.

LOOK: a good egg has a plump upright yolk which is yellow/orange and sits on a compact, firm, jelly-like white. Blood spots are normal so leave or remove with a knife tip.

HOW TO
SEPARATE EGGS

1. Get 3 bowls.

2. Crack the egg sharply on the side of a bowl or counter edge.

3. Hold it over a bowl. Pull the two halves apart with your thumbs, letting the yolk settle in one half of the shell as the white spills down.

4. Pass the yolk backwards and forwards between the halves until the white has gone.

5. Drop the yolk into the second bowl. Tip the white into the third.

6. Separate your next egg into the first bowl and repeat the process.

OR DO IT BY HAND: Crack the egg and drop it into a bowl. Tip it into your clean cupped hand which is held over another bowl. Let the white drip down through your fingers. Place the yolk in another bowl.

EGG STORE

KEEP IN THE BOX

For protection, to remind you of their sell-by-date and to stop porous shells absorbing other tastes and smells

KEEP COOL

Sit the box away from any heat source in the kitchen so you can use them directly (always use eggs at room temperature) or keep them in the fridge

HOW TO MAKE
ESSENTIAL MAYONNAISE

Sit a large bowl on a tea towel. Add **2 EGG YOLKS**, a pinch each of **SALT** and **SUGAR**, 1 good **TSP MUSTARD** and beat together using a balloon whisk. Measure **175ML GROUNDNUT OR SUNFLOWER OIL** and **50ML MILD OLIVE OIL** into a jug. Start to drip-trickle it over the yolks, beating constantly, adding it in a very slow drizzle so it emulsifies. Once it starts to thicken properly, stop and add **1 TBSP WHITE WINE VINEGAR** or lemon juice. Continue to beat, adding the oil a little more steadily. Once it's all in, add a further **1 TBSP VINEGAR** or juice and **1 TBSP HOT WATER**. Give it a final beat and adjust the seasonings. Flavour with garlic, wasabi, mustard, ketchup, or dill.

MAYO TIPS Make sure all your ingredients are at room temperature. To save a mayo that splits, tip another yolk into a bowl and add the split mix ½ a teaspoon at a time, whisking all the while.

EGG AND DAIRY DOCTOR

EGGS AND DAIRY PACK THEIR FAIR SHARE OF BONE-STRENGTHENING **CALCIUM AND PROTEIN** MAKING THEM PRIME FOODS FOR VEGETARIANS. Eggs, hard and semi-hard cheeses are high in *Vitamin A* WHICH SUPPORTS VISION, SKIN AND IMMUNE SYSTEM, **VITAMIN B2** which is good for the skin, eyes and nervous system and **VITAMIN B12** which supports the immune system and the manufacture OF RED BLOOD CELLS. EGGS, YOGHURT AND MANY CHEESES CONTAIN **PHOSPHORUS** for healthy teeth and bones. EGGS CONTAIN **ZINC** which boosts fertility and *Iron* WHICH HELPS TRANSPORT OXYGEN ROUND THE BODY.

The level of SATURATED FAT in eggs is LOW so ignore previous advice about restricting consumption on health grounds WATCH HIGH LEVELS OF SALT AND SATURATED FAT in cheese; luckily it's a rich food so you don't need a lot.

CHEESE BOARD

Cheesemaking is an ancient art enjoying a revival; work out what's best for a cheeseboard or for cooking. Buy and store it well.

HARD

These are mature cheeses which have a hard dense texture and which vary in strength from mild to palate-scorching. Varieties include **VINTAGE CHEDDAR**, **AGED GOUDA** and **GRUYÈRE**, **EMMENTHAL** and **MANCHEGO**. **PARMESAN** and **PECORINO** are the driest and have a very long shelf-life. They're expensive but you don't need a lot: grate them into your cooking and over finished dishes.

SEMI-HARD

Here you've got a huge range of affordable, amiable cheeses which vary in strength, taste and texture. Many melt well: some work best uncooked with fruit, bread and celery, chutney, or with a bit of fruit cake or in a salad.

CHEDDAR: A tasty, versatile cheese which works for all manner of eating and cooking. Choose fully flavoured or substitute with an alternative cheese like double gloucester or red leicester if you prefer it milder.
LANCASHIRE: A lovely, tangy cheese which melts well and holds its flavour in cooking: get it creamy, tasty, or crumbly. It's good in risottos, burgers and Welsh rarebit.
GRUYÈRE: A nutty Swiss cheese with a bit of an edge which melts well. It's great in fondues, tarts, soufflés, with eggs, and works in potato dishes.
CHESHIRE: Melts well, a crumbly milky tasting white cheese.
RACLETTE: Swiss melting cheese; good with potatoes and for dipping.
WENSLEYDALE: A mild slightly tart cheese which works best eaten as is or in salads.
EDAM AND GOUDA: Dutch cheeses, Edam is lower in calories. Gouda has a stronger flavour and is a better melt. Both are good in salads and for snacking.

BLUE

A distinctive style of cheese with a blue line and macho reputation. Varieties include **STILTON** – the king of English cheeses – and the cave-aged **ROQUEFORT**. Some, like **GORGONZOLA** can be quite palate-challenging but others, like **CAMBOZOLA** can be soft and subtle. Try before you buy…

SOFT

A range of seductive spreadable cheeses including brie, camembert and taleggio with a bloom and ooze to them.
BRIE: A soft fruity creamy cheese which should ooze out onto the plate when ripe: its edible rind should be white and firm and the cheese itself pale yellow and creamy. Eat with wine and crackers. It does melt so experiment with it. Brie de Meaux is best.
CAMEMBERT: A crumbly soft item which gets creamier. Enjoy with a crunchy baguette and fruit and nuts, or try baked whole with wine and herbs, or breadcrumbed and deep-fried.
TALEGGIO: Melts into a thick tasty cream without splitting. Slice it onto puff pastry tarts, over potatoes and onto steaks and burgers.

FRESH

MOZZARELLA: Traditionally made from buffalo's milk, most mozzarella is processed and packaged in brine. Melted, it has a unique stringy quality. Serve with fresh basil and tomatoes or use it sliced or grated on pizzas, in pastas or bakes. Get blocks of denser cooking mozzarella for grating into lasagnes etc.
FETA: Cube or crumble it into Greek salad with chopped tomatoes, olives, cucumber and a sharp dressing. Use to stuff peppers, tomatoes, courgettes.
RICOTTA: Made from the liquids of the cheese, it should be creamy. Use for puddings or stuffing cannelloni and pasta dishes.
MASCARPONE: Not really a cheese but a cream cheese-style cream. Use for sauces, in cheesecakes and for tiramisu.

GOAT'S

There are hundreds of different types out there ranging from mild to pungent, creamy to crumbly. It's shaped in logs, cones, wheels, crottins. Get it fresh or rolled in herbs, ash, mixed with herbs and garlic. Crumble into salads. Slice it to melt on tarts, pizzas, use to stuff vegetables, or breadcrumb and deep-fry.

CHEESE ETIQUETTE
WHERE TO GET IT, WHAT TO LOOK FOR & HOW TO STORE

THE SPECIALIST CHEESE SHOP: get free samples and advice on what's best. Find out what's in season (cheeses have them). Expect a range of artisan cheeses from home and away; can get expensive…

THE GOOD SUPERMARKET: caters for great value cooking cheeses; try before you buy only works at the cheese counter. Check labels for cheese information.

Cheese checklist
◀ look for fat/sodium levels if it matters to you;
◀ strength of flavour should be graded (key for cooking cheese);
◀ check sell-by date;
◀ check suitability for vegetarians (rennet-free is the way forward);
◀ and the type of milk used (anyone who is pregnant, ill, very young must avoid cheese made with unpasteurised milk).

Looking for the best
It's best to get cheese freshly cut from a whole piece rather than pre-packed. The outer rind of the hard and semi-hard cheeses should be intact. The paste should look calm and pleasant, neither dry nor sweaty; the rind of soft cheeses should be evenly coloured – surface mould is normal on some cheeses.

STORAGE
Cheese hates extremes: it's best kept in a box in the garage, larder, cellar, windowsill or the warmest part of the fridge (salad drawer or butter section). Chill fresh cheeses. Re-wrap any cheese sold in cling film: replace with baking/greaseproof paper and then cling film to preserve. Hard cheeses can last for weeks but don't let them dry out. Soft cheese may need an extra few days to ripen – use your judgement. Always give eating cheese a couple of hours to return to room temperature.

FRIENDS

EGGS
ANCHOVY, ASPARAGUS, BACON, BASIL, BEETROOT, BREAD, CHEESES, CHILLI, CHORIZO, CHUTNEYS, CINNAMON, CREAM, CRESS, CUCUMBER, DILL, HAM, HONEY, LEMON, LETTUCE, MAYONNAISE, MUSHROOMS, MUSTARD, ONIONS, OLIVES, PARSLEY, PASTA, PICKLES, PEAS, POTATOES, PRAWNS, ROCKET, SOY, SMOKED HADDOCK, SMOKED SALMON, SAUSAGE, SPINACH, TARRAGON, TOAST, TOMATOES, WATERCRESS

CHEESE
APPLES, ASPARAGUS, AUBERGINE, AVOCADO, BACON, BEEF, BREAD, CABBAGE, CARROT, CAULIFLOWER, CELERY, CHICORY, CHICKEN, CRACKERS, CREAM, CUCUMBER, GARLIC, GRAPES, LEMON, LETTUCE, LIME, MANGO, MUSHROOM, NECTARINE, ONION, ORANGE, PASTA, PEACH, PEAR, PORK, POTATOES, PRAWNS, SPRING ONION, TOMATO, WALNUTS, WATERCRESS, WHITE WINE, WHITE FISH

1 BOILED

BOILED EGG AND TOASTED SOLDIERS

FAST

FEEDS 1

INGREDIENTS

2 large hen's eggs (at room temperature)
a pinch of salt for the water
2 slices toast
softened butter, for spreading
salt and pepper

——— CHANGE IT UP ———

Switch the toast for asparagus spears. Snap
the woody ends from a few bits of seasonal
English asparagus and peel the stalks. Boil
for 3–4 minutes. Dip as per toast.

TIPS
1. If eggs crack in the water, add a tablespoon of any vinegar to seal them. **2.** To hard-boil a hen's egg, cook in boiling water from cold for 10 minutes. Cool under running water to stop the yolks discolouring.

Enjoy your egg in its purest form; boil simply for a set amount of time to create one of the most delicious and indulgent ready-meals ever. Soldiers are compulsory.

PREP Fill a small pan with enough water to cover the eggs. Bring it to the boil. Add the salt.

COOK Lower the eggs into the pan using a large spoon or a pair of tongs. Increase the heat so the water returns to the boil. As soon as it does, reduce it to a gentle boil. Set your timer. For a very soft egg, cook for 4 minutes; for medium, cook for 5; for a firm white and moist still runny yolk, cook for 6. Adjust the timing if using smaller eggs. If cooking eggs from chilled allow 30 seconds extra. Remove immediately at the end of your chosen cooking time.

PLATE Spoon the eggs into cups on a plate. Bang the top of the first egg with a spoon to crack it. Peel the shell off. Or cut it across with a knife. Repeat with the second or it will continue to cook. Spread butter on the toast. Cut it into soldiers. Put a little salt and pepper on the plate. Get dipping.

BONUS BITES

LUXURY DUCK'S EGGS AND FRIED SOLDIERS
Bring a pan of water to boil as above. Lower 2 duck eggs into it. Set the timer for 6 minutes once it returns to the boil. Meantime, melt a little butter in a frying pan. Cut 2 slices of firm white bread into sticks as wide as they are deep. Fry them, turning, until crisp and a bit smoky. Sit the eggs in cups. Serve as above with the fried soldiers for dipping.

SWEET SOFT-BOILED QUAIL'S EGGS AND SOLDIERS ON SALAD
Boil 150g baby new potatoes for 10 minutes or until tender. Drain. Meantime, grill 2 streaky bacon rashers until crisp. Make up a honey mustard (p26) or walnut dressing (p33). Remove crusts from a slice of white bread. Dice it into 5mm bits. Heat a little olive or walnut oil in a pan and fry the dice till crisp. Set a small pan of water to boil. Add 6 quail's eggs. Boil for 2 minutes for soft-boiled or 3–4 minutes for hard-boiled. Cool in running water, crack at their rounded ends, neatly peel the shells off and slice in half across. Throw the potatoes into a bowl with 2 handfuls of soft green salad leaves and toss with 1–2 tbsp of dressing. Crumble the bacon on top. Add the soldier croutons and the sliced quail's eggs and drizzle over more dressing to finish.

GLORIOUS SCRAMBLE

2 scrambled

 FAST

FEEDS 1

INGREDIENTS

3 large hen's eggs (at room temperature)
a pinch of cream of tartar
25g butter
salt and pepper

TIP
Soak your used pan in hot water immediately with a dash of vinegar so the egg remains don't stick.

Here's an unusually gentle way to prepare your scrambled eggs: using the oven means you've got more control over the texture and more time to make toast. You can multiply this up pretty easily so if you've got loads to feed it's a good 'un.

PREP Preheat the oven to 170°C/Gas 3. Get an ovenproof bowl ready. Crack the eggs into a large mixing bowl. Add the cream of tartar. Beat with a balloon whisk for 30 seconds.

Meantime, put a heavy-bottomed saucepan onto a low heat (18–20cm is good). Add the butter to melt.

Tip the eggs into the pan. Stir constantly with a wooden spoon for 30 seconds, or until lumps just begin to form. Transfer to the ovenproof bowl.

COOK Bake the eggs in the bowl for 8–9 minutes, or until as creamy as you like. Stir the mix once after 4 minutes. Keep an eye out and test it so it doesn't over-cook.

PLATE Add salt to taste. Pile the egg immediately onto hot buttered toast, muffins or bagels. Add black pepper. It's also perfect with the great full English breakfast (baked sausages, baked mushrooms, baked tomatoes and baked beans).

BONUS BITES

SCRAMBLE IN A PAN WITH STIR-INS

Beat 3 large eggs in a bowl. Add 2 tsp cream, a pinch of salt and a little pepper. Gently heat 3 tsp butter in a small heavy-bottomed pan until melted. Add the eggs and reduce the heat to very low. Stir the eggs once every 20 seconds or so using a wooden spoon. The egg ribbons gently as it cooks. Remove from the pan the second it's done so it doesn't overcook. Sprinkle with a few grains of vanilla salt and a little thyme, ideally. For stir-ins: Just as your egg is almost set as you like it, stir in any of the following to melt or heat through: thin slivers of smoked salmon, crispy bacon pieces, a few drained capers, a tiny bit of grated cheddar or gruyère cheese, a little diced, fried chorizo, a couple of sliced mushrooms fried in garlic butter, a bit of shredded cooked mackerel, a sprinkle of chopped dill or tarragon.

3 FRIED

EGG BANJO

 FAST   **FEEDS 1**

INGREDIENTS

2 slices good white bread
  (bought or homemade, p202)
softened butter, for spreading
tomato ketchup/brown sauce
1 tsp good olive oil
  (or flavourless oil of your choice)
1 tsp butter
1 large egg (at room temperature)

TIPS

1. For over-easy eggs, flip with a spatula after 1 minute and cook for a further minute before serving.
2. For compact fried eggs, crack them low in the pan slowly.

── CHANGE IT UP ──

1. For a bacon and egg banjo, fry 2 rashers of back bacon in the pan. Remove and keep warm in a preheated oven before adding the egg to the pan and cooking in the bacon fat until done. Slap into a roll with the bacon.
2. For a veggie banjo, fry 4 button mushrooms in a little oil at the same time as the egg.
3. To make egg banjo for a crowd, crack 4 eggs into 1 tbsp hot oil. Cover with a lid. Reduce heat to medium/low. Cook for 3–5 minutes.

AKA the Fried Egg Sandwich. To enjoy the full banjo effect, take a good bite and strum the yolk off your front using one hand while you hold the sandwich up and out to the side with the other.

PREP Spread both your bread slices with butter (be liberal or restrained to taste) and one with sauce. Heat the oil and butter in a small pan over a medium heat. It needs to be hot enough for your egg to bubble and spit as it hits the fat, but don't burn it.

COOK Get your egg in: tap it sharply against the side of the pan. Tuck both thumbs into the natural crack you've created and pull the shell apart so it slips neatly out into the hot fat. Or crack it into a cup and pour it in.

Let it settle for a few seconds. Tip the pan at an angle so the fat runs down. Using a teaspoon, spoon the hot buttery juices over the egg for 1 minute or until it's done: the white firm, the yolk cooked underneath but still runny on top with a very light transparent film over it. Whip it out with a spatula the second it's done. Bang it onto the sauced slice of bread. Sandwich it.

PLATE Get stuck in.

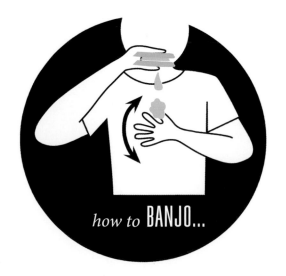

how to **BANJO...**

PERFECT POACHED EGGS AND PANCETTA ON POTATO CAKES
WITH HOLLANDAISE SAUCE

FEEDS 2

INGREDIENTS

2 large eggs
a little groundnut or other flavourless
 oil for lining
4 strips of pancetta/streaky bacon
POTATO CAKES
2 medium potatoes
25g onion
salt and pepper
1 tbsp olive oil
a knob of butter
HOLLANDAISE SAUCE
3 egg yolks
1 tsp caster sugar
1 tbsp water
1 tbsp white wine vinegar
1 tbsp lemon juice, plus extra to finish
175g clarified butter (p141)
 or soft butter
salt and pepper

TIP

Add finely chopped tarragon/basil to leftover hollandaise and reheat gently over a pan of hot water. This sauce is also great with steak/ griddled chicken/white fish/asparagus.

——— CHANGE IT UP ———

1. For eggs benedict, make the hollandaise sauce and keep it warm. Poach the eggs as above or use the frying pan method below. Toast 2 sliced muffins/bagels. Spread with soft butter. Add a slice of ham, a poached egg and cover with sauce.
2. For salmon benedict, use a slice of smoked salmon instead of ham.
3. For mushroom benedict, brush a portobello mushroom with olive oil and cook on a hot griddle for 2 minutes per side. Lay on a toasted muffin and top with a poached egg and hollandaise.

Once you're down with the perfect poached egg and a silky sexy hollandaise you're well on your way to veteran status.

PREP Potato cakes: At least 1 hour before eating, boil the potatoes whole for 10 minutes or until just softening but still a bit firm. Remove. Drain. Cool. Just before cooking, peel and grate coarsely into a bowl along with the onion. Season and mix lightly with a fork. Set aside.

COOK EGGS: Line 2 cups/ramekins with large pieces of cling film, leaving plenty to spare. Brush lightly with oil using a pastry brush and crack an egg into each. Pull the film up and twist to make them watertight. Plop into a pan of simmering water for 3 minutes to poach until the whites are set and yolks still runny. Untwist to touch and check (twist and return if you need to). Cool immediately in chilled water, still in the cling film, so the eggs stop cooking.

HOLLANDAISE: Put a pan of water on to heat. Get a large heatproof bowl that can fit into the top without touching the water. Add the egg yolks, sugar, water, vinegar and lemon juice. Sit it into the pan. Reduce the heat to a bare minimum (if it's too hot your sauce will scramble) and beat continuously with a balloon whisk. The mix will be thin at first but thicken to the point where the whisk leaves a trail on the surface. This will take 3–8 minutes. Be patient.

Take it off the heat. Add the butter while still whisking. For clarified butter, pour and whisk in a small steady trickle so the mix doesn't curdle. For soft butter, add ½ teaspoon at a time, whisking each bit in before adding the next. Season with salt and pepper and squeeze over a little extra lemon juice to finish. Keep the sauce warm; it can't be reheated. Sit it in a bowl, film covered over a pan of hot water off the hob. Stir it regularly. If it curdles, bang a new egg yolk into a clean bowl and whisk your sauce in bit by bit to pull it back.

Put a frying pan on to a medium/high heat. Add the oil/butter. Get two large cookie cutters or chef's rings. Sit them on a board. Stuff each with potato cake mix. Carefully transfer to the pan to cook for 3 minutes. Turn with the help of a spatula. Fry until crisp and cooked through. (If you don't have any cutters don't worry, just go free-style instead). Remove from the pan and keep warm.

Fry the pancetta in the same pan for 1–2 minutes per side until crisp. Sit it on kitchen paper. Reheat the eggs: put a pan of water on to simmer. Plop the eggs in for 1–2 minutes. Remove with a slotted spoon and remove the cling film.

PLATE Place the potato cakes on plates. Layer with the pancetta, sit the poached eggs on top and spoon over a good dollop of hollandaise.

—— BONUS BITE ——

FRYING PAN POACHED EGGS

Two-thirds fill a small frying pan with water. Add a pinch of salt, bring to the boil and reduce to a simmer. Crack the egg straight in (or pour it in from a cup) and leave to cook for 3–4 minutes, until the white is set and the yolk runny. Lift it out on a slotted spoon. Drain off water. Trim the white with scissors if you need to. Sit on hot buttered toast and season. Or team with a griddled portobello mushroom, fried vegetarian/pork sausage and fried tomato for an all-day breakfast.

A SIMPLE OMELETTE

 FEEDS 1

INGREDIENTS

3 large free-range eggs
2 tsp water
  (optional, but makes it lighter)
1 tsp chopped flat-leaf parsley
1 tsp chopped tarragon leaves
1 tsp chopped chives
3 tsp butter/olive oil/clarified butter
  (p141)
salt and black pepper

TIP
Using clarified butter (p141) means you can get your pan hotter for a faster and tastier result as it has a higher smoking point than regular butter.

CHANGE IT UP

1. For a cheese omelette, add 1 tbsp finely grated cheddar/parmesan to the egg mix (with or without the herbs) and sprinkle another 2 tbsp over the mix as you season it. Use a spatula to fold it over and slide it out onto a plate.
2. For a cheese and ham omelette, fill with a thin slice of good ham torn roughly and a good grating of gruyère or cheddar to taste.
3. For a mushroom omelette, make up some hot mixed mushrooms (p25). Spread over the omelette base and fold before sliding out.
4. For a blue cheese and onion marmalade omelette, crumble 30g stilton or other blue cheese and mix with 1 tbsp warm caramelised onion (p80) or a good onion marmalade (p144). Fill the omelette just as it's ready.

You can measure a cook by their omelette. Keep it simple and the method fast. Get it out while it's still slightly underdone and be subtle with the filling.

PREP Crack the eggs into a bowl. Add the water. Beat lightly with a fork for a few seconds to combine well but no more. Beat in the herbs. Put a plate on to warm.

COOK Bang the butter into an omelette pan on high heat (16–20cm base for a 3 egg omelette). As soon as it foams, shoot the egg mix in and get to work.

Give the mix a quick stir with a fork so it spreads across the base. Then use it to draw the outer setting edges of the omelette up towards you so the liquid egg runs down to the edge and underneath to set itself. It helps if you tilt the pan away from you. Do this a few times, working very quickly around the pan until the omelette is done. It should have a softly-set base, a soft top that's a bit runny still (it'll cook as you fold it) and should take less than a minute. Season it very lightly and quickly with salt and pepper (salting early can toughen the egg).

Roll it out of the pan for maximum softness. Take it away from the heat and tilt it down towards your plate. Tease the edge nearest the handle with the fork or a spatula so it flips over and rolls out.

PLATE Omelettes won't wait, so have a salad dressed and ready with maybe some chips or fried garlic and rosemary potatoes, or just good bread.

BONUS BITE

CLASSIC OMELETTE ARNOLD BENNETT
Heat 150ml milk in a pan with a peeled, halved shallot and a few black peppercorns. Add 150g smoked haddock (un-dyed is best) and simmer for 5 minutes or till soft. Remove the fish. Use a fork to break it into flakes and check for bones. Set aside. Make up a hollandaise sauce (p160). Preheat the grill. Make a 3 egg omelette following the method above, making sure it's still very soft. Cover it with flakes of fish and spoon the hollandaise over the top. Bang under the grill for a few seconds until it glazes and browns a little and sprinkle with chives to finish.

CRÊPE COMPLET

FEEDS 4

INGREDIENTS

110g plain white flour
a pinch of salt
1 large egg
300ml milk
1 tbsp melted butter, plus extra for
    frying
YOUR CHOICE OF FILLING

——— CHANGE IT UP ———

1. Mix your crêpe up by filling it with the following ingredients... **Savoury:** torn ham and grated gruyere, fried mushrooms and tarragon, smoked trout, dill and sour cream. **Sweet:** maple syrup, sugar and lemon juice, hot blueberries, strawberries and ginger cream, raspberries and ice-cream, sliced banana and Nutella.
2. To up the nutrients, replace 25g of the white flour with buckwheat flour.

TIP

It's common for the first crêpe to stick. Throw it away if it happens. No shame.

········ TIME SAVER ········

Make the batter up to 24 hours ahead. Add a splash of water and re-whisk before using.

——— BONUS BITE ———

BAKED CHICKEN & MUSHROOM CRÊPES
Make up a bèchamel sauce (p185) and the crêpes as above. Shred 175g leftover roast chicken. Slice and fry 450g mushrooms in ½ tbsp oil and 1 tsp butter with a little garlic and tarragon until soft. Preheat the oven to 200°C/Gas 6. Lay the crêpes flat out and grate a little cheddar or gruyère over each. Lay a mix of mushrooms and shredded chicken down the centre, adding dabs of sauce. Roll and place seam down in a greased dish. Cover with remaining sauce and sprinkle with extra cheese. Bake for 30 minutes till golden.

Here's a French way with a classic British breakfast (wrap it in a crêpe) and some other lovely fillings. Enjoy anytime. I made 200 of these for a party once.

PREP Sift the flour and salt into a bowl. Make a well in the centre. Crack the egg into it with a good splash of milk. Start to beat the flour into the liquid using a balloon whisk or wooden spoon. Add the remaining milk slowly, beating as you go, to get a smooth batter. Add the melted butter. Pour the batter into a jug. Set aside.

COOK Put a crêpe pan or large shallow frying pan onto a high heat. Coat with melted butter using a silicone brush (or put a bit in and swirl to coat) so your crêpe won't stick. Working fast, add 2–3 tablespoons of batter to the pan or pour the equivalent from a jug or ladle. Swirl the pan to coat evenly and achieve a thin crêpe. Cook for 1 minute or until the base browns up. Turn it with a metal spatula (run underneath to loosen first) or stand back from the hob and toss it high into the air with a forward movement so it turns. Catch it in the pan. Cook for another minute. Slide it, flat, onto a sheet of greaseproof paper. Make the rest and layer them up with more paper. Make up your filling of choice and fill and fold as described.

PLATE Get stuck into these as they are or team with a salad of your choice.

═══ FILLINGS ═══

1 EGG AND BACON
Grill 4–8 bacon rashers for 2 minutes per side. Keep warm. Fry 4 large eggs in 2 tsp each of butter and oil as per egg banjo for a crowd (p158). Put crêpes onto warm plates. Tear the bacon into small pieces. Divide and scatter down the middle of each crêpe. Top with an egg. Add a dollop of ketchup. Flip the sides over to cover.

2 SAUSAGE AND APPLE
Bake 4 good fat pork (or vegetarian) sausages at 200°C/Gas 6 for 20 minutes or till done. Core and slice 2 small eating apples into sixths and fry as per filling 3. Fill the centre of each crêpe with sausage and apple and fold the edges in.

3 CARAMELISED APPLE AND BLACK PUDDING
Fry 2 slices of black pudding in a little oil for 1–2 minutes per side till cooked. Keep warm. Core and slice 2 small eating apples into sixths. Fry in 2 tsp butter for 1 minute per side. Sprinkle with 1 tsp sugar. Cook 1 minute per side longer. Alternate crumbled black pudding and apple down the middle of each crêpe. Fold the edges in. Serve with maple syrup.

4 HAM AND CREAM CHEESE
Spread a thin layer of cream cheese over each crêpe. Add a thin slice of ham to the centre of each and flip the sides over to cover.

FAST FRITTATA WITH BUTTERED SPINACH AND INSTANT TOPPINGS

 FAST FEEDS 1-2

A frittata is a flat Italian omelette; this one packs layers of flavour.

INGREDIENTS

100g baby spinach
20g butter
50g parmesan/vegetarian equivalent
3 large free-range eggs
1 tbsp olive oil

INSTANT TOPPINGS
1. 50g feta cheese, crumbled
2. a handful of rocket and a few shavings of cheddar/parmesan
3. 6 chopped cherry tomatoes in a few drops of dressing
4. 3 slices of air-dried ham/crispy pancetta

── BONUS BITES ──

AUBERGINE, FETA AND DILL FRITTATA

Fry 8 x ½ cm slices of aubergine in a little olive oil, turning once, till brown and soft. Remove. Add a sliced shallot to the pan and cook till it just softens. Crumble and semi-mash 100g feta cheese in a bowl, adding 5 beaten eggs, a handful of torn dill, ½ tsp dried mint and a pinch of black pepper. Heat a little olive oil in an omelette pan and add half the mix. Layer the aubergine in and cover with the rest. Cook on a very low heat for 10 minutes or till the base is set but the top is slightly runny. Drizzle 1 tbsp oil over the top and sit under a preheated grill for 2 minutes or until just set and lightly golden.

ROASTED BROCCOLI FRITTATA

Toss 300g broccoli florets in 1 tbsp olive oil with 2 pinches each of sea salt and cumin and a pinch of chilli flakes. Roast in a preheated oven at 200°C/Gas 6 for 10 minutes. Beat 5 large eggs, a pinch of pepper and 20g finely grated parmesan/cheddar together. Add the egg and broccoli to a heated omelette pan with 1 tsp oil. Fry on a low heat for 5 minutes or until the base is set but the top is still a bit runny. Sprinkle with 10g extra parmesan, dab with butter and sit under a preheated grill for 2 minutes until set and lightly golden.

PREP
Prep your choice of topping so you're good to go. Preheat a grill.

COOK
Cook the spinach: empty it into a pan with 2 tablespoons water. Stir to wilt it for 2 minutes. Drain it into a sieve. Press any excess moisture out with a spoon. Tip it into a bowl, season lightly. Stir in 1 teaspoon of the butter. Set aside. Finely grate the parmesan or other hard cheese.

Mix the frittata: crack the eggs into a bowl and beat with a fork. Add half the cheese and all the buttered spinach. Put your 16–20cm base omelette pan on to high heat. Add the oil. Once it's hot, add the egg/spinach mix. Reduce the heat to low after 20 seconds.

Leave to cook on low for 1–2 minutes or until the base is just set and the top still runny. Sprinkle with the rest of the parmesan and dot with butter. Finish under the grill for 1–2 minutes until browned at the edges with the top glazed, golden and puffy.

PLATE
Slide it onto a plate and add your choice of toppings. Eat with bread, piles of dressed green salad and a plate of sliced tomato dressed with oil, lemon juice and sliced shallots.

CHEESE SOUFFLÉS WITH
ONION MARMALADE

FEEDS 6

INGREDIENTS

25g butter, plus extra for greasing
10g parmesan, grated (optional)
200g cheddar
35g plain white flour
½ pint milk
1 tbsp cider
3 very large eggs, separated (p153),
    plus an extra white
1 ¼ tsp Dijon mustard
2 tsp lemon juice
a shake of Worcester sauce
a good pinch of cayenne
salt and pepper
4 chives, snipped (optional)
1 x onion marmalade (p144)

TIP
Add an extra egg white or two to the mix if
you like to make for a lighter soufflé.

CHANGE IT UP

For a mixed cheese soufflé, replace a third
of the cheddar with either gruyère or
parmesan.

BONUS BITE

ONE BIG SOUFFLÉ: For one big soufflé for
sharing, grease a 1.5 litre soufflé dish with
melted butter as above. Sprinkle and coat
with grated parmesan, if you like. Spread
1–2 tbsp of onion marmalade, a bit of
homemade tomato sauce or cooked buttered
spinach across the base of the dish. Fill
with the basic soufflé mix and sprinkle with
grated cheese. Bake for 40–45 minutes until
ready as above.

*Special; but don't let the word soufflé put you off. They're easy enough
to make. As for taste they're lovely, light and cheesy with a delicious
sweet onion base. Get them onto the table straight from the oven:
perfect for dinner parties.*

PREP Organise 6 x 7cm individual soufflé dishes. Grease them well with a
little melted butter. Apply with a pastry brush using upward strokes
so the soufflés rise well. If using Parmesan, divide between the dishes. Shake
and tap it round to coat them well. Finely grate the cheddar.

COOK Make a thick white sauce: Melt the butter to foaming point in a
heavy-based pan on a gentle heat. Add the flour and stir to make
a paste using a wooden spoon. Stir for 2 minutes as the paste cooks. Remove.
Use a balloon whisk to beat the milk and cider into the paste very gradually
so the sauce you create is ultra-smooth. Return to a low heat and stir until the
sauce thickens. Set aside for 1 minute. Preheat the oven to 200°C/Gas 6.

Beat the egg yolks straight into the white sauce with the mustard, lemon juice,
Worcester sauce, cayenne, salt, black pepper and chives if using. The base mix
has to be well seasoned to counteract the bland white. Add the grated cheddar,
saving enough to sprinkle over the tops later. Combine well.

Whisk the 4 egg whites with an electric hand whisk or balloon whisk. (If you've
used the latter for your sauce, dunk it into boiling water and dry it well.) Once
the whites can stand in stiff peaks, stir one heaped tablespoon into the egg yolk
mix to loosen it, using a spatula. Tip the rest on top and fold them in gently
with as few cutting, scooping movements as you can get away with. If the odd
bit of white remains, that's fine, but don't over-mix it.

Spoon 1 teaspoon of the onion marmalade quickly into the base of each
dish. Use a larger spoon to fill each dish with the soufflé mixture to within
½ cm of the rims. Run a clean thumb tip round the edge of each to help shape
traditionally. Top with the remaining cheese.

Bake for about 10 minutes without opening the oven door. The soufflés should
be well risen, golden, pretty firm on top but soft in the centre. (To be honest,
you need to wobble them a bit to test and you probably won't know if they're
just right until you get your spoon in.)

PLATE Sit the soufflés on small plates, with teaspoons on the side. Tell
everyone to get their spoons down to the oniony bit at the bottom
so they can mix it up.

EASY LEMON SOUFFLÉS AND APRICOT SAUCE

FEEDS 6

INGREDIENTS

25g melted butter, for coating
1–2 tbsp sifted icing sugar, for dusting
1½ tsp good apricot preserve/jam
5 large free-range eggs (at room temperature)
150g caster sugar or vanilla sugar
1 large juicy lemon
55g ground almonds
APRICOT SAUCE
6 tbsp apricot preserve
water
1 tsp butter
a good squeeze of lemon juice

—— CHANGE IT UP ——

Replace the apricot preserve with homemade lemon and passion fruit curd (p216) or shop-bought lemon or orange curd.

✳✳✳✳ CASH SAVER ✳✳✳✳

Bang used, dried vanilla pods into caster sugar to store for instant vanilla sugar

TIP

If the egg whites collapse because you over-whisk them, just whisk in another egg white to save them.

These go fast, believe me. Within 3 minutes of getting them out of the oven during first testing, all six had disappeared and there were very burnt but happy mouths all round.

PREP Coat 6 x 7cm individual soufflé dishes lightly with melted butter using a pastry brush with upward strokes. Dust the insides with a little icing sugar. Spoon the jam into the base of each one. Preheat the oven to 180°C/Gas 4.

Bang and roll the lemon on a surface to soften it a bit for better juicing. Wash and dry it well. Grate finely. Cut in two and squeeze as much juice out as possible.

Using clean hands, separate the eggs into two grease-free bowls. Using a balloon or an electric hand whisk, whisk the egg yolks until fluffy. Start to add the sugar, a bit at a time, whisking, until you have a thick mousse. Still whisking, add the zest, juice and ground almonds. Stop as soon as they're in. Boil a kettle.

Remove the blades from your whisk. Dunk them or the balloon whisk into boiling water to remove the grease then dry well. Whisk the egg whites to the stiff peak stage.

Stir a tablespoon of whites into the mousse to loosen. Tip the rest in. Fold in very gently with a spatula to preserve air. Divide the mix between dishes, coming to within ½ cm of the tops. Shape with your thumb around the edges.

COOK Cook for 20 minutes or until very well risen and golden on top. Wobble to judge it as for cheese soufflés. Meantime, melt the preserve in a pan on a very gentle heat with the butter and as much water as you need to thin it a little. Add lemon juice to taste. Pour into a jug.

PLATE Serve soufflés on a plate with a teaspoon and a jug of sauce to pour into the centres at the table.

FRENCH EGG, CHEESE AND BACON TART

FEEDS 6

INGREDIENTS

225g plain white flour
½ tsp fine salt
110g chilled butter or
    55g butter/55g lard
2 tbsp chilled water
1 tbsp soft butter for greasing
FILLING
160g back bacon rashers
1 tbsp butter
140g gruyère cheese
6 egg yolks
400ml double cream
salt and pepper
a pinch of nutmeg

TIPS

1. To reduce the chance of breaking the pastry as you shape it into the tin, break off a spare bit and use to press the case gently into place.
2. To remove the tart from the tin, carefully break off any overhang clinging to the rim. Sit the tart on top of a jar. Holding the tin firmly, push down so the rim is released. Slide the tart onto a plate or board to take to the table.

········· TIME SAVER ·········

Reheat extra the next day or take into work and microwave. Freeze any extra. Defrost before reheating thoroughly.

In other words, quiche lorraine, and made the proper French way. It's rich and sumptuous so please make it.

PREP Sift the flour and salt into a large bowl. Cube the butter/lard and rub into the flour between your fingertips until it resembles fine breadcrumbs. Add the water gradually, mixing together with a fork, till you have a pliable dough that's neither dry nor sticky. By machine: pulse the flour, salt and butter until fine. Pour in the water gradually, pulsing between additions. Roll the dough into a ball, then flatten into a disc. Wrap in cling film and chill for 1 hour.

Preheat the oven to 220°C/Gas 7. Rub a tablespoon of soft butter over the base and sides of a 23 x 3cm loose-bottomed tart tin to help the pastry cook/prevent sticking. Remove the pastry from the fridge. Leave it to soften a little before rolling it out on a lightly floured board and fitting it to your tart tin, leaving an overhang (p201). Prick the base of the pastry very lightly all over with a fork so it won't rise as it bakes.

Filling: Lay your bacon rashers on a board. Remove any rind with a sharp chef's knife. Cut it into thick crossways strips on the diagonal or snip with kitchen scissors. Melt the butter in a frying pan on medium heat. Once it's foaming, scatter the bacon bits in. Fry for a few minutes, turning, until they're cooked but not crisp. Spoon onto kitchen paper and set aside.

Slice the cheese thinly and spread it evenly across the pastry base. Scatter the bacon pieces evenly over the top so every slice will get some. Beat the yolks in a bowl with a fork, adding the cream, seasoning and nutmeg till well incorporated. Pour the mix over the cheese and bacon.

COOK Bake for 20 minutes then reduce to 180°C/Gas 4 for another 20 minutes, or until the filling has set and is browned on top. Remove. Cool for 10 minutes.

PLATE Slice the tart into portions at the table using a cake slice or very sharp knife. Serve with boiled new potatoes, a carrot and orange salad, or boiled new potatoes and a green salad with honey mustard dressing.

········· TO GO WITH ·········

CARROT AND ORANGE SALAD

Coarsely grate 350g peeled carrots. Mix with 1 peeled, chopped orange and 3 chopped dates. Toss in 3 tbsp olive oil, 1 tbsp lemon juice and a pinch each of salt and sugar. Sprinkle with a few chopped cashew nuts.

LEEK, TARRAGON, CHEDDAR AND SOUR CREAM TART

FEEDS 6

INGREDIENTS

225g plain white flour
½ tsp fine salt
110g chilled butter (or 55g butter/55g lard), plus extra for greasing
25g strong cheddar
2–3 tbsp chilled water
1 egg white for sealing
FILLING
500g leeks
25g butter
1 tbsp olive oil
50ml water
225g strong cheddar
110ml double/whipping cream
160g sour cream
½ –1 tbsp chopped tarragon
4 large eggs
salt and pepper

TIP
Use uncooked rice or dry beans instead of ceramic beans for baking blind.

My favourite tart; sweet, soft leek works a treat in the creamy cheese base. Using lard in your shortcrust pastry gives it a crumblier texture than all-butter. A top eat with friends and family.

PREP Make the pastry. By hand: Sift the flour and salt into a large bowl. Cube the butter or butter/lard mix. Rub it lightly into the flour between your fingertips until it resembles fine breadcrumbs. Finely grate the cheese. Stir it into the mix with a fork. Add the water gradually, mixing with the fork for pliable dough that's neither dry nor sticky (add more flour or water to get it right). Don't over-handle the pastry at any stage as it spoils the texture. Roll the dough lightly into a ball then flatten it into a disc. Wrap in cling film and chill for 1 hour. By machine: Pulse the flour, salt, cheese and butter until fine. Add the water gradually, pulsing between additions until a dough forms. Stop and test with your fingers to check it's not too dry. Roll, wrap and chill.

Preheat the oven to 180°C/Gas 4. Sit the pastry on a floured board and leave to soften a little. Grease a 23 x 3cm loose-based fluted tart/quiche tin. Roll the pastry out in a circle to fit the tin plus 5cm extra. Without stretching the pastry, roll the pin under it and lift it over and down into the tin. Support the edges with one hand. Press into the base and sides for a close fit without it cracking. Use spare pastry to fill any holes/breaks, leaving an overhang on the edges in case it shrinks. Prick the surface lightly with a fork.

COOK Cut a piece of greaseproof paper and lay it into the pastry to protect the base and sides. Fill it with baking beans and bake blind for 10–20 minutes, till the sides are hard and lightly coloured. Remove the paper and beans and brush lightly with egg white. Bake again for 4 minutes. Cool.

Meantime, make the filling: Trim, wash and dry the leeks. Slice the white and palest green parts across in 1cm slices, discarding the tough dark green leek. Melt the butter with the oil in a large frying pan on a low heat. Add the slices of leek and leave to sweat for 2 minutes. Add the water, cover with a lid and sweat for a further 3 minutes or until soft but not browned, turning carefully if you need. Season to taste and leave to cool.

Grate the cheese finely and spread half of it evenly over the tart base. Tip the rest into a bowl with the cream, sour cream and tarragon. Mix with a fork. Beat the eggs. Stir them into the mix. Arrange the softened drained leek evenly over the cheese, cut side down. Pour the cream mix evenly over the top and carry it carefully to the oven. Bake it for 40 minutes or until the filling is puffy and golden brown. Remove. Leave it to settle for 10 minutes.

PLATE Sit the tart on a plate or board. Cut it into slices at the table. Serve with cooled baby potatoes tossed in mayonnaise, a green salad with honey mustard dressing (p26) or a carrot and orange salad (p169).

PASTA, NOODLES, RICE AND *Couscous*

Everyone remembers their first cooking disaster. Mine was a batch of pasta dough. Too many eggs died in vain that day, escaping from the well of flour I'd made, ending up splattered all over the kitchen floor. I was nine. I sulked for a bit and then got over it. Now I've got the method sorted it's a slicker operation and every so often I'll make ravioli (bought ones are too dry) or a lovely dish of homemade pasta. But I won't lie. I generally use the dried stuff for every day. A lot of the produce out there is really excellent and, like all the other staples in this chapter, it's easy to cook and so fast. The key to the basics is to get the cooking method right: pasta needs to boil in loads more water than you'd think to stop it sticking. Some varieties of rice need rinsing before they cook to keep them fluffy, while others want to hold on to their starch to keep the grains glutinous. Couscous needs a little bit of help once it's prepped. The very simplicity and blandness of these basics means they will play a key supporting role in your cooking – pile in the flavours and enjoy yourself.

BAGGING YOUR PASTA
A Buyer's Guide

FRESH FROM THE DELI An expensive delicious treat and fast-cooking. FROM THE SUPERMARKET Hmm…'fresh' pre-packed is a bit faster to cook than dried but costs more and often thickens in cooking and so eats heavily.

DRIED FROM THE DELI Get the best artisan brands and adventurous shapes and varieties (squid ink/beetroot etc.). These cost a bit more but eat well.
FROM THE SUPERMARKET Brilliant range and value in most. Dried pasta can be better than fresh and it's the ultimate convenient fast food. It's fast to cook (ok, a bit longer than 'fresh') and cheap. Try out shop own brands (some are excellent) or get a good readily available artisan variety.

VARIETIES Pastas (dried and fresh) are made with or without egg. Pasta with egg takes a bit longer to cook and is richer, so you don't need so much per person. Brown pasta is healthier (more fibre and magnesium) but a heavier eat. Buy buckwheat, corn, rice or soy based pastas to avoid gluten. Filled pasta is expensive to buy and is often dry, heavy and disappointing. So make your own (p182).

PASTA STASH

Fresh pasta will last 2–4 days in the fridge.

Dried pasta lasts 2 years or 1 year if made with egg (it's brittle, so store carefully).

Prepared pasta dishes for baking freeze well. Defrost then cook.

Toss 50g pine nuts in a dry pan to toast very lightly for 2–3 minutes till golden (not brown). Blitz in a processor with 1 garlic clove, 50g basil, 75g parmesan, and the juice of ½ a lemon for just a few seconds. Add 125ml good olive oil in a steady trickle for a thick green sauce. Season.

SHAPES

Long pastas (spaghetti, linguine, angel hair etc.) work best with light sauces.

Short pastas (penne, farfalle, fusilli, macaroni etc.) work best with heavier sauces.

Ridged and hollow pastas are better at holding on to a sauce.

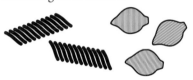

Baby pastas are designed to bang into soups for balance, difference, texture and value.

PASTA COOKING ACTION

TIMING Cook it just before serving (don't pre-cook and reheat). Fresh pasta cooks in 1–2 minutes. Fresh stuffed 2–6 minutes (filling- and size-dependent) Dried 8–15 minutes. Check the packet for exact timings.

BIG PAN Get one with a lid (catering/hardware/Asian shops have bargains).

WATER Boil up at least 1 litre of water per 100g of pasta in a covered pan. Pasta needs lots of room to spread or it sticks. The water must be boiling before you add the pasta.

SALT Add 10g per litre of water to bring out the flavour just before you add the pasta.

OIL If you're cooking lasagne, add a bit to the water to prevent sticking.

STIR Stir the pasta once as you add it to the pan to prevent sticking.

TESTING Cook for the designated cooking time but test minutes before it's due. Fish a bit out and bite it. It should taste tender but not mushy. Italians call it 'al dente' but get it as you like it. If it's to be baked into a dish (lasagne/macaroni) give it a bit less time at this stage.

DRAINING Tip into a colander or sieve to drain. Save a bit of pasta water to loosen your sauce if it needs it. Tip the pasta back into the warm pan.

DRESSING Add a little oil, butter or reserved pasta cooking water. Add some or all of your sauce to coat or pile it onto the served pasta.

ALMOST INSTANT PASTA DRESSINGS

Stir the following into freshly cooked pasta…

butter, grated parmesan and black pepper

grated lemon zest and juice, cream or crème fraîche

hot olive oil flavoured with sliced garlic and diced chilli

oil-based salad dressing

a good pesto sauce

PASTA FRIENDS

ANCHOVIES, BACON, BASIL, BUTTER, CHEESE SAUCE, CHILLI, COURGETTES, CREAM, CRÈME FRAICHE, EGGS, GARLIC, LEMONS, OLIVE OIL, OLIVES, ONIONS, MASCARPONE, MOZZARELLA, MUSHROOMS, NUTMEG, PANCETTA, PARMESAN (OR VEGETARIAN EQUIVALENT), PARSLEY, PASSATA, RAGU, RICOTTA, ROASTED VEGETABLES, SAUSAGES, SPECK, SPINACH, TOMATOES, WINE

Noodle & FRIENDS

BEANSPROUTS, BLACK BEAN SAUCE, BROCCOLI, CHICKEN STOCK, CHILLIES, CHINESE LEAF, CORIANDER, FISH SAUCE, GARLIC, GINGER, GREEN BEANS, HOISIN SAUCE, LEMONS, LIMES, MALT VINEGAR, MINT, MISO, MUSHROOMS, ONIONS, OYSTER SAUCE, PEPPERS, PLUM SAUCE, RICE VINEGAR, RICE WINE, SESAME OIL, SOY SAUCE, SPRING ONIONS, SWEET CHILLI SAUCE, SWEET BLACK VINEGAR, TERIYAKI SAUCE, TOFU, WATER CHESTNUTS

USE YOUR NOODLE
– WHAT TO GET FOR THE JOB –

You'll find a brilliant range of dried noodles in your local supermarket. Asian shops and Chinese supermarkets stock a huge range and at good prices.

EGG NOODLES Found in the chilled cabinet or dried into nests or sheets. Get them thin, medium or thicker to taste. Boil noodles (following pack instructions) and add to stir-fries or bang in soups. Fresh are wok-ready but more expensive and have a shorter shelf-life.

RAMEN NOODLES Thin Japanese egg noodles good for stir-fries/soups/salads.

SOBA NOODLES Taste nutty and are darker than normal noodles. Cook and serve cold in a dressing for salad.

UDON These wide, white noodles are great for soups and Asian stews.

CELLOPHANE NOODLES *(aka Chinese vermicelli/glass noodles)* Pretty bland, fine shreds of noodle designed to absorb flavours. Don't boil but soak for a few minutes (see the packet) before using in soups, salads and stir-fries. You can also deep-fry without soaking for crispy noodles.

RICE AND GRAINS

Store grains in airtight containers in a dark cupboard. Use within a year.

EASY-COOK RICE Not the nicest but the fastest. It's steamed before milling so long grains will stay separate during cooking.

AMERICAN ALL-PURPOSE RICE Your standard white or brown long-grain rice.

BASMATI RICE Top choice for curries and pilaf and a finer aromatic grain.

THAI FRAGRANT/JASMINE Good with Chinese, Thai and curry dishes and great for salads.

STICKY RICE Traditional with Thai dishes served in the bowl or rolled into small balls. Sticky rice needs soaking overnight or for as long as you can before cooking.

RISOTTO RICE Supermarkets and delis stock a range of different varieties (vialone nano/carnaroli/arborio) of this short grain to make creamy risotto. Never rinse it.

COUSCOUS Shelved with grains in the store but actually a pre-cooked pasta that just needs soaking in liquid to prepare it. Eat hot with vegetable and meat stews (tagines) or flavour and spice it up for salads.

BULGUR WHEAT Great with Eastern salads.

QUINOA A nutritionally perfect, gluten-free, super-grain and complete protein which can be used instead of rice and couscous.

POLENTA Great either served wet (like mash) with flavours like herbs/butter/grated cheese/garlic added or set and brushed with oil, then grilled and served with a tomato or meat sauce or roast griddled vegetables. Instant polenta cooks in 5 minutes (check pack for instructions).

||||||||||| THE RICE COOKER |||||||||||||

FREESTYLE METHOD Bring a large pan of lightly salted water to the boil. RINSE easy cook/American/basmati rice under cold water in a sieve to prevent sticking. Add to boiling water. Stir once. Cook it, uncovered, on a rolling boil. Test a few grains to check they're tender. Easy-cook, test at 5 minutes. American and basmati, test at 8. Brown rice takes 15–20 minutes. Rinse just-tender rice in a sieve with boiling water from the kettle. Sit the sieve back on the pan. Cover. Leave for 3 minutes. Fluff it up. **ABSORPTION METHOD** For Thai/jasmine/sticky rice. Add 2½ parts water to 1 part rice a pan with a little salt. Stir once. Cover. Simmer on very low heat for 10-15 minutes until swollen and tender. Leave for 10 minutes before decanting.

RICE SPECIALS

1 STIR-FRY RICE
Cook basmati, jasmine or American rice following your method of choice (see above). Cool rapidly and chill immediately so it's safe to use. Don't leave it around at room temperature. Stir-fry from cold so the grains stay separate.

2 STUFFED VEG
Mix cooked and cooled rice with spices/herbs/oils/grated cheese/cream/sautéed shallot/seasoning/lemon zest/meat ragu etc. Stuff into hollowed out tomatoes, peppers or courgettes, drizzle over olive oil and bake in a preheated oven at 180°C/Gas 4 until the veg are soft and the stuffing is piping hot.

3 *Pilaf* Tip basmati rice into a bowl and cover with cold water. Rinse and change 6 times over an hour or until clear. Fry 2 diced shallots and garlic in oil or butter till soft. Add the rice. Turn for 2 minutes or till coloured. Add chicken or vegetable stock (twice the liquid to volume of rice) and simmer over a low heat for 10–15 minutes. Season and add finely chopped herbs. Eat with lamb kebabs (p124), griddled harissa mackerel (p142) or chicken in piri-piri sauce.

RICE FRIENDS

AUBERGINES, BACON, BEANS, BEEF, BROCCOLI, CHEDDAR, CHICKEN, CHILLI, CHILLI SAUCE, CREAM, EGG, GARLIC, GREEN VEGETABLES, HARISSA, HOISIN SAUCE, LAMB, LEMON, MINT, MUSHROOMS, OILY FISH, ONION, PARMESAN, PARSLEY, PEAS, PORK, RAGU, SHALLOT, SOY SAUCE, SPRING ONIONS, STOCK, WHITE WINE

STAPLES NUTRITION

GRAINS AND STAPLES SHOULD MAKE UP ⅓ OF YOUR PLATE. Whole grains are nutritionally superior to processed grains as they contain more fibre and other nutrients.

PASTA IS A COMPLEX **CARBOHYDRATE**
It releases energy slowly, keeping blood sugar levels steady, making it ideal for athletes and for EVERYDAY ENERGY NEEDS. IT'S LOW IN FAT AND CONTAINS ADDED **FOLIC ACID** AND **IRON** WHICH TACKLES ANAEMIA AND GIVES MENTAL FOCUS. It's easy to digest and the starch relaxes the body making it good for insomnia and a mood enhancer.

BROWN RICE IS A RICH SOURCE OF **PROTEIN** *for* GROWTH, **CARBOHYDRATE, FIBRE,** *Vitamin B1,* **NIACIN** AND **IRON** – WHITE HAS LESS.

BULGUR WHEAT IS PACKED WITH **B VITAMINS**

QUINOA IS A PERFECT **PROTEIN** SO PARTICULARLY GOOD FOR VEGETARIANS AND WHEN CASH IS SHORT. Balance staples with loads of vitamin-rich vegetables and your choice of fish, meat, eggs and cheeses.

SPAGHETTI WITH EASY TOMATO SAUCE

 HEALTHY · FAST

FEEDS 4

Simple as you like – and trust me you will like. This sauce is perfect on spaghetti (though it goes well with other pasta shapes too) and works in many different scenarios. Get the seasoning right to balance any acidity…

INGREDIENTS

440g dried spaghetti
salt and pepper
a glug of olive oil
a knob of butter
a handful or two of freshly grated
    parmesan (or vegetarian alternative)
a few basil leaves (optional)
EASY TOMATO SAUCE
3 tbsp olive oil
2 garlic cloves, peeled and finely sliced
a pinch of chilli flakes/crumbled dried
    chilli
2 x 400g cans of chopped/whole plum
    tomatoes
a good pinch of sugar
a squeeze of lemon juice or a drop of
    balsamic vinegar (optional)

—— CHANGE IT UP ——

1. Try tearing in a few fresh basil leaves as you finish the sauce, or swirling a teaspoon of pesto (p172) through it before serving.
2. For a chilli tomato sauce, sweat off 1–2 finely diced red chilles for 3 minutes before adding to the sauce in place of the chilli flakes.
3. For a thicker tomato sauce, sweat off a finely chopped onion for 5–10 minutes before adding the chilli flakes and garlic.
4. If you like it creamy, blitz the cooked sauce with a stick blender or in a food processor with 2 tbsp mascarpone or cream cheese until smooth.

PREP Make the sauce: Put a heavy-bottomed pan over a gentle heat. Add two-thirds of the oil then the garlic and chilli flakes. Let it warm through to soften the garlic for 2 minutes or so (colouring will turn it bitter). Add the chopped tomatoes directly. If using whole plum tomatoes, squish them in with your fingers or break them up with a wooden spoon. Add the sugar and season with salt and pepper. Stir well. Bring to the boil then lower to a simmer and cook for 10–20 minutes.

PREP Meantime, cook the pasta: Put a large, covered pan of water with a pinch of salt and a glug of oil on to boil. Add the pasta and cook until *al dente* (p173 or check your packet for timings).

Finish the sauce: Season to taste, add a little more sugar if it's sharp or a drop of lemon juice or balsamic to brighten it. Add the remainder of the olive oil.

Drain the pasta into a colander. Tip it straight back into the pan and add the butter and a little black pepper. Stir in the sauce.

PLATE Stick a large fork into the pasta. Twirl to hook a reasonable amount. Lift and place onto plates or into warm bowls. Or grab it out with a pair of tongs. Scatter over some parmesan, top with a few basil leaves, if you like, and serve with bread or garlic bread (p178) and a rocket salad with balsamic dressing (p28).

BONUS BITES

CHILLI AND BACON TOMATO SAUCE
Blitz a can of chopped tomatoes. Fry a handful of diced bacon/pancetta with 1 diced small onion, a diced chilli and a diced garlic clove. Add the tomatoes and cook as before.

RAW TOMATO SAUCE
Chop a handful of good vine or cherry tomatoes. Spoon out the seeds and roughly chop. Marinate in a mix of 2 tbsp olive oil and 1 tbsp wine vinegar with a few torn basil leaves or a bit of chopped parsley to taste. Alternatively, toss with a few chopped olives, ½ tsp drained capers and a drizzle of olive oil. Leave for 30 minutes. Toss into hot spaghetti.

STIR-IN SPAGHETTI CARBONARA

FAST

FEEDS 2

Here the heat of the pasta cooks the egg yolks and pulls everything together into a beautifully creamy sauce. A must-have dinner.

INGREDIENTS

a pinch of salt
a glug of oil
2 large egg yolks
25g freshly grated parmesan/pecorino cheese, plus extra for serving
1 tbsp milk
200g spaghetti
freshly ground black pepper
a few crispy garlic breadcrumbs (optional, p201)

BACON AND MUSHROOM STIR-IN

70g unsmoked bacon/pancetta
a knob of butter
2 tbsp oil
6 small button mushrooms

SMOKED SALMON STIR-IN

a little freshly chopped dill (or dried)
50–100g mild smoked salmon
lemon wedges

PREP Put a large pan of water on to boil for the pasta, adding the salt and oil. Now, prep your choice of stir-in. For the bacon and mushroom: cut the bacon/pancetta into strips. Heat the butter and oil in a frying pan, add the meat and cook until it releases fat and is lightly browned. Remove. Slice the mushrooms. Add to the pan and stir until soft but holding shape. Season lightly. Set aside. For the salmon: Finely chop the dill and slice the fish into strips. Make the garlic breadcrumbs, if using.

Beat the egg yolks in a bowl. Add the grated cheese and milk.

COOK Add the spaghetti to the boiling water and cook until *al dente* or as you like it (see p173 or check your packet for timings). Drain well. Throw the pasta back into the pan. Add the egg and cheese mixture immediately along with your choice of stir-in. Stir well to coat the strands.

PLATE Twirl spaghetti into bowls or plates. Add plenty of black pepper. Scatter with parmesan and/or crispy garlic breadcrumbs and serve with garlic bread. Serve the salmon with lemon wedges to squeeze over.

**** CASH SAVER ****
Substitute cubes of leftover post-roast gammon for the bacon pieces.

.... TO GO WITH ....

GARLIC BREAD

Preheat the oven to 220°C/Gas 7. Slash a baguette, diagonally, with a bread knife, but keep it intact. Mix 110g soft butter, a 125g ball of mozzarella cheese, 75g grated cheddar, 3 crushed garlic cloves, a squeeze of lemon juice, a little pepper and 2 tbsp chopped parsley together in a bowl. Spread the mix into each slash, smearing any last bits over the top and wrap in foil. Sit on a baking tray (or chill/freeze it until needed) and bake for 20 minutes, until baking hot and crisp but nicely sticky inside.

SPICY SAUSAGE PENNE

FEEDS 4

INGREDIENTS

450g penne
a pinch of salt
a glug of oil
freshly grated parmesan, for serving
SAUCE
1 tbsp olive oil
4 good spicy sausages (ideally Italian
    but Toulouse or chorizo work)
2 onions, finely chopped
6 garlic cloves, crushed
2 good pinches of chilli flakes/
    1 red chilli, finely diced
125ml red wine
1 x 400g can of chopped tomatoes
2 pinches of dried oregano
1 tsp sugar
1 tbsp tomato purée
1–2 tsp chilli sauce or harissa paste
    (optional)
50g cubes of mozzarella or 2–3 tbsp
    double/sour cream (optional)
a handful of fresh parsley, chopped
    (optional)

—— CHANGE IT UP ——

For a vegetarian alternative, replace the
sausage with one large chopped aubergine.
Cook the onion till soft then add the garlic
and cubed aubergine. Fry it gently for
15 minutes before adding the wine and
continuing as above.

TIP

If you've over-estimated the amount of pasta
you need for any dish, transform it into a
salad for the next day. Toss it in a bit of oil or
salad dressing or stir some pesto (p172 or a
good bought one) in there and add whatever
else you fancy.

*Get yourself a few spicy sausages and crumble them up into a few
basic store cupboard ingredients; you've got yourself a punchy sauce in
less than half an hour. It's also great with ribbon pastas like tagliatelle.*

PREP Make the sauce: Put a large frying pan or casserole over a medium
heat. Add the olive oil. Slice the sausage open, extract the meat and
crumble into the pan. Cook, stirring, for a few minutes until coloured on all
sides. Add the onions, garlic and chilli flakes/diced chilli, lower the heat and
cook, stirring, for 10 minutes. Add the wine, bring to the boil and cook until
the wine has evaporated.

Add the tomatoes, oregano, sugar and tomato purée, lower the heat and
simmer for 15 minutes, stirring sometimes. Taste and adjust the seasoning,
adding the chilli sauce/harissa, if using, to taste. Leave to simmer over a very
gentle heat, adding a splash of water to the sauce if it is looking too thick.
Meantime, put a large, covered pan of water with a bit of salt and oil on to boil.

COOK Add the penne to the boiling water. Cook until *al dente* (p173 or
check your packet for timings). Drain well.

If using cream, stir into the sauce. Stir the sauce into the pasta, adding
mozzarella cubes and parsley, if using.

PLATE Tong the pasta out onto plates or pasta bowls. Top with parsley.
Serve with parmesan, red wine, good bread and salad.

ASPARAGUS
RAVIOLI

TURN OVER
FOR RECIPE

ASPARAGUS RAVIOLI

FEEDS 4

INGREDIENTS

300g strong white bread flour, plus
    extra for rolling out
salt and black pepper
3 large eggs
1 tbsp olive oil
2 tbsp freshly grated parmesan

FILLING

300g fresh asparagus
3 tsp ricotta
3 tsp mascarpone
3 tsp freshly grated parmesan
½ tsp finely grated lemon zest
½ garlic clove, peeled and crushed
3 tsp fine fresh breadcrumbs (p201)
a squeeze of lemon juice

SAUCE

1 tbsp butter
a good squeeze of lemon juice
a few sage leaves, finely sliced

——— BONUS BITE ———

TOMATO RAVIOLI

Blitz up 150ml easy tomato sauce (p176)
in a food processor and mix together with
6 tsp breadcrumbs and 8 tsp grated parmesan.
Season to taste and use to fill the ravioli.

BUTTERNUT SQUASH RAVIOLI

Preheat the oven to 200°C/Gas 6. Cut, peel
and weigh out 300g of butternut squash.
Roughly chop into cubes, toss in oil and roast
in the oven for 15 minutes or fry gently until
soft. Cool then blitz in a food processor until
smooth. Add 50g grated parmesan,
½ tsp nutmeg, the grated zest of 1 lemon and
a squeeze of lemon juice and stir to combine.
Season to taste and use to fill the ravioli.

A milestone on your journey to veteran status: making your own pasta dough does take a bit of time but the results are spectacular. Use a (not costly) hand crank pasta machine to get your pasta silk-thin.

PREP Make the pasta. By hand: Take a large bowl and sift the flour and half a teaspoon of salt into it. Crack the eggs into a hollow in the middle then add the oil. With your hand in a claw shape, move from the centre outwards in a clockwise motion, mixing everything together to form a soft dough. By machine: Mix and pulse the dry ingredients in a food processor adding the egg and oil gradually through the funnel. Sit the dough on a floured board and knead like bread (p200) for 10 minutes till silky smooth, adding a bit more flour if still a bit sticky. Cover and leave for 1 hour or wrap in cling film and chill until needed.

Filling: Put a frying pan of water on to boil. Bend the asparagus spears to break them off at their woody ends and discard. Add to the pan and boil for 2–3 minutes until just tender. Drain, roughly chop and leave to cool, then put into a processor and blitz with the cheeses, lemon zest and garlic until just blended. Stir in the breadcrumbs and season for a stuffing that can just hold its shape (add more breadcrumbs if too wet, or a little extra water or lemon juice if too stiff).

Roll the pasta. By machine: Divide the dough into 6 pieces. Cover 5 with a tea towel and flatten the remaining piece with your hand. Put the roller on your pasta machine onto its widest setting. Roll the piece through. Guide then catch it with your other hand as it emerges. Fold in two and repeat. Now, reduce the width setting on the machine. Lightly dust the pasta with flour to ensure smoothness then roll it through it again. It will thin out and become silky smooth. Repeat until you're on the tightest setting, flouring lightly between each rolling so it doesn't tear. Repeat with the rest. Leave for 10 minutes.

By hand: Cut the dough in two. Flatten into rounds. Roll the first piece out and away from you with a rolling pin. As you pull it stretch it back with your other hand. Use the pin to flip it over and quarter turn. Repeat till paper thin.

Make the ravioli: Lay your first piece of pasta on a table or clear, clean surface. Place heaped teaspoons of filling down the centre of the sheet to the halfway point, leaving a good space between each one. Brush a square around each mound using egg wash. Now, fold the other half of the pasta over the top. Press down gently around the mounds to seal and exclude the air. Cut around the mounds with a 7cm biscuit cutter or free-style with a knife. Repeat with the rest. Let them dry for 20 minutes if you have time.

COOK Bring a large pan of salted water to the boil and add a little oil. Meanwhile, melt the butter for the sauce gently in a pan. Add the lemon juice and sage, stir and season to taste. Cook the ravioli a few at a time, for 2–3 minutes. Remove carefully with a slotted spoon and drain.

PLATE Divide the ravioli between warmed plates or bowls. Spoon over the sauce and scatter over the parmesan. Serve with bread to mop up the juices.

CLASSIC OLD-SCHOOL MACARONI CHEESE

FEEDS 4

INGREDIENTS

1 small onion, peeled
6 black peppercorns
850ml milk
225g macaroni/penne
50g butter, plus extra for baking
50g plain white flour
1 tsp English mustard
a good squeeze of lemon juice
200g strong cheddar, grated
salt and black pepper
a shake of Worcester sauce/
    mushroom ketchup (optional)

TOPPING

50g white bread
½ garlic clove, peeled
a bit of parsley
a bit of grated lemon zest

—— BONUS BITE ——

SWISS-STYLE BAKED MACARONI

Preheat the oven to 200°C/Gas 6. Boil 125g
potatoes for 5-10 minutes until just soft.
Drain. Meantime, fry 50g bacon cubes in a
pan for 5 minutes, until they release their
fat and crisp up. Remove from the pan then
add the potatoes to cook till just colouring.
Cook 130g macaroni as before. Make up
the béchamel sauce following the technique
above, but with 600ml milk, 25g each of
butter and flour and 50g each of gruyère and
cheddar cheese. Add a glug of white wine or
kirsch if you like before adding the cheese.
Stir the pasta, sauce, bacon and potato
together, tip into a dish, scatter with a little
extra cheese and bake for 20–30 minutes.
Eat with apple purée.

*This old-school favourite is packed full of flavour. If you're short on
time don't bother to infuse the milk. Use a strong cheese.*

PREP Start your sauce: Put the onion, peppercorns and milk into a pan
and heat to the point of boiling. Remove from the heat and leave for
30 minutes for the flavour to infuse. Strain though a sieve and set aside.

Meantime, cook the pasta. Bring a large pan of salted water to the boil. Add the
pasta. Cover. When it boils again, take the lid off and cook until *al dente* (p173
or check your packet for timings). Drain. Preheat the oven to 200°C/Gas 6.

Melt the butter in a heavy-based pan. Add the flour. Stir rapidly with a wooden
spoon over a low heat for 2 minutes to cook out the flour. Remove from the heat.

Very gradually, beat the flavoured milk into the paste with a balloon whisk or
spoon until absolutely smooth. Return to the heat and stir until the mix boils
and thickens, adding a splash more milk if necessary. Lower the heat and gently
simmer for 5 minutes. Add the mustard, lemon juice and cheese and season to
taste, adding a dash of Worcester sauce/mushroom ketchup if you like.

COOK Mix the pasta and sauce together. Tip into a large buttered dish
or a few small ones. To make the topping, blitz the bread with the
garlic and parlsey. Add the lemon zest and scatter over the top. Dot with butter
or a few drops of oil and bake for 20–30 minutes, until bubbling and golden.

PLATE Spoon into bowls and enjoy on the sofa. Or serve up with roasted
whole vine tomatoes (p78) or zingy tomato green beans (p51).

NOW TRY THIS...

TOMATO AND OLIVE LASAGNE

HEALTHY FAST FEEDS 3

Lasagne's a great crowd pleaser; layer up ragu with lasagne and béchamel sauce and everyone's happy (p85). For something less obvious (but lovely), give this a go. The pungent sauce packs a delicious punch.

INGREDIENTS

6–10 lasagne sheets
   (dried/chilled/homemade)
75–100g freshly grated parmesan
110g mozzarella, diced
a few crispy garlic breadcrumbs
   (p201, optional)

TOMATO SAUCE

3 tbsp olive oil
a knob of butter
3 pinches of chilli flakes
4 garlic cloves, peeled and crushed
2 x 400g cans of chopped tomatoes
½ tsp sugar
a good pinch of dried oregano
150g pitted black olives
3 tsp capers, drained
6–8 anchovies (optional)
fresh basil (optional)
salt and pepper

BÉCHAMEL SAUCE

25g butter
25g flour
600ml milk
1 tsp English mustard
a good squeeze of lemon juice
50g strong cheddar
25g parmesan
salt and pepper

TIP
Salted anchovies from a tin or jar can be used directly. For a milder taste, soak them in milk for 30 minutes, then drain.

PREP If using fresh lasagne: Make, roll and cut the pasta to shape and size following the instructions for ravioli (p182). Cover with a floured tea towel. Dry for 1–2 hours before using.

For the tomato sauce: Put a medium pan on to a low heat and add the oil and butter. Add the chilli and garlic and cook for 2 minutes before adding the tomatoes, sugar and oregano. Simmer gently for 10 minutes. Add the olives, capers, anchovies and basil, if using, and season to taste.

For the béchamel sauce: Melt the butter in a heavy-based pan. Add the flour. Stir rapidly with a wooden spoon over a low heat for 2 minutes. Remove from the heat. Slowly pour the milk into the paste, bit by bit, with a balloon whisk or spoon until absolutely smooth. Return it to the heat and stir until the mix boils and thickens, adding a little extra milk if it needs it. Lower to a gentle simmer and cook for 5 minutes. Add the mustard, lemon juice, cheese and season. If using dried pasta sheets, soak in cold water for 10 minutes. Drain well.

Preheat the oven to 200°C/Gas 6. Layer up your lasagne: Grease a shallow ovenproof dish. Smear a little of the béchamel sauce across the base. Cover with a layer of pasta, then a layer of tomato sauce. Add some grated parmesan and diced mozzarella before layering up again in the same way. Finish with a layer of pasta and top with the béchamel sauce, a handful of grated parmesan, a little extra grated mozzarella or garlic breadcrumbs, if using.

COOK Cover with foil and bake for 30 minutes, uncovering for the last 10, until the cheese has melted and the top is golden brown. Remove from the oven and leave to settle for 5 minutes before digging in.

PLATE Spoon onto plates or into bowls. Eat with a sharply dressed rocket salad and a bit of bread to mop up the juices.

BONUS BITES

AUBERGINE AND COURGETTE LASAGNE
Make the tomato sauce as above but omit the olives, capers and anchovies. Slice 2 aubergines and 3 courgettes lengthways into strips, brush lightly with oil and griddle both for 5–10 minutes until softening. Add the veg slices to the lasagne when layering up as before.

MUSHROOM AND TARRAGON LASAGNE
Soak a handful of dried porcini in hot water for 20 minutes. Drain and cut into small pieces. Lightly fry 450g of mixed mushrooms (e.g. chestnut/portobello/oyster) with 1 crushed garlic clove, a few tarragon leaves and the porcini in a little butter and oil. Add 2 tbsp double cream, a sprinkling of grated nutmeg, a squeeze of lemon juice and season to taste. Layer béchamel, lasagne, mushrooms, parmesan, béchamel etc. and bake as above.

SPINACH AND RICOTTA CANNELLONI

FEEDS 4

INGREDIENTS

6–10 lasagne sheets
   (dried/chilled/homemade)
   or 12 small dried cannelloni tubes
4 tbsp double/whipping cream
a few good handfuls of grated
   parmesan/cheddar/mozzarella
SAUCE
2–3 tbsp olive oil
1 medium onion, peeled and finely
   chopped
3 garlic cloves, peeled and crushed
a good pinch of chilli flakes
2 x 450g cans of chopped tomatoes
1 tsp sugar
1 tsp balsamic vinegar
salt and black pepper
STUFFING
250g spinach leaves
1 x 250g tub ricotta
2 small egg yolks
grated lemon zest, to taste
grated nutmeg, to taste (optional)
40g freshly grated parmesan
salt and pepper

—— CHANGE IT UP ——

1. For a creamy cannelloni, top the bake
   with béchamel sauce (p185).
2. For a change of flavour, swap the balsamic
   vinegar for 1 tsp vodka instead.

TIP
Use the spinach mix to stuff ravioli (p182) or
whiz it up in a food processor and add it to
easy tomato sauce (p176).

Another classic baked pasta dish and a sophisticated blend of flavours. These pasta tubes are best made using either fresh or dried sheets of lasagne. Soften them up and roll them round the stuffing before saucing and baking. Skip the nutmeg if you're not keen on the flavour.

PREP For fresh lasagne: Make, roll and cut the pasta to shape and size (p182). Cover with a floured tea towel. Dry for 1–2 hours.

Make the sauce: Put a pan on to heat and add the oil. Tip in the onion, garlic and chilli and cook on a low heat until very soft, not coloured, about 5–8 minutes. Add the tomatoes, sugar and balsamic vinegar and season to taste. Bring to the boil, then reduce the heat to simmer over a very low heat for 30 minutes, stirring occasionally. Set aside.

Make the stuffing: Wash the spinach but don't drain it. Bang it into a large pan with 2 tablespoons of water on a very low heat. Turn with a spoon as it wilts right down over 3–4 minutes. Tip it into a colander to drain, and squeeze to remove excess moisture. Cool and roughly chop. Tip it into a bowl, add the remaining stuffing ingredients and mix well, adjusting the seasoning to taste.

Preheat the oven to 200°C/Gas 6.

If using dried own or bought lasagne, put a large pan of salted water on to heat. When it boils, add the sheets and cook for 1 minute until just softening and pliable. Drain. Cut into large squares if you need. Otherwise, get your pliable bought sheets or no-cook tubes for stuffing. Stuff or wrap-round: Divide the filling between your fresh lasagne squares. Roll up into tubes and sit seam-side down in a single layer in a greased ovenproof dish. Alternatively, spoon the mix into your cannelloni tubes. Pour your tomato sauce evenly over the lot. Drizzle with cream and sprinkle with grated cheese.

COOK Bang your cannelloni straight into the oven and bake for 20–30 minutes, or till hot all through and bubbling.

PLATE Spoon onto plates from the dish on the table. Enjoy with classic green salad, a plate of sliced tomatoes and shallots drizzled in olive oil and some good bread for mopping the sauce up.

BONUS BITE

BIG MAC AND CHEESE
Sweat off 1 chopped onion and a crushed garlic clove in oil till soft. Add 300g minced beef/pork, season with salt and pepper then fry for 10 minutes. Cool. Mix with 250g ricotta, 50g freshly grated parmesan and 50g mozzarella. Wrap into lasagne sheets or stuff into tubes before covering with tomato sauce and cooking as above.

CHAR SIU PORK
ON SOFT NOODLES
WITH BEANSPROUTS

FEEDS 2

INGREDIENTS

1 x 400–500g plump pork fillet
2 tbsp runny honey
a splash of water
MARINADE
1 tbsp granulated sugar
1 tbsp yellow bean curd sauce
1 tbsp oyster sauce
1 tbsp Shaoxing rice wine
1 tbsp red chilli bean curd
a splash of sesame oil
a pinch of Chinese five spice
NOODLES
3 nests or sheets of egg noodles
2 tbsp groundnut oil
a splash of sesame oil
1 garlic clove, peeled and thinly sliced
a handful of beansprouts
2 tsp soy sauce

—— BONUS BITE ——
PORK RAMEN

Mix 1 tsp caster sugar, 1 tbsp malt vinegar,
1 tbsp sweet chilli sauce, 2 tbsp fish sauce,
1 tsp tomato ketchup and a bit of finely diced
red chilli in a bowl to make a finishing sauce.
Set aside. Bring 850ml chicken stock to the
boil with ¼ star anise, a peeled and finely
sliced thumb-sized piece of ginger and 3
garlic cloves. Cover and leave to simmer for
at least 20 minutes. Strain the stock, season
to taste (adding a dash of soy if you like)
and return to the heat. Add a good handful
of chopped Chinese leaf/iceberg lettuce
and simmer for a minute. Add a couple of
bundles of ramen noodles to the stock and
cook for 1 minute or till done. Divide the
noodle broth between serving bowls and top
with sliced char siu pork, a few beansprouts
and 2 sliced spring onions. Serve with the
finishing sauce.

Racks of barbecued char siu pork hanging from hooks in the windows of London's Chinatown are one of my earliest food memories. It's definitely worth a trip to your Asian supermarket to stock up on ingredients for this. You could get away without the red bean curd here but hold out for the yellow if you can. Try it on bowls of rice if you're out of noodles.

PREP
Make the marinade: mix all the ingredients together in a large non-metallic dish.

Remove the pork fillet from its packaging if necessary. Pat dry and trim off any fat/membrane with a filleting knife. Sit the meat in the dish, and turn it in the marinade so that it is evenly coated. Chill overnight, or for at least 5 hours.

Remove the pork from the fridge at least 30 minutes before cooking to give it time to get to room temperature. Preheat the oven to 220°C/Gas 7. Boil a kettle.

COOK
Pour the boiling water into a roasting tin and sit on a low shelf in the oven. Remove the pork from the marinade and sit on a metal rack on the shelf directly above the tin. Cook for 10 minutes. Lower the temperature to 180°C/Gas 4 and brush the meat with marinade to stop it drying out. Give it another 5–10 minutes until cooked through, but not dry. Remove from the oven and set aside to rest for 5 minutes.

Preheat the grill to high. Mix the honey and water to make a glaze. Brush it over the pork. Grill for 3–4 minutes, turning once, until the edges char very slightly. Remove and set aside.

Cook the noodles in boiling water according to the packet instructions. Drain. Heat the oils in a wok. Throw in the garlic and bean sprouts, tossing and stirring for 2 minutes, or till cooked. Add the noodles and toss till hot. Add the soy sauce.

To make a sauce, put the marinade into a saucepan with a few tablespoons of water from the tin in the oven. Boil thoroughly for 2 minutes.

PLATE
Carve the pork into slices. Heap the noodles into bowls and lay the meat over the top. Drizzle with the sauce to finish.

ASIAN NOODLES AND STIR-FRY VEG IN SAUCE

FEEDS 2

INGREDIENTS

150g egg noodles
100g broccoli
1 small onion, peeled
2cm piece of fresh ginger
2 garlic cloves, peeled
1 red chilli
4 shiitake mushrooms
1 fat head of pak choi
50g green beans
125ml chicken/vegetable stock
   (p49/p15)
2 tsp cornflour
1 tbsp groundnut oil
1 tsp sesame oil
1 tbsp soy sauce
2 tbsp oyster/blackbean/plum sauce
salt and pepper

—— CHANGE IT UP ——

1. For a chicken stir-fry, chop bits of chicken breast/thigh into bite-sized bits. Toss in a bit of soy, rice wine and a pinch of sugar. Leave for a bit. Stir-fry in 1 tbsp each of groundnut/sesame oil for 3-4 minutes until white all through. Remove. Cook the vegetables as before and stir in with the noodles to finish.

2. For a tofu stir-fry, marinade as above and throw on top of the cooked noodle dish.

A simple, fast, throw-together meal with some lovely flavours.

PREP Cook the noodles: put a large pan of water on to boil. Throw the noodles in. Turn off the heat and leave for 2–3 minutes until cooked (or follow the packet instructions). Drain well. Refresh in cold water. Set aside.

Prep the veg: Wash the the broccoli and divide into florets. Slice the onion into half moons roughly 1–2mm thick. Peel and grate the ginger. Slice the garlic and deseed (p16) and slice the chilli. Slice the mushrooms. Wash the pak choi and separate the leaves. Wash and trim the beans.

Warm the chicken/vegetable stock in a small pan. Spoon two tablespoons of the stock out into a cup, add the cornflour and stir it in.

COOK Stir-fry: Heat the groundnut and sesame oils in a wok. Add the onion, beans and broccoli, toss and stir-fry for 2 minutes. Add the garlic, ginger, and mushrooms. Stir-fry for 2 minutes. Add the pak choi and cook for 1 minute. Add the soy, chilli, and chosen sauce. Cook for a minute. Add the stock and cornflour mix and season. Let it bubble to thicken. Stir the noodles in to coat and cook through.

PLATE Tip into bowls and enjoy as it is with cups of green tea, or serve alongside char siu pork (p187).

VEGETABLE KORMA
WITH BASMATI RICE

FEEDS 3-4

INGREDIENTS

8 cardamom pods
1 tsp ground cumin
1 tsp ground coriander
1 tsp turmeric
1 small cinnamon stick
300g basmati rice
3 garlic cloves, peeled and crushed
a thumb-sized piece of fresh ginger,
*   peeled and grated*
1 red chilli, deseeded (p16) and diced
1 tbsp groundnut oil
25g butter
2 medium onions, peeled and sliced
1 small aubergine, chopped
200g butternut squash, peeled and
*   cubed*
1 floury potato, peeled and cubed
200g canned chickpeas, drained
350ml water/vegetable stock (p15)
110g okra, trimmed and sliced across
a small handful of green beans,
*   trimmed and sliced*
150ml whipping/double cream
4 tbsp yoghurt
a handful of fresh coriander, chopped
a good sprinkle of garam masala
salt and pepper
1 tbsp ground almonds
a good squeeze of lemon juice

Here the delicate fluffy rice complements a subtle creamy korma. Prep everything up in advance and it's easy. If you don't do dairy, make up the tomato-based curry at the bottom of the page instead.

PREP Organise your spices: Bash the cardamom lightly and add to a dish with the cumin, coriander, turmeric and cinnamon stick. Rinse the rice in a sieve under running water. Set aside. Put cold water into a pan ready to boil later. Set the garlic, ginger and chilli to one side on a plate. Prep the veg.

COOK Put a large pan on to heat. Add the oil and butter. Fry the onion for 5 minutes, or till soft but not coloured. Add the garlic, ginger and chilli and cook, stirring, for 2 minutes. Tip in the spices and stir for 30 seconds as they release fragrance. Stir in the aubergine, squash, potato and chickpeas.

Add the water/vegetable stock and bring to the boil. Reduce the heat and simmer on low for 10 minutes, or until the squash is just tender. If it's looking dry, add a splash more water.

Put the pan of rice water on to boil, covered. Add the rice. Reduce the heat. Cover and simmer for 10 minutes (p175) or as the packet directs.

Meantime, add the okra and beans to the curry. Cook for 5 minutes or till tender. Stir in the cream, yoghurt, chopped coriander and garam masala and season to taste. Simmer gently for 5 minutes. Taste again and adjust the seasoning if needed. Add a few ground almonds for a slightly thicker texture and/or a little lemon juice to get the right acidity.

Test the rice for doneness – it should be soft and plump. Drain into a sieve. Sit the sieve back into the pan and cover with the lid for 2 minutes.

PLATE Tip the rice into a bowl and fluff it up with a fork. Serve with the korma as is, or with poppadoms, naan bread (p130), mango chutney, honey mint raita (p130), and other meat curries.

BONUS BITES

TOMATO VEGETABLE CURRY
Fry 1 finely chopped large onion, a little grated ginger, 3 crushed garlic cloves and 2 deseeded and diced red chillies till soft. Add 2 chopped tomatoes and the spices as above and cook for 3 minutes. Add 8 tbsp passata and 225ml water with 200g cubed butternut squash, a handful of cauliflower florets, 400g canned chickpeas and a few sliced okra. Simmer gently for 20 minutes. Uncover. Simmer for a further 10 minutes to thicken. Taste and season. Finish with a large handful of fresh coriander, 1 tbsp lemon juice and 1 tsp garam masala and serve with rice.

STICKY RICE WITH
THAI VEGETABLE CURRY

FEEDS 3

INGREDIENTS

250g Thai sticky rice/jasmine rice
200g aubergine
1 medium onion, peeled
150g new potatoes, scrubbed
200g butternut squash, peeled and
    seeds removed
75g fine green beans
100g carrot, peeled
150g mushrooms
110g tofu and 1 tbsp soy (optional)
1 tbsp groundnut oil
2 x 400ml cans of low-fat coconut milk
a small handful of cashew nuts
    (optional)
a squeeze of lime juice
a handful of fresh coriander/torn basil
    leaves (optional)
1 lime, cut into wedges
CURRY PASTE
10 small green chillies
5 fat garlic cloves, peeled
groundnut oil
2 lemongrass stalks
2 shallots, peeled and chopped
a thumb-sized piece of fresh ginger,
    peeled and grated
80g fresh coriander (leaves and stalks)
3–4 dried kaffir lime leaves/
    1½ tbsp lime juice
grated zest of ½–1 lime
1 tsp salt
2 tsp ground coriander
½ tsp ground cumin

········· TIME SAVER ·········

If you find yourself tight for time you can always sub in 2 tablespoons of a good shop-bought curry paste instead – just add 4 dried kaffir lime leaves to the pan at the same time as the onion to boost the flavour.

Sticky rice is my favourite; I go for its glutinous texture and the way it works with a sauce. For this gorgeous meat-free curry, you can easily make your own paste (not by hand – you'll need a blitzer or grinder).

PREP Soak the rice ahead: Measure into a bowl and cover with cold water. Leave overnight or for as long as you've got (even 20 minutes makes a difference).

Make the paste: Wash, dry and trim the tips of the chillies. Blitz in a food processor with the garlic and a tablespoon of groundnut oil. Sit the lemongrass on a board. Bash with a rolling pin to bruise then chop as finely as you can. Add and blitz. Add the shallot and ginger. Blitz again. Add the remaining ingredients and enough groundnut oil to blitz into a thick paste.

Sort the rest: Slice the aubergine and thinly slice the onion. Cut the potatoes and butternut squash into bite-sized chunks. Trim the beans and cut in thirds. Thinly slice the carrot and mushrooms. Cube the tofu, if using, and toss in the soy. Set aside. Drain the rice and tip into a saucepan with 350ml cold water.

COOK Heat the oil in a wok or large pan. Add the onion. Cook very gently, stirring, to soften without colouring. Add 2 tablespoons of the curry paste and continue to cook, stirring, for a minute or two as it releases its fragrance. Add the carrot and aubergine. Cook and stir for 5 minutes or until the aubergine is softening. Add the coconut milk and increase the heat until it almost boils. Reduce to low, add the squash and potato and simmer for 10 minutes, or until the squash is tender.

Meantime, cook the rice. Bring to the boil, cover and simmer for 10–15 minutes. It's done when the water is absorbed fully. Check it regularly.

Finish the curry: Add the mushrooms, beans and a few of the cashews, if using. Cook for a further 10 minutes or until tender. If the sauce looks like reducing too much, add a splash of water or vegetable stock. Stir frequently. Just before serving, squeeze in a bit of lime and stir through a little chopped coriander or basil if you like. Taste and adjust the seasoning. Add the tofu, if using, to a pan with a little oil and fry for 3–4 minutes, turning, till well browned.

PLATE Tip the curry into a large bowl. Top with coriander, cashews and tofu. Serve on your sticky rice with bits of lime for squeezing.

BONUS BITES

EGG FRIED RICE AND BACON
Add 1 tbsp groundnut oil and ¼ tbsp sesame oil to a heated wok with a handful of frozen peas and cook for 1–2 minutes. Add a handful of cubed pancetta or char siu pork (p187) and cook until it's hot and crisping up. Beat 2 eggs and pour into the dish with 200g cold cooked basmati rice and 2 sliced spring onions, stirring continuously. Cook till piping hot. Season and serve with a bit of fresh coriander and a finishing sauce of a little hoisin/plum sauce mixed with water.

COUSCOUS, ORANGE, FETA
AND BEETROOT SALAD

FEEDS 2-3

INGREDIENTS

4 beetroot
2 tbsp olive oil
salt and pepper
225g instant couscous
300ml boiling water
1 large orange
a handful of pine nuts
a small handful of fresh parsley
a small handful of fresh mint
1 x honey mustard dressing (p26)
110g feta cheese
COURGETTE TZATZIKI
4–6 tbsp Greek yoghurt
1 garlic clove, peeled
½ a small courgette, grated
a small handful of chopped mint
1 tsp sugar
a squeeze of lemon juice
a pinch of salt
½ tbsp olive oil

—— CHANGE IT UP ——

Substitute a good Lancashire, goat's or simple salad cheese for the feta. Replace the tzatziki with hummus.

—— BONUS BITE ——

LAMB TAGINE WITH COUSCOUS

Cube 200g lamb steaks. Fry off till browned in olive oil. Remove. Fry a sliced onion and 2 crushed garlic cloves till soft. Add a pinch of cayenne and 1 tsp each of cumin, coriander, ground ginger and cinnamon. Stir for 2 minutes. Return the lamb. Add 450g canned chopped tomatoes, 220g canned chickpeas, 1 tbsp tomato purée, 4 chopped dried apricots, salt, pepper and a little honey. Simmer for 30–40 minutes. Pile onto hot couscous and top with lots of chopped coriander and a few chopped almonds.

Here's a tasty bit of salad to take your couscous places. This pre-cooked grain can be rather dull, so treat it to lots of herbs, spices, fruit and strong flavours. This combination will set your palate alight.

PREP Preheat the oven to 220°C/Gas 7. Peel and chop the beetroot into large chunks. Roll them in half the oil on a baking tray and season with salt and pepper. Cook for 20 minutes, or until tender.

Meantime, cook the couscous. Tip the grain into a heatproof dish, pour over the boiling water and remaining oil and cover with a tea towel. Leave for at least 5 minutes. Uncover and fluff it up with a fork to lighten and separate the grains a bit.

Segment the orange: sit it on a board. Using a paring or small serrated knife, slice the top and base away. Now, holding it firmly, cut down each of the segment lines towards the middle of the fruit to release the wedges of flesh from the membrane. Remove and leave them whole or chop them. Lightly toast the pine nuts in a dry pan for a minute or until just brown. Chop the herbs. Make up the dressing. Mix the tzatziki ingredients together in a bowl.

Cut the beetroot into bite-sized pieces. Stir a bit of dressing, the pine nuts and herbs into your couscous and season with salt and pepper.

PLATE Bang the couscous into a handsome bowl. Top with the orange segments and beetroot. Crumble over the cheese and drizzle over the rest of the dressing. Serve with the tzatziki, a bit of good brown bread and butter or some warm pitta.

BEETROOT RISOTTO

FEEDS 2

INGREDIENTS

225–275g whole beetroot
2 shallots, peeled
2 fat garlic cloves, peeled
850ml chicken/vegetable stock
    (p49/p15)
35g butter
a splash of olive oil
175g vialone nano/carnaroli/arborio
    risotto rice
3/4 small glass of white wine
a little fresh thyme (optional)
salt and black pepper
juice of ½ a lemon
50g freshly grated parmesan
a knob of butter

STIR-INS
50g crumbled blue cheese
1 tablespoon mascarpone, cream or
    crème fraîche
a few baby spinach or rocket leaves

TOPPINGS
blue cheese and herb croquettes
    (see overleaf)
a handful of freshly grated parmesan/
    crumbled Lancashire/goat's cheese
2 tbsp sour cream/natural yoghurt
a few caramelised walnuts
½ tbsp horseradish cream

With its shocking colour and sound flavour, this one's quite the exhibitionist. I love the layers of flavour and texture that the stir-ins and toppings give the risotto here, but keep it nice and simple if that's how you like it. Serve as a main course, a starter or as a lovely little extra alongside a nice bit of beef or oily fish like salmon or mackerel.

PREP Cut any leaves away from the beetroot, wash them, pop them in a pan and cover with cold water. Boil till tender and easily pierced with a knife – allow 20 minutes for smaller beet. Set aside to cool.

Dice the shallots and garlic with a small sharp knife. Pour the chicken/vegetable stock into a pan, bring it to the boil then lower to a simmer.

Peel the beet. Chop and blitz in a processor with 4 tablespoons of hot stock or use a stick blender to make a thick, smooth purée. Prep your choice of stir-ins/toppings.

COOK Put a second pan on to heat. Add the butter and oil. Once hot, add the shallot and garlic, stirring with a wooden spoon. Reduce the heat to low and cook very gently for 5 minutes, till the onion softens.

Tip the unwashed rice into the pan and stir well to coat it. Cook for a minute, stirring. Increase the heat. Add the wine and stir till it's almost absorbed, then add a large ladle full of hot stock immediately. Add the thyme, if using. Reduce the heat to medium so the mix keeps bubbling a bit but doesn't cook too fiercely as it absorbs the new liquid. Once absorbed, add another ladle of stock and keep stirring. Repeat until the stock is just about used and the rice is just about cooked (test a grain – the end result wants to be soft but with a tiny bit of texture and the risotto itself should neither be stiff and dry nor wet and soupy), about 15–20 minutes. Add salt, pepper and lemon juice.

Stir in two-thirds of the beetroot purée. Taste and adjust the seasoning. Add the rest of the purée now (or add later as a topping) plus your choice of stir-ins and half the parmesan. Stir in the butter to make it glossy. Taste and adjust. Turn off the heat, put the lid on the pan and leave to rest for 3 minutes.

PLATE Spoon the risotto into warm shallow bowls and finish with the remaining parmesan and your choice of toppings.

TO GO WITH
CARAMELISED WALNUTS
Heat ½ tsp butter in a frying pan. Throw in a handful of walnut halves. Toss to sauté for 1–2 mins until lightly brown and toasted. Tip onto kitchen paper. Sprinkle with a bit of fine salt and caster sugar.

ONION RISOTTO

FEEDS 3

INGREDIENTS

3 large mild/white onions, peeled
110g parmesan, plus extra to serve
50g butter, plus extra to serve
2 fat garlic cloves, peeled and crushed
1.2 litres chicken/vegetable stock
    (p49/p15)
300g risotto rice
150ml Noilly Prat (or other vermouth/
    dry white wine)
100ml double cream
salt and black pepper
a squeeze of lemon juice
a few grains of vanilla salt (optional)
a little fresh thyme

—— CHANGE IT UP ——

For a delicious cappuccino effect, add a
teaspoon or two of coffee before serving.
Or soak a couple of crumbled Amaretti
biscuits in coffee and scatter at the bottom
of the bowls.

It's a contradiction, this dish – delicate, yet fully flavoured. In a word, yummy. Using milder white onions makes it nice and sweet.

PREP Slice the onions thinly. Grate the parmesan so you can chuck it in later without abandoning your stirring

COOK Heat a large heavy-bottomed pan. Add the butter. Throw in the onions and garlic. Stir to coat in butter then cook very gently on a low/medium heat for up to 10 minutes until very soft and translucent. Don't let them colour or it will spoil the flavour.

Put the pan of stock on to boil then reduce to a simmer. Half-cover with a lid.

Once the onions are soft, increase the heat slightly. Add the unwashed rice. Stir to coat the grains for 2 minutes. Increase the heat. Add the Noilly Prat and stir until absorbed. Add a single ladle of hot stock. Stir continuously until absorbed, then add another ladle and repeat. Continue to add stock, stirring until absorbed before repeating, for 15–20 minutes until the grains of rice swell and the mix is creamy. You may need all, more or a bit less liquid (if you need more, add a bit of hot water or a splash more wine).

When it looks and feels done (still a bit soupy with the rice softened, but not mushy) add the parmesan and two-thirds of the cream, black pepper and a little salt to taste. Add a little more cream or a squeeze of lemon juice if you feel it needs it. Cover and leave to settle for 2 minutes.

PLATE Spoon into warm bowls. Sprinkle with vanilla salt, if using, thyme, parmesan and dot each with a dab of butter. Serve with extra parmesan for grating at the table.

TO GO WITH

BLUE CHEESE AND HERB CROQUETTES

Mix a bit of fried shallot, a pinch of dried sage or diced fresh and some crumbled blue cheese like dolcelatte/stilton. Roll into 4 mini-logs, about 2.5 cm. Roll in flour, dip in beaten egg and coat in breadcrumbs. While the risotto is resting, fry the croquettes in groundnut, vegetable or sunflower oil for a minute or so per side until golden outside, melting inside. Drain on kitchen paper and serve on top of the risotto.

A POST-ROAST CHICKEN RISOTTO

FEEDS 2

INGREDIENTS

meat stripped from your post-roast
    chicken (p54)
600ml chicken stock (p49)
50g parmesan, plus extra to serve
a small/medium onion, peeled
25g butter
1–2 garlic cloves, peeled
175g risotto rice
1 small glass white wine (or more
    stock)
a bit of chopped tarragon/thyme/
    rosemary/sage, to taste
juice of ½ a lemon
a knob of butter, plus extra for serving
1 tbsp cream/mascarpone/crème
    fraîche
salt and black pepper

Can a roast bird be as good the second time around? Yes it can with this one...

PREP On roast chicken day: Enjoy your meal. Strip off the extra meat. Cover and chill. Make up your chicken stock using the carcass following the instructions on page 49.

On risotto day: Remove the meat from the fridge to get to room temperature. Bring the stock to a simmer in a pan. Grate the parmesan and chop the onion.

COOK Melt the butter in a larger, heavy-bottomed pan on a gentle heat. Add the onion and crush in the garlic. Cook for 5 minutes or until soft and translucent. Fling the unwashed rice in and stir well to coat. Add the wine, increase the heat and cook until it evaporates.

Add the first ladle of hot stock, stirring until it's absorbed, then add another without ever flooding the rice. Continue to add stock in this way – adding any chopped herbs as and when you like – until the risotto is almost done (the grains of rice should be creamy and the mix a bit soupy). Add most of your chicken, a bit of lemon lemon juice and the parmesan. Stir in extra butter, cream/mascarpone/crème fraîche. Season, taste and adjust the balance.

PLATE Spoon the risotto into warm bowls. Top with the remaining bits of chicken, some extra grated parmesan and a few extra fresh herbs.

BREAD AND CAKES

Baking's where it all began for me: the smell of fresh bread, the licking of the bowl, the general mess of it all. I was a hooked virgin cook. But then it got serious. Baking's an exact science. So you've got to treat it with respect. It's all about the relationship between fat, sugars, flour, baking powder or yeast; the shape and size of the tin or the spoon, the temperature of the eggs, measuring liquids exactly and the heat of the oven. Get these things right and you're on your way to cookie heaven and other good places. Something as simple as a loaf of fresh bread with a crisp crust and a soft sweet crumb will stun the most discerning of palates. As for the cakes and the pizzas – I've included some classics…so you be the judge.

★ BAKING HEROES ★

✶✶✶✶✶✶✶✶ FLOURS ✶✶✶✶✶✶✶✶

PLAIN FLOUR: Use for biscuits, scones, cakes, a few quick breads, pastry and alternative pizza dough. It has no raising agent of its own. Plain wholemeal flour can be substituted for white where specified in a recipe. It tends to produce a heavier texture but the husk of the grain is there so there are health benefits.

SELF-RAISING FLOUR: Comes in white and wholemeal. Already contains a raising agent. Don't confuse with plain flour!

STRONG BREAD FLOUR: Contains a much higher level of gluten than standard white flour. This is activated by the kneading process and allows the bread to rise. Use for loaves and pizzas. Strong brown/wholemeal bread flour has a stronger taste and makes a denser but healthier loaf.

MULTI-GRAIN FLOUR: Mixes up the grains for a varied taste and texture. Has no raising agent.

CORNMEAL, OATS AND OATMEAL, **SPELT**, *Buckwheat*, **RYE FLOUR**, KAMUT, *Bulgur* and other grains all provide their own different tastes and textures. Once you know your flours and recipes try combining different types of whites and browns.

✶✶✶✶✶✶✶✶ RAISING AGENTS ✶✶✶✶✶✶✶✶

YEAST For bread, buns, pizzas and dough. It comes in three guises (see below). Use whichever's convenient. If substituting dried for fresh, use half the amount (e.g. for 10g of fresh yeast use 5g dried/quick-acting).

FRESH YEAST: A living organism. Get it from health food shops and some bakers/supermarkets. It can be rubbed straight into the flour, though it is usually activated before use. To activate, sit it in a small bowl. Cream it with a spoon. Add a bit of the warm (not hot) water specified in your recipe. Cover and leave for 10 minutes until it produces a frothy head. If the water is too hot (over 30°C) you will kill the yeast.

DRIED YEAST: Needs activating before use. Add the specified amount to a bit of measured water with ½ tsp sugar or honey. Stir, cover and leave to froth.

EASY-BLEND QUICK-ACTING YEAST: Although sometimes I activate it first, this can be added directly to your dry ingredients. If in doubt, read the packet instructions. Check the use-by date. Always have some in.

AIR: Introduced by SIFTING FLOUR, WHISKING EGGS, RUBBING IN and CREAMING. It's preserved by careful FOLDING IN and OPENING AND CLOSING THE OVEN DOOR GENTLY.

BAKING POWDER: A mix of acid and alkali and the most common raising agent. It works by interacting with the liquid in your dough or batter, producing carbon dioxide which fills the air pockets you've created when beating/creaming your mix. It reacts again when it meets the heat of your oven so you get a double-rising effect. Check the use-by date. It loses potency after a year; store in a dry place.

BICARBONATE OF SODA: (AKA baking soda or bread soda) an alkali which reacts with the acid ingredients in your batter/mix/eggs/treacle/lemon juice to create gases. These in turn reacts with the gluten in your flour which expands and your baking rises. Don't confuse it with baking powder.

★★★★★★★★★★ SUGARS ★★★★★★★★★★★

CASTER: Finer than granulated so perfect for baking.

GOLDEN CASTER: Ok for baking and has a more distinctive flavour.

DEMERARA: A crunchy sugar useful in biscuits and for topping cakes.

LIGHT BROWN: Useful in cookies and fruit cakes.

DARK BROWN: A strong dense flavour good for ginger cake and strong fruit cakes.

ICING: Use for some biscuits and for icings, buttercreams, dusting. Needs sifting to remove lumps.

HONEY: A distinctive flavour so use judiciously.

BLACK TREACLE: Great for gingerbreads, ginger biscuits and breads.

★★★★★★★★★★ EGGS ★★★★★★★★★★★

SIZE MATTERS. Get it right. If you use a small egg when large is specified your proportions are wrong.

ALWAYS Bake with eggs at room temperature. Use the best you can: a good egg will flavour and colour your baking.

★★★★★★★★★★ FATS ★★★★★★★★★★★

BUTTER: Great for taste and colour and natural. Unsalted is best. Use at room temperature for ease and speed unless cold is specified in the recipe (as in most pastry).

MARGARINE: Use instead of butter if you must.

OILS: Use tasteless oils in cakes/muffins – save olive oil for bread and pizza.

★★★★★ WATER (AND OTHER LIQUIDS) ★★★★★

MEASURE these absolutely accurately. If you get it wrong your cake or bread won't rise properly or have the right texture. **THE CLUE'S IN THE RECIPE.** Some cakes want to be **'SOFT DROPPING'** (falling off the end of your spoon) and you'll need to judge that by adding more liquid until it does. Water is equally important for dough. Don't just slosh it in. **BE ACCURATE.** However, flours vary in their absorption rate so you may need to add more or less to get the right consistency.

QUICK
Flaky pastry

Wrap 175G BUTTER in foil and stick in the freezer for an hour. Chill a mug of WATER. Sift 225G FLOUR and a PINCH OF SALT into a bowl. Grate the butter coarsely into the flour, peeling the foil back as you go. Mix them lightly with a fork. Now add 2 TBSP WATER, mixing until you get a smooth firm dough. Add more water if needed. Pull it into a smooth ball, working lightly, and wrap in foil/film. Chill for 30 minutes before using.

DOCTOR BAKER

ALL FLOUR CONTAINS

PROTEIN
CARBOHYDRATE

AND EASILY ABSORBED

Calcium

for healthy teeth and bones.
WHOLEMEAL FLOUR IS HIGH IN

VITAMIN B1 **IRON**
MAGNESIUM
ZINC & FIBRE
WHICH HELPS
PROTECT AGAINST
both heart and bowel diseases
and in controlling weight.
MULTI-GRAIN AND WHOLEMEAL
FLOURS CONTAIN ESSENTIAL

FOLATE

Oats are full of slow-release energy
and will keep you going for longer,
while seeds and nuts are rich in

PROTEIN IRON
Phosphorus ## ZINC
CALCIUM NIACIN
AND B VITAMINS

DATES, DRIED FIGS AND
APRICOTS ARE ALL HIGH IN

FIBRE & slow-release
energy, while
CHOCOLATE IS FULL OF

IRON

WHICH HELPS FIGHT ANAEMIA
AND BOOSTS FEEL-GOOD FACTOR.

— TAKE THE HEAT —

Never put your baking into a cold
oven or one that hasn't reached
the right temperature. Preheat
means just that. Inaccurate oven
temperature is the main cause of
a cake sinking.

THE KNEAD TO KNOW
BREAD TECHNIQUES

MixINg You could use a spoon but why not use your hand? Get in touch with the dough and utilise your hand heat. Mix everything in a large bowl or sift the flour and salt onto a clean surface. Make a well in the centre. Add the yeast and liquid. Draw the flour in and mix till you have a ball of dough.

KNEADING A work-out for the gluten in the flour which makes it elastic so the gases can stretch it and the dough will rise. Do it by hand or machine. By machine: You need a free-standing mixer. Bang the dough in and mix for 8 minutes or till its elastic. By hand: Roll the dough into a rough ball. Slap it onto a floured surface. Flour your hands. Push and stretch the dough away from you. Then flip the just stretched portion back onto the main ball and press down. Rotate the ball round. Repeat the process for 10 minutes or until it feels smooth and elastic.

PROVING
Shape the dough into a ball. Brush lightly with oil. Sit it in a large bowl. Cover with a damp tea towel. Sit it in a warm draught-free place until it doubles in size (1 hour plus, temperature dependent). Poke it. If your finger leaves a hole, it's ready. You can leave it, covered, in the fridge for 8 hours if it suits. The longer the rise the better the flavour.

KNOCK IT BACK Scoop the risen dough onto a surface. Knead and punch it for 2 minutes to redistribute the air and for best-textured bread.

SHAPE Shape the bread to fit your oiled loaf tin or bang on a tray.

SECOND RISE Most loaves need another rise once shaped. Consult your recipe.

Finishing Shiny glaze – brush with egg wash before baking and again 5 minutes before the bread is done. Natural look – dust with a bit of flour. Buttery – brush with melted butter when it's hot out of the oven. Olive oil – brush with oil before baking and 5 minutes before it's done.

TESTING FOR DONENESS Test every loaf. Take it out of the tin with a tea towel. Tap the base. It should sound hollow and feel light. Put it back, without the tin, if it needs longer/sounds dull and feels doughy. Cool on a rack.

STORING In a tin. It gets stale fast if you chill it. Freeze fresh as soon as it cools.

SHELF *Life*

Store your dry ingredients in sealed containers in dry cupboards.

Check the pack if you don't bake often.

Sugar lasts indefinitely.

Watch out for wildlife. Weevils breed in flour, sugar, oats etc so check; they're tiny but visible.

Flour has limited shelf-life.

CREAMING Beat soft butter and sugar into a light, white, airy cream. Use a wooden spoon or mixer but finish with the spoon. Beat for 5 minutes to aerate.

RUB IN Literally rub the butter into the flour using your thumbs and fingertips. Hold your hands high over the bowl as you do to add air.

FOLD IN Develop a cutting and folding action with a large metal spoon as you incorporate new ingredients into a delicate mix. Think figure of eight.

SIFTING Putting flour/cocoa/icing sugar/raising agents through a sieve to aerate.

DONE YET?

SPONGES
Look for a golden brown cake that's risen well and shrinking away from the sides of the tin slightly. If you press lightly in the middle the sponge springs back.

OTHER CAKES
Test by piercing the centre with a cocktail stick/toothpick/wooden skewer. It should come out clean.

TIN TALK SIZING & LINING

TURNING OUT RUN a sharp thin knife smoothly between the edge of the tin and the cake. SIT a rack on top of the cake. PROTECT your hands with a tea towel. Holding cake and rack, INVERT so the cake shifts to the rack. REMOVE the tin. PEEL the paper off. TURN it upside down to cool and so it doesn't mark too much. COOL on the rack and store in an airtight container.

SIZE Match recipe to tin size if you want your cake to work.

GREASE Rub with soft butter or flavourless oil (vegetable/groundnut).

LINE To protect from heat and prevent sticking. For the base, sit tin on greaseproof/baking paper. Draw round it with a pencil. Cut and lay in. For the sides, fold paper in half lengthways. Wrap round the tin. Mark the length plus a bit. Cut and fit in. For a loaf tin all-in-one: cut paper to twice the size of the base. Put tin in the centre. Cut diagonal lines to each corner. Tuck paper into the tin to fit and line completely.

BREADCRUMBS

SOFT & FRESH: Slap stale bread in a processor or tear and blitz with a stick blender - blitz to the texture you want. **DRIED:** Preheat the oven to 180°C/Gas 4. Spread breadcrumbs on a tray and cook until golden brown/dried out. **PANKO STYLE:** lay slices out on a tray overnight or till dried out. Bash or crumble to crumbs. **FRIED:** Put fresh crumbs into a pan on a very low heat with a bit of oil/butter (crushed garlic and herbs if you want) and cook until crisp. Use to sprinkle on pasta instead of parmesan and to top gratins.

CLASSIC
WHITE LOAF

MAKES 1 LARGE OR 2 SMALL LOAVES

INGREDIENTS

450g strong white bread flour
2 tsp fine salt
1 x 7g pack easy-blend yeast
50g butter, in cubes, plus extra for
    greasing
250ml milk
1 tsp runny honey
1 large egg (at room temperature)
groundnut oil, for brushing
a little flour/beaten egg, for finishing
    (optional)

—— CHANGE IT UP ——

1. Nip off good plum-sized bits of dough
and shape into rolls. Leave to rise. Brush
with egg wash, sprinkle over poppy/sesame
seeds and bake for 10–15 minutes. 2. For a
pesto and olive loaf, add 1 tsp pesto with the
liquid, a few chopped green olives before
you finish kneading and brush with olive oil
or an olive oil/pesto mix before baking.

—— BONUS BITES ——

• Add the following to half the bread mix.
• Cook in a 450g loaf tin.
HERB, CHEESE AND BACON LOAF
By hand: Add ½ tsp mustard powder, ½ tsp
dried oregano and 50g grated cheddar to
the flour before you add the liquid. Add 4
rashers of cooked, crumbled streaky bacon
to the dough just before you finish kneading.
By machine: Add all the extras as you begin
kneading. Brush the loaf with thinned
marmite/vegemite or grated cheddar/
gruyère and bake as before.
SIMPLE WHOLEMEAL LOAF
Mix 700g wholemeal flour with 2 x 7g
sachets fast-action dried yeast, 1 tsp fine
salt, 1 tsp sugar or honey, 425ml warm water
and 1 tbsp olive oil. Proceed as for white
loaf. Bake in 2 greased 450g tins for 20–30
minutes at 230°C/Gas 8.

Unless you've got an artisan bakery nearby you won't be finding bread like this very easily. It's sweet, flavoursome, has an unbeatable texture and accommodates a range of great flavours. Ok, it takes a while to get to the table but most of that is actually down-time, when you can be getting on with other things…

PREP
Sift the flour and salt into a bowl. Add the yeast and butter. Rub everything together between your fingers and thumbs until the fat and yeast are incorporated. Warm the milk in a small pan. Add the honey. Keep it lukewarm. Make a hollow in the flour. Beat then add the egg. Pour in 200ml of the milk and mix with your hands or a wooden spoon for dough that's soft, warm, and not too sticky. Add more milk if you need it. Pull it into a warm ball and sit it on a floured board.

Knead it by machine: Put the dough in the bowl of a mixer and knead with the dough hook for 8 minutes until it's smooth and elastic. Or do it by hand: pressing, stretching, folding, turning and slapping it roughly for 10 minutes (p200) until glossy and pliable.

Let it rise: Roll the dough into a ball and brush it with a little groundnut oil. Slap it into a large bowl. Cover with a damp tea towel. Leave it in a warm, draught-free place till it doubles in volume (about 1 hour).

Knock it back: Once risen, bang the dough back on the board. Knead and punch it for 2 minutes. Grease a 900g loaf tin. Use your hands to shape your dough into a rectangle the length of the tin but a bit wider. Fold the two sides under to create a seam and to a size that will fit the tin. Cover and leave to rise for a further 20 minutes.

Use a sharp knife to make a 3cm-deep cut down the centre of the loaf for the split effect. Leave it for a final rise, about 10 minutes. Meantime, preheat the oven to 230°C/Gas 8.

Finish the loaf: Either sprinkle with flour, brush with egg or keep it plain.

COOK
Bake for 20–30 minutes. Turn it out of the tin. Tap the base to test for doneness. It should feel crisp and sound hollow. Put it back if it needs extra time. Cool on a rack.

PLATE
This loaf slices beautifully. Cut it up and use for sandwiches or toasting. Enjoy with soup, or cut up into soldiers for boiled eggs.

HEALTHY SEED MULTI-GRAIN

MAKES 1 LARGE LOAF

INGREDIENTS

450–500g multi-grain brown flour
½ tsp salt
1 x 7g packet easy blend yeast
1 tsp caster sugar or honey
300ml warm (not hot) water
1 tbsp olive oil, or sunflower/rape/
  flaxseed
a small handful of mixed seeds
  (pumpkin/sunflower)

—— CHANGE IT UP ——

For cinnamon toast, toast and spread
with a mix of soft butter, caster sugar and
cinnamon.

—— BONUS BITE ——

FAST BLACK TREACLE BREAD

Grease 2 x 900g loaf tins. Mix 2 x 7g sachets
easy-blend yeast with 150ml warm water,
1 tbsp black treacle and 1 tbsp honey. Cover
and leave for 10 minutes till frothy. Mix
together 450g wholemeal bread flour, 450g
white flour and 1 tsp salt in a bowl. Add the
frothed liquid plus 700ml warm water and
stir to make a soft, loose dough. Spoon it
into the tins. Cover with a tea towel. Leave
to rise above the surface of the tin. Bake at
200°C/Gas 6 for 30–40 minutes or till the
base sounds hollow when tapped. Cool.
Makes great toast and lasts well.

Multi-grain and multi-dimensional – this one packs flavour and nutrition.

PREP Tip the flour, salt, yeast and sugar into a large bowl. If using honey, stir it into the warm water to dissolve. Add the water to the flour mix. Stir with your hand or a wooden spoon to form a rough dough. Add the oil and knead it in to the mix for a minute.

To knead by machine: Slap the dough into your mixer bowl. Knead with the dough hook for 8 minutes. If the mix seems too sticky, add extra flour at the start, but don't make it too dry/stiff. By hand: Slap the dough onto a lightly floured board and knead for 10 minutes, until smooth and elastic.

Prove the dough: roll it into a ball and brush with a little oil. Put it into a bowl to rise; it should double in volume. Cover with cling film or a damp tea towel. Leave it somewhere warm for an hour and check its progress occasionally.

Knock it back: slap the dough back onto the board. Knead for 2 minutes. Bang it into a very well-greased non-stick tin. Scatter the seeds on top. Cover and leave for 20 minutes.

COOK Meantime, preheat the oven to 220ºC/Gas 7. Bake for 30–40 minutes. Remove from the tin and tap the base to test for doneness. It should sound hollow. Cool on a rack.

PLATE Slice for toast or sandwiches. It makes for a good high-energy breakfast bread and travels well for a picnic or lunch box.

BANG-IT-TOGETHER SODA BREAD (OR MUFFINS)

MAKES 1 LARGE LOAF
OR 8 MUFFINS

INGREDIENTS

500g plain white flour (not bread flour), plus extra for the tray
425ml buttermilk
1 tsp salt
1 heaped tsp bicarbonate of soda
1 tsp runny honey

TIP

If you don't have any buttermilk to hand, squeeze 1½ tbsp lemon juice into the same quantity of milk and leave for 15 minutes out in the kitchen before using in its place. Alternatively, use plain yoghurt soured with 2 tsp lemon juice.

—— CHANGE IT UP ——

1. For brown soda bread, use 500g plain wholemeal flour or half white, half plain. Add a beaten egg and a glug of sunflower or light oil to the mix too.

2. Customise your breads. Add raisins or sultanas, chocolate chips, dried or fresh blueberries or savoury extras like olives and herbs to white soda breads – oatmeal, oats, seeds or any dried fruits to brown breads.

So fast, so simple. Slice or split open and get lavish with the butter.

PREP Preheat the oven to 230°C/Gas 8. Sprinkle a little extra flour on a baking tray.

Sift the flour, salt and bicarbonate into a bowl. Make a well in the centre.

Add the buttermilk and honey. Beat it together with a wooden spoon or use your hand, starting from the well and working outwards, drawing the flour in.

The dough should be soft, not stiff (or you'll get a dry, heavy bread), nor should it be too sticky. Add more milk/flour as you judge it. Pull it into a ball.

Sit it on a lightly floured board. Pat it gently into a 5cm-wide circular loaf. Use a sharp knife to cut a deep cross (5cm) over the loaf so it marks into 4 quarters. Sit it on the tray. For muffins: Grease and flour the holes of a large muffin tin. Cut and shape the dough to fit and fill 8 holes.

COOK Bake the loaf for 15 minutes. Reduce the heat to 200°C/Gas 6 for another 20–30 minutes. Tap the base to test for doneness. It should sound hollow. Turn it upside down to cook for another few minutes if it doesn't. Cool on a rack. Cook the muffins for 5 minutes at 230°C/Gas 8, then reduce to 200°C/Gas 6 and cook for a further 10–15 minutes. Test as for the bread.

PLATE Eat on the same day smothered in butter, with cheese, cold meats, soup, honey, cream cheese or jam.

BONUS BITES

BANG IT IN THE PAN BREAD
Using half the quantity above, make up the soda bread into a dough as before. Pat out to fit a large frying pan (about 23cm). Heat the pan. Fry for 10–15 minutes per side till crusty and the crumb is cooked.

LAGER LOAF
Sift 250g plain flour, 1 level tbsp baking powder and 1 tsp salt into a bowl. Add 1 level tbsp granulated sugar, 110g finely grated strong cheddar and 2 tsp dried herbs of your choice. Pour 340ml lager in slowly, beating as you go. Spoon into a well-greased 450g loaf tin and bake in a preheated oven at 190°C/Gas 5 for 40 minutes or till cooked through. Eat warm or cold.

PIZZA

MAKES 4 REGULAR PIZZAS

INGREDIENTS

450g strong white bread flour
1 tsp fine salt
2 x 7g sachets easy-blend yeast
1 tsp caster sugar
300ml warm water
2 tbsp olive oil, plus extra for greasing
TOMATO SAUCE (OPTIONAL)
1 tbsp olive oil
4 garlic cloves, peeled and diced
1 x 400g can of chopped tomatoes
1½ tsp sugar
1 tbsp tomato purée
salt and pepper

········· **TIME SAVER** ·········

Make more dough than you need, roll out as bases and freeze on trays. Remove. Store in freezer bags until needed. Top and bang in the oven, giving them an extra 2 minutes.

───── **BONUS BITES** ─────

PISSALADIÈRE

Make quadruple amounts of caramelised onion (p80) adding 4 crushed garlic cloves, 2 tsp brown sugar and ½ tsp balsamic vinegar. Roll the dough out to fit a large rectangular baking tray. Top with the onion, 2 pinches of oregano/thyme, a handful of black olives and 12 drained anchovy fillets. Cook as before for 15–20 minutes.

LOW-FAT CRISPY DOUGH

Sift 300g plain white flour, 50g white bread flour and ¾ tsp fine salt into a large bowl. Add ½ tsp caster sugar. Measure 125ml semi-skimmed milk and 175ml hot water into a separate bowl. Add 2 x 7g sachets of easy-blend yeast to the liquid. Cover with a tea towel. Leave to froth for 10–15 minutes. Pour into the flour mix, add 25g extra plain white flour and mix for a very soft, slightly sticky dough. Knead, rise, knock back and roll as before. Top with lighter toppings.

Pizza's all about getting the simple things right: you want quality dough, an excellent tomato sauce (or other tasty base), a delectable topping and a very hot oven. Find the dough and the sauce on this page – turn over for toppings. This quantity makes 4 regular, 6 small or 1 large tray bake pizza. Vary it to suit the occasion.

PREP Sift the flour and salt into a bowl. Add the yeast and sugar. Boil 100ml of the water and mix with the 200ml of cold. Check the temperature – it should be comfortable to the finger. Add to the flour with the olive oil. Mix everything with your hands or a wooden spoon to get a soft smooth dough that's neither too wet nor dry. Add extra flour or water if you need to.

Pull the dough into a ball and knead by either throwing it into the bowl of a mixer and processing with the dough hook for 8 minutes or sitting it on a lightly floured board and kneading by hand (p200) until smooth and elastic.

Place the ball of dough in a large bowl and brush it lightly with olive oil. Leave in a warm place covered with a damp tea towel or cling film until it doubles in size – approximately 1 hour.

Meantime, make your tomato sauce, if using. Heat the olive oil in a pan on a very low heat. Add the garlic, sweat and stir for a minute without browning. Add the chopped tomatoes, sugar and tomato puree and season to taste. Increase the heat to medium. Simmer for 10–15 minutes, stirring occasionally. Taste to judge acidity, adding more sugar and adjusting seasoning if needed. Set aside.

Knock the risen dough back and knead for another 2 minutes on the floured board. Divide into four pieces. Sit one piece on the board, covering the rest with a tea towel so they don't dry out. Flatten it with the palm of your hand. Make indentations with your finger 1 cm from the outside to create a rim all the way around. Flip the dough over. Put one hand in the middle. With the other, gently stretch the dough out, rotating the pizza as you go. Now get a rolling pin and roll out, turning it 45 degrees between each roll to keep it circular. Get it as thin as you can. Repeat with the remaining pieces. Leave the pizza bases to rise again for a further 5 minutes.

COOK Preheat the oven to its highest temperature. Place your pizza bases on oiled baking trays. Spread tomato sauce thinly over each, if using, leaving a 1–2 cm rim. Cover with your topping of choice (see overleaf for inspiration). Shove your baking tray into the oven. Cook until golden and crisp (about 8 minutes, depending on the thickness of the dough and your choice of topping).

PLATE Finish with any extras such as grated parmesan, rocket leaves, olive oil or as dictated by your chosen recipe.

GARLIC

FETA AND CARAMELISED ONION

FUNGHI

SALAMI AND FIG

PIZZA TOPPINGS

GARLIC AND TOMATO

Make up some garlic butter by creaming together 70g soft butter in a bowl with 1–2 crushed garlic cloves. Spread thinly over two-thirds of each base using the back of a spoon or a spatula. Spread tomato sauce over the remaining thirds. Drizzle with a little oil and scatter over a little sea salt. Bake for 4–6 minutes or until cooked.

FETA AND CARAMELISED ONION

Make up some caramelised onion (p80). Smudge the base with mascarpone then the tomato sauce. Dot over the caramelised onion, add some crumbled feta, a bit of oregano, a few dabs of garlic butter (see right) and a drizzle of olive oil. Cook for 6–8 minutes or till golden and bubbling.

COURGETTE AND GOAT'S CHEESE

Smear your pizza bases with a layer of mascarpone. Grate 1 medium courgette and scatter over the bases with cubes of goat's cheese to taste, sea salt and black pepper, dabs of garlic butter and a drizzling of olive oil. Add parmesan shavings when cooked.

CHERRY TOMATO

Scatter 6 sliced cherry tomatoes over each pizza base. Drizzle over olive oil. Sprinkle over a little sea salt. Bake for 6 minutes. Add more salt, a drizzle of oil and a little rocket or basil before serving.

MARGHERITA

Cover your pizza bases with tomato sauce. Sprinkle over 150–200g diced mozzarella and a pinch each of dried thyme and oregano. Dot with a handful of olives and drizzle lightly with olive oil. Bake. Add grated parmesan.

FUNGHI

Heat a little olive oil and a knob of butter in a pan. Cook 2 diced garlic cloves for a minute without browning. Add 2 handfuls of thinly sliced white/chestnut mushrooms. Cook for a minute. Add a glug of white wine, season and cook for another minute. Top your bases with either a smudge of tomato sauce or a smeared covering of mascarpone. Cover thinly with the mushrooms. Scatter with diced mozzarella, a good pinch of oregano and a drizzle of olive oil. Finish with a few strands of caramelised onion if you like. Sprinkle with a little sea salt. Cook for 6–8 minutes until bubbling.

SALAMI AND FIG

Smear the bases with the tomato sauce. Place as many torn pieces of salami as you like evenly over the top. Place blobs of fig relish or a few slices of fresh fig. Scatter each pizza with a few 1cm cubes of mozzarella, a few chilli flakes and a handful of torn basil. Drizzle with olive oil. Cook for 6–8 minutes or till golden and bubbling.

POLLO

Slice and shred a good handful of cold roast chicken. Smear your bases lightly with tomato sauce and top evenly with a good scattering of diced mozzarella, crumbled blue cheese and the chicken. Sprinkle over a few leaves of torn tarragon, season and drizzle with olive oil, making sure the chicken has some coverage so it doesn't dry out in the scorching heat. Slap the tray in the oven for 6–8 minutes or until crisp and golden. Remove. Top with a few rocket leaves and shavings of parmesan.

DOUBLE CHOC CHIP GINGERS AND CHOC CHERRY SOUR COOKIES

MAKES 12 BISCUITS

INGREDIENTS

75g butter, softened
140g plain white flour
150g caster sugar
1 tsp vanilla extract
grated zest of ½ a small orange
1 medium egg
50g dark chocolate
DOUBLE CHOC CHIP
1 level tbsp cocoa powder
CHOC GINGERS
25g crystallised ginger, diced
CHOC CHERRY SOURS
25g dried sour cherries, halved

So many cookies are just so-so – these cookies are just so good. Thinner than most, they make a beautiful base for more daring flavours. So, make the mix, add your option.

PREP Preheat the oven to 180°C/Gas 4. Grease 2 large baking trays.

Tip the butter into a bowl. Break it up with the wooden spoon. Sift in the flour. Add the sugar, vanilla extract and orange zest. Beat the egg. Bang it in. Beat everything together using a wooden spoon until smooth.

Sit the chocolate on a board. Use a long sharp chef's knife to dice it into small bits. Add it all to the mix. Now prep and add your chosen extra, sifting the cocoa powder over the mix if making the double choc chip option.

Work into the base mix with a metal spoon or fork.

COOK Drop heaped teaspoons of mixture well apart on the trays to allow for spreading (you may need to cook in batches). Bake for 8 minutes or until they are crisping at the edges. Remove. Leave on the trays for 3 minutes. Run a metal spatula very carefully underneath to loosen them. Leave for another 4 minutes before removing to a rack to cool.

PLATE Enjoy with a cuppa.

BONUS BITE

CHOCOLATE FLORENTINES
Preheat the oven to 180°C/Gas 4. Grease two large baking trays. Lightly toast 50g flaked almonds in a dry frying pan on a very low heat for a minute, stirring, until very pale brown. Remove. Melt 50g butter in a pan and combine with 50g caster sugar, 2 tsp runny honey and 1 tsp grated lemon or orange zest in a pan on low heat. Cool in a bowl for 5 minutes. Add 50g sifted plain white flour, 10g chopped raisins, 30g finely chopped mixed peel and 40g roughly chopped glacé cherries and stir lightly until well combined. Using your fingers, shape and squeeze the mix into 12 blobs. Space them well apart on the baking trays, flattening them slightly with your fingers, and bake for 8–10 minutes, until golden-edged but not dark. Rest on trays for 2 minutes. Slide a metal spatula underneath. Remove to cool on a rack. Melt 110g milk/white/dark chocolate in a bowl over a pan of water (p226). Spoon a little of the melted chocolate onto the flat side of each cooled cookie. Leave for 5 minutes. Repeat, using a fork to make wavy lines in the chocolate for effect if you want to. Leave to set.

VANILLA CUSTARDS

MAKES 12 BISCUITS
(OR 6 AS CUSTARD CREAMS)

INGREDIENTS

175g butter, softened
75g icing sugar
½–1 tsp vanilla extract
175g plain white flour
50g custard powder
**CUSTARD CREAM FILLING
(OPTIONAL)**
50g butter, softened
110g icing sugar, sifted
3 drops vanilla extract
1–2 tbsp raspberry jam (or whatever
   jam you fancy)

—— CHANGE IT UP ——

For lime custards, make a lime buttercream
by adding the finely grated zest and juice
of ½ lime and a squeeze of lemon
to the custard cream filling.

—— BONUS BITE ——

SHORTBREAD ROUNDS OR HEARTS

Cream 175g butter and 50g caster sugar as
above. Sift in 150g plain white flour and
25g custard powder. Beat together, adding
1 tsp vanilla extract. Pull into a firm dough
with your hands. Roll out to ½ cm thick on
a floured board. Cut out 12 x 6cm rounds
or hearts, re-rolling between. Sit them on
a greased baking tray, prick lightly all over
with a fork and sprinkle with caster sugar.
Bake as above until pale gold. Cool on tin
for 5 minutes. Add more sugar. Sandwich
as above or with whipped cream, jam and
raspberries. Or enjoy plain.

An alternative take on a favourite biscuit; it's kind of chic but it takes you back in time and puts a smile on your face…

PREP Preheat the oven to 180°C/Gas 4. Grease a large baking tray.

Cream the mix: Tip the butter into a large bowl. Break it up with a wooden spoon. Beat for a few seconds. Sift in the icing sugar and beat for a good few minutes until soft and creamy white. Beat in the vanilla extract. Sift in the flour and custard powder.

Mix with a fork until integrated. Draw into a ball with your fingers. Divide into 12. Roll each bit lightly between your hands to shape into a ball. Sit them well apart on the baking tray. Use a fork to press down very lightly into each one, first one way, then the other to flatten slightly and cross-hatch the surface.

COOK Bake for 10–15 minutes or until pale golden. Don't let them brown.

Cool for 2 minutes then run a metal spatula under and transfer to a rack. Cool completely. Store in an airtight container until needed.

For custard creams: Beat the butter in a bowl. Add the icing sugar and vanilla extract and mix until soft. Spread 6 biscuits with the jam, then cover with the icing. Sandwich with the remaining biscuits.

PLATE Pile them up and get stuck in…

GINGER CHILLI LIMES

MAKES 12 BISCUITS

INGREDIENTS

150g butter, softened
200g caster sugar
50g Demerara sugar
1 tbsp golden syrup
1 small egg, beaten
250g plain flour
1 tsp baking powder
½ tsp bicarbonate of soda
3 tsp ground ginger
a pinch of cinnamon (optional)
a small pinch of chilli flakes
½ tsp salt
grated zest of ½ a lime

—— CHANGE IT UP ——

For chocolate ginger chilli limes, melt 110g dark or milk chocolate very slowly in a bowl over a pan of barely simmering water. Spread a little over the base of the cooled gingers. Leave to set before eating.

TIP
Store ginger biscuits separately as other biscuits can pick up their flavour.

A delicious ginger biscuit with an exotic twist...great with a cup of tea.

PREP Preheat the oven to 180°C/Gas 4. Grease 2 large baking trays.

Tip the butter into a bowl. Beat it for a few seconds with a wooden spoon. Add the sugars and cream together until the mixture is soft and very pale. Add the golden syrup. Add the egg and beat furiously. Sift the flour, baking powder, bicarbonate, ginger and cinnamon into the bowl.

Add the chilli flakes, salt and lime zest. Using a large metal spoon, fold the mix together, cutting down into it then folding gently in figure-of-eight movements until it amalgamates.

Roll the mix into 12 walnut-sized balls. Place well apart on the trays to allow for spreading (you may need to cook in batches).

COOK Bake for 15–20 minutes or till golden brown. Remove. Leave on the trays for 2 minutes. Slide a metal spatula carefully under to loosen them and transfer to a rack. Leave to cool. Store in an airtight container until needed.

PLATE Pile onto a plate. Also good with coffee!

BONUS BITES

GINGER SNAPJACKS
Preheat the oven to 190°C/Gas 5. Melt 110g butter gently in a pan. Remove. Mix in 110g oats, ¾ tsp ground ginger, 75g soft light brown sugar and 10g semolina. Spoon into a well-greased 28 x 18cm shallow tin, pressing the mix to fit. Bake for 15 minutes. Cut into 12 with a sharp knife after a few minutes and leave to cool in the tin. These biscuits are thin and delicate, so lift them carefully with a metal spatula.

GINGER BRANDY SNAPS
Preheat the oven to 160°C/Gas 3. Melt 50g granulated sugar, 50g butter and 65g golden syrup in a pan. Remove. Mix in 50g sifted plain white flour, 2 level tsp ground ginger, 1 tsp lemon juice. Space 4 tsp of mix well apart on a very well greased tray and bake for 8 minutes or till golden. Remove. After 1 minute run a spatula underneath. Roll each one around a wooden spoon handle. Remove after a minute. Cook and roll remaining mix. Cool. Enjoy as they are or roll in melted chocolate.

BUTTERMILK
SCONES

MAKES 8

INGREDIENTS

225g self-raising flour
½ tsp baking powder
½ tsp salt
50g soft butter
50g caster sugar
*150ml buttermilk, plus extra for
  brushing*
granulated sugar, for finishing

TIP
Use a wine glass if you don't have a cutter.
Re-flour the cutter every time for a cleaner
cut and a better rise.

········ TIME SAVER ········
Freeze cooked scones on a baking tray for
20 minutes. Seal in freezer bags. Thaw and
reheat for 10 minutes at 180°C/Gas 4 for
8–10 minutes. Freeze uncooked scones as
above. To cook, thaw as long as it takes the
oven to pre-heat. Bake for the regular time
plus another minute or two.

*Using buttermilk in your scones raises their game – team them with
jam and clotted cream for a classic cream tea.*

PREP
Preheat the oven to 220°C/Gas 7. Grease a baking tray. Sift the flour,
baking powder and salt into a large bowl. Add the butter. Rub it into
the flour between your fingers and thumbs, lifting the mix high over the bowl
as you do so, until it looks like fine sand. Keep it light (over-handling scones
makes them heavy). Add the sugar and two-thirds of the buttermilk. Mix with
a fork. Add more buttermilk until you have a soft (not wet) dough. Draw it
together with your fingers and knead it very lightly for a second until you get a
smooth ball.

Sit the dough on a floured board. Pat it out very lightly into a rough circle
approximately 2.5cm thick. Cut out the scones using a floured 6.5 cm cutter,
pressing down sharply without twisting. Lift the scones out cleanly and place
on a tray. Re-roll the scraps and repeat, re-flouring the cutter. Brush the scones
with extra buttermilk and sprinkle with sugar.

COOK
Bake for 15 minutes until risen and golden. Cool on a rack.

PLATE
Split in two when warm or cold. Serve butter, jam or fruit curd and
clotted or whipped double or whipping cream.

BONUS BITES

ORANGE, LEMON AND SULTANA CUT-AWAY SCONES
Preheat the oven to 220°C/Gas 7. Grease a large baking tray. Sift 500g self-raising flour, a
pinch of baking powder and a pinch of salt into a large bowl. Rub 175g butter into the flour,
then mix in the grated zest of ½ a lemon and ¼ orange, 2½ tbsp caster sugar and 75g sultanas/
dried fruit, with a fork. Add as much of 2 large beaten eggs as you need to form a soft smooth
dough. If too dry, add a splash of milk. Sit on a lightly floured surface, pat out as above and
cut into triangular scones with a sharp, floured knife. Sit them on a tray. Brush the tops with a
little milk and a sprinkle of sugar. Bake for 10–12 minutes.

MULTI-TOP CHEESE, ONION AND OLIVE SCONES
Fry a finely chopped onion gently in olive oil until golden. Cool. Preheat the oven to 200°C/
Gas 6. Grease 2 baking trays. Sift 225g plain white flour, 2 heaped tbsp baking powder, a pinch
of salt, ¾ tsp cayenne and 1 tsp mustard powder into a bowl. Rub 25g butter into the mix with
your fingers. Add the onion, a few chopped black olives, 110g grated strong Cheddar cheese
and a beaten egg. Mix together with a fork. Add 6 tbsp milk to the mix gradually. Pull the
dough into a soft ball, pat out lightly on a lightly floured board until 2.5cm thick and cut out
as above. Brush the tops of the scones with a little egg/grated cheddar/pesto or a spreading
of mustard, and bake in the oven for 15–20 minutes. These are good warm, split, spread with
cream cheese or butter. Make and serve with soup for a good lunch.

VICTORIA SPONGE CAKE WITH LEMON AND PASSIONFRUIT CURD & CREAM

FEEDS 8

INGREDIENTS

225g soft butter, plus extra for greasing
4 medium eggs
225g self-raising flour
225g caster sugar
2 tsp vanilla extract
a pinch of salt
1–2 tbsp milk (if required)
a little sifted icing sugar or caster sugar
    for finishing

CURD
juice and grated zest of 2 large lemons
110g caster sugar
50g butter
2 large eggs, beaten
2–3 passionfruit, halved

CHANTILLY CREAM
200ml double cream
1 tbsp icing sugar
a few drops of vanilla extract

·········· TIME SAVER ··········

Save on your prep time by adding 1 tsp
baking powder to the sponge mix. Bang it all
into a bowl/mixer. Beat for 5 minutes or till
well creamy. Bake as above.

────── CHANGE IT UP ──────

1. Fill with your choice of jam/whipped
cream/sliced strawberries/peaches/
raspberries.
2. For a gluten-free Victoria sponge, preheat
the oven to 160°C/Gas 3. Whisk 6 medium
eggs and 150g caster sugar together till pale
and fluffy, then fold in
150g sifted rice flour, 1 tsp xanthum gum
and 3 drops of vanilla extract. Divide
between two greased and lined sandwich
tins and bake for 20–30 minutes.

This old girl still has it: keep her classic or be bold with a more unusual filling. Start with all the ingredients at room temperature, and it's always light and gorgeous.

PREP Preheat the oven to 180°C/Gas 4. Grease two 18cm sandwich tins. Line their bases. Beat the eggs together in a small bowl. Sift the flour onto a plate.

Cream the mix: Slap the butter into a large bowl and break it up with a wooden spoon. Add the sugar. Beat them together furiously for 4–5 minutes until creamy, white and airy. Now add the egg, a little at a time, beating continuously (too fast and it may curdle). If it starts to look grainy, beat even harder, adding 2 teaspoons of flour. Add the vanilla extract. Hold a sieve high over the mix. Sift the flour and salt into the bowl a bit at a time.

Fold it in lightly: use a large metal spoon to cut into the ingredients and fold them together with a few gentle scooping figure-of-eight movements. Once amalgamated, the mixture should drop softly off the end of the spoon (fold in a little milk if it looks too thick). Divide between the tins, smoothing to the edges very lightly but not pressing down. Keep the air in there.

COOK Bake for 20–25 minutes. The cakes are done when they're high, golden and spring back when touched in the middle (don't test too soon). Open and close the oven door carefully. Remove and run a knife round the edges to loosen and take them out of the tins (p201). Peel the lining paper away in strips and very carefully. Leave to cool on a rack before filling.

Meanwhile, make the curd filling. Sit a large bowl over the top of a pan of barely simmering water. Add the lemon juice, zest, sugar and butter. Melt slowly. Stir to dissolve the sugar. Add the beaten eggs. Stir constantly with a wooden spoon on a low heat for a few minutes until it thickens and coats the back of the spoon. (If it starts to split, sit the bowl in cold water and beat wildly). Remove from the heat. Scoop out the pulpy insides of the passionfruit and stir into the mixture. Leave to cool.

Just before filling, make the chantilly cream: Whisk the cream in a cold bowl until it starts to thicken. Sift the icing sugar and add with the vanilla. Whisk till light and airy, not stiff or grainy. Taste and adjust till you like it.

Using a metal spatula, spread the flat side of one of the sponges with curd. Cover with chantilly cream and sit the second sponge on top. Sprinkle with caster or icing sugar.

PLATE Sit the cake on a large plate. Cut into slices…enjoy.

BONUS BITES

CHOCOLATE VICTORIA
Replace 1 tbsp of the cake flour with cocoa powder. Make a chocolate icing by melting 50g chocolate (p226) and adding to 110g creamed butter mixed with 225g icing sugar and 2 tsp milk. Use to cover.

FRUIT VICTORIA
Add 2 tsp grated lemon/orange zest to the mix with 1 tbsp lemon/orange juice. Ice with lime buttercream (p212).

COFFEE VICTORIA
Add 50g finely chopped walnuts and 1–2 tbsp cold coffee to the cake mix instead of milk. Ice with coffee buttercream (p219).

SPONGE DROPS

MAKES 12-16

INGREDIENTS

4 medium eggs (at room temperature)
100g caster sugar
125g self-raising flour
50g cornflour
3 drops of vanilla extract
icing sugar, to serve
FILLING
3–4 tbsp jam or lemon curd
1 x chantilly cream (p216)
a punnet of raspberries or strawberries

········ **TIME SAVER** ········

To speed up the whisking process, sit the
eggs and sugar in a heatproof bowl over a
pan of very gently simmering water.

—— **BONUS BITE** ——

SWISS ROLL

Grease and line a Swiss roll tin/2 sandwich
tins, bringing the paper up over the edges.
Sprinkle well with caster sugar. Whisk 110g
caster sugar with 4 eggs as above till stiff
and foamy. Very gently fold in ½ tsp vanilla
extract, 2 tbsp warm water, grated zest of 1
lemon and 110g sifted plain flour. Pour into
the tin. Bake for 12–15 minutes at 190°C/
Gas 5; it should be high, golden and just
firm. Sprinkle sugar over another piece
of paper. Remove the cake from the oven.
Loosen the edges. Invert onto the sugared
paper. Remove the tin and the paper. Spread
with lemon curd. Use the paper to roll it up.

*Think Swiss roll but in a much neater package. These whisked baby
sponge cakes are great piled with jam, cream and fruit for a sweet tea.
Sort out your technique before moving on to the real deal – Swiss roll
is an impressive favourite.*

PREP Preheat the oven to 180°C/Gas 4. Grease and line 2 baking trays
with baking paper.

Crack the eggs into a large bowl. Add the sugar. Whisk them into a
mousse with an electric hand whisk or in a mixer until pale, thick, stiff and
voluminous. Once the beaters leave a thick trail on top of the mix it's done.
This could take about 8 minutes.

Sift over the flours and add the vanilla extract. Using a large metal spoon, fold
them together very gently in figure-of-eight movements until combined. Take
care to keep it light and airy.

Spoon tablespoons of the mix onto the trays, keeping them well apart to allow
for spreading. Slice the strawberries, if using.

COOK Bake for 9–10 minutes or until the drops are risen and have crispy
golden brown tops. Leave to cool on the trays. Make and chill the
chantilly cream.

PLATE Spread the jam or curd onto the flat sides of half the drops. Top
with cream and raspberries or sliced strawberries. Sandwich with
the remaining drops and dust with icing sugar. Alternatively, top every one of
them. Pile onto a plate with extra whole berries.

SINFUL CHOCOLATE COFFEE CAKE AND ICINGS

FEEDS 8

INGREDIENTS

150g dark chocolate (70% is best),
*   broken into squares*
1 tsp instant coffee granules
125g butter, softened
125g caster sugar
5 eggs, separated
*   (at room temperature)*
75g self-raising flour
1½ tsp baking powder
a pinch of bicarbonate of soda
2 tbsp cocoa powder
finely grated zest of ½ a medium orange
1 tbsp brandy/rum/amaretto
1 tsp vanilla extract
1 tbsp water

—— CHANGE IT UP ——

1. Decorate further to suit any event. Add your choice of candles/fresh cherries/crumbled chocolate flake/chocolate curls/pick 'n' mix sweets/grated chocolate. **2.** For a simple finish, sift 2–3 tbsp icing sugar over your naked cake. **3.** For a chocolate chilli cake, add 1 tbsp chilli flakes to the mix.

—— BONUS BITE ——

CHOCOLATE TORTE

Make the cake up as above. Melt 2 tbsp apricot jam or marmalade gently in a pan. Brush it over the top and sides as it comes out of the oven. Cool. Just before icing, melt 180g dark chocolate, 125g unsalted butter and 1 tbsp golden syrup in a bowl over a pan of water, stirring as it melts. Pour over the cake for a smooth finish.

Rich, decadent and blissfully tempting. Adapt with your choice of gorgeous icings, cloak it in chocolate or leave plain. Dress it up or keep it tasteful. To fill and cover your whole cake, just double up the icing.

PREP Preheat the oven to 160°C/Gas 3. Grease and line the base and sides of a 22cm loose based/spring form tin with baking paper.

Put a small pan a third full of water on a very low heat. Sit an ovenproof bowl on the top, leaving the base clear of water. Add the chocolate pieces and coffee granules and leave until the chocolate has melted (do not stir). Once it's liquid, remove from the heat and stir to dissolve the granules. Let it cool.

Meantime, tip the butter into a large bowl and break it up with a wooden spoon. Add the sugar. Beat for 5 minutes or until the mix is pale, light and fluffy.

Beat the egg yolks. Add them to the mix with the cooled chocolate. Stir well. Sift in the flour, baking powder, bicarbonate of soda and cocoa powder. Add the orange zest. Fold the mix together very lightly with a large metal spoon till incorporated. Stir in the brandy, vanilla extract and water.

Whisk the egg whites in a large clean bowl until stiff, then stir 1 tablespoon into the chocolate mix to loosen it. Add the rest, folding lightly and gently to incorporate. It will resist at first but it will come together. Don't overwork it. Pour into the tin and tip to spread it evenly.

COOK Bake for 45 minutes. Test for doneness – a skewer/toothpick inserted into the middle should come out clean. Remove from the oven and cool on a wire rack for 10 minutes in the tin. Don't worry if the top cracks. Run a blunt knife about the edge of the cake to loosen, release the spring and place a rack or plate over the cake. Invert it. Remove the base. Peel off the lining. Re-invert onto a rack and leave to cool completely.

PLATE Cut the cake in half with a serrated knife. Lift the top half away and lay on the rack. Fill and top with your chosen icing. Slice and eat.

━━━━━━━━━ **ICINGS** ━━━━━━━━━

1 **COFFEE BUTTERCREAM**
Cream 110g softened butter till smooth. Sift 175g icing sugar and beat into the butter gradually till beautifully light. Beat in 2–3 tsp cold strong black coffee, tasting and adjusting. Spoon and smooth a third of the icing over the cut side of one half. Dollop the rest of the icing on the top. Smooth and swirl with a spatula or use a fork to peak and pattern extravagantly.

2 **CHOCOLATE FUDGE**
Melt 110g butter with 1 tbsp strong black coffee and 3 tbsp water. Let it cool a bit. Sift 275g icing sugar and 25g cocoa powder into a bowl. Beat in the butter mix until thick and smooth. If it starts to look odd, add a bit of cold water. Divide between the middle and top as above.

LIME, LEMON AND ELDERFLOWER DRIZZLE CAKE

FEEDS 6

INGREDIENTS

165g self-raising flour
a pinch of baking powder
10g ground almonds
175g butter, softened
170g caster sugar
2 large eggs (at room temperature)
    beaten
grated zest of 1 large lemon
grated zest of 1 large lime
a splash of elderflower cordial
2 tbsp lime juice
1 tbsp lemon juice
3 tbsp milk
DRIZZLE
3 tbsp icing sugar
juice of 2 fat limes
juice of ½ a lemon

——— CHANGE IT UP ———
To make lemon and lime poppy seed
cake, follow the main recipe, using 175g
self-raising flour and omitting the ground
almonds. Add 3–4 tbsp poppy seeds at the
final folding in.

This is a much zingier version of a typical lemon drizzle cake, and much better for it. Make sure to taste both mix and the drizzle and adjust for a good strong bright flavour. Use granulated instead of icing sugar if you like your topping a bit crunchier.

PREP Preheat the oven to 160°C/Gas 3. Grease and line the base and sides of a 900g loaf tin. Sift the flour and baking powder into a bowl. Add the almonds and set aside.

Tip the butter into a separate bowl and break it up with a wooden spoon. Add the sugar and beat furiously for 5 minutes or till pale, light and very creamy. Dribble the beaten egg bit by bit into the mix, beating wildly to incorporate. If it looks like it is splitting, add a bit of flour and keep going.

Sift the flour/almonds into the bowl (tip in any bits which stay in the sieve).

Add the zests. Using a large metal spoon, cut and fold the mixture together with large, light figure-of-eight movements until just combined. Fold in the cordial, juices and milk very gently. Check you have a soft dropping (off the end of the spoon) consistency. Taste the mix. Add a little more juice or milk as appropriate.

COOK Ease the mix gently into the tin. Bake for 50 minutes or till well risen, golden brown and springy to the touch. Test for doneness – a skewer/toothpick inserted into the middle should come out clean. Remove from the oven. The cake will probably lose height but don't worry.

Have the drizzle ready to go. Sift the icing sugar into a bowl, add the juice and mix. Taste to check that it's very zingy, adding more of either citrus juice if it isn't. Prick the hot cake all over with a toothpick/thin skewer. Pour the drizzle evenly over the top. After 10 minutes, use the paper to lift the cake out of the tin. Sit it on a rack. Peel the paper away. Leave to cool.

PLATE Enjoy on the same day with a cuppa. It lasts for 3 days in an airtight container and freezes well.

YORKSHIRE TEA LOAF

FEEDS 12

INGREDIENTS

425ml boiling water
2 Yorkshire teabags
200g raisins
100g currants/sultanas
75g caster sugar
30g crystallised ginger, diced
grated zest of ½ a small orange
grated zest of ½ a lemon
60g glacé cherries
30g walnuts, roughly chopped
2 medium eggs, beaten
270g plain white flour
½ tsp mixed spice

—— CHANGE IT UP ——

1. For an earl grey and fig loaf, switch the Yorkshire tea bags for earl grey tea bags and add 6 chopped dried figs to the raisins and sultanas before proceeding as above.

2. For a rum and orange loaf, omit the tea. Mix 350ml boiling water with 50ml orange juice and 25ml dark rum and use this to soak the sultanas and raisins. Add the 50g chopped dates to the tea mixture when adding the remaining fruit and proceed as before.

3. For a tea, prune, date & walnut loaf, add 50g chopped dates to the soaking fruit before adding 30g each of chopped dates and walnuts when adding the remaining flavourings.

I love Yorkshire tea. I love cake. The relationship was inevitable. This one's so easy and delightfully fruity. Get it going the night before.

PREP Pour the boiling water into a measuring jug. Add the teabags. Let it brew for 5 minutes. Discard the bags. Pour the hot tea into a heatproof bowl with the raisins and currants and leave to cool, covered, overnight or for at least 6 hours.

Preheat the oven to 150°C/Gas 2.

Grease and line a large loaf tin (20 x 10 x 7cm). Add the sugar, ginger, zest, a mix of halved and whole glacé cherries and the walnuts to the tea mixture. Stir well, mixing in the beaten eggs.

Sift the flour and mixed spice into the mix. Beat everything together and pour into the tin.

COOK Bake for about 1½ hours, until risen and golden brown. Stick in a toothpick/skewer to test – it should come out clean (double-check. It might have just hit a cherry). Give it longer if it needs it. Leave it to rest on a rack for 15 minutes. Remove from the tin to cool. Peel off the lining paper.

PLATE Slice when cold using a serrated knife. Eat as it is or spread with butter and top with slices of Wensleydale, cheddar or Lancashire cheese. Have it plain with coffee or tea, or enjoy as part of a picnic lunch with celery, cheese, bread and pickles.

GINGER APPLE LOAF WITH BUTTERSCOTCH ICING

FEEDS 8

Unashamedly attention-seeking; you've got sweet butterscotch fudge and a moist gingery cake with just a hint of lovely healthy apple.

INGREDIENTS

175g self-raising flour
3–4 tsp ground ginger
a pinch of cinnamon
½–1 tsp mixed spice
50g soft brown sugar
50g soft butter
2 medium eggs
½ tbsp black treacle
1½ tbsp golden syrup
1 large eating apple, diced into 1cm
    cubes
15g crystallised ginger, diced
    (optional)
150ml milk
1 tsp bicarbonate of soda

BUTTERSCOTCH ICING

75g butter
100g brown sugar
60ml cream
125g icing sugar
½ tsp vanilla extract
a few pieces of crystallised ginger
    (optional)

—— CHANGE IT UP ——

1. Add 30g whole glacé cherries to the mix.
2. Grate in half a carrot and add together with 15g finely chopped walnuts.

PREP Preheat the oven to 180°C/Gas 4. Grease and line the base of a large loaf tin (20 x 10 x 7cm).

Sift the flour, ginger, cinnamon and mixed spice into a large bowl. Add the sugar. Add the butter in bits then incorporate by rubbing it in between your fingertips. Beat in the eggs, treacle and golden syrup using a wooden spoon to make a smooth batter. Stir in two-thirds of the apple and the crystallised ginger, if using.

Heat the milk in a saucepan until just boiling. Remove from the heat and pour slowly into the batter, stirring as you go. Stir in the bicarbonate of soda.

Pour the mix into the tin and scatter the remaining apple pieces over the top.

COOK Bake the cake for 40–60 minutes or until a toothpick/skewer comes out clean. Cool it in the tin for 15 minutes and then turn it out. Strip away the lining paper. Leave on a rack to cool completely.

Meanwhile, make the icing by melting the butter and sugar over a low heat, stirring until the sugar has dissolved. Slowly add the cream, stirring, and continue to cook until the mix is thick and glossy. It will spit but that's fine. Remove from the heat. Leave to cool then sift over the icing sugar and add the vanilla. Beat well until smooth.

Once the cake is completely cooled, smother it with the icing. Smooth it out with a spatula for a polished look or keep it rough and rustic. Decorate with a few extra pieces of ginger sliced on the diagonal, if you're using it.

PLATE Serve as a whole and slice in front of guests, or just nick a slice every now and then for a perfect complement to a cup of tea.

BONUS BITE

CHOCOLATE APPLE MUFFINS

Sift 200g plain flour, 2 tsp baking powder, ½ tsp bicarbonate of soda and 25g cocoa powder into a bowl. In a separate bowl beat together 2 eggs, 75g caster sugar, 2 tbsp sunflower oil, the grated zest and juice of ½ orange and 150ml cold milk. Add this mixture to the flour, whisking together with a fork, until you have a lumpy batter. Add 50g broken chocolate buttons and half an eating apple, cut into chunks. Spoon into 8 muffin cases and bake for 15 minutes at 200°C/Gas 6 until risen and firm. Cool on a rack.

RASPBERRY RIPPLE
CHEESECAKE

FEEDS 12

INGREDIENTS

BASE
225g ginger biscuits
50g butter
RIPPLE
150g raspberries
2 tsp caster sugar
FILLING
900g soft cream cheese
  (at room temperature)
225g caster sugar
2 tsp vanilla extract
200ml sour cream
125ml double cream
4 tbsp plain white flour
1 tbsp cornflour
4 eggs (at room temperature)
juice of 4 limes, plus grated zest of 2
juice of 1 lemon
255g white chocolate, melted

✳✳✳✳   CASH SAVER   ✳✳✳✳

Use frozen raspberries; or buy cheap in
summer and freeze your own.

·········· TIME SAVER ··········

The base and purée can be made a day
ahead. Just refrigerate until needed.

TIP
For a clean edge to your cheesecake slices, cut with a sharp knife you've dipped in hot water then dried.

Here's your traditional New York Cheesecake, but the raspberry ripple takes it somewhere else. Watch out for cracks…enjoy!

PREP Base: Break the biscuits up a bit then pulse/blitz them in a food processor until fine, or tip into a freezer bag and bash them with a rolling pin. Melt the butter gently in a pan. Remove from the heat, add the fine crumbs and stir well. Press the mix down over the base of a 20cm loose-bottomed cake tin. Chill.

RIPPLE: Tip the raspberries and sugar into a small pan. Heat very gently, stirring till the fruits fully release their juices. Tip the mix into a sieve over a bowl. Push the fruit through with the back of a wooden spoon, discarding the seeds left in the sieve. Scrape any extra puree left on the other side of the sieve. Set aside.

Preheat the oven to 170°C/Gas 3 (low heat means less chance of cracking).

FILLING: Get a big mixing bowl. Add the cream cheese and stir to loosen it up with a wooden spoon. Stir in the sugar, vanilla extract, sour and double cream, then sift the flour and cornflour over the mix. Stir together using a metal spoon. Don't beat it.

Crack the eggs into a bowl and beat well with a fork. Dribble them into the mix gradually, stirring rapidly with the wooden spoon until fully absorbed. Add the lime zest and lemon and lime juice.

Break the chocolate into bits, tip into a heatproof bowl, sit over a pan of barely simmering water (with the base clear) and leave until melted. Remove from the heat and stir till smooth. Cool for a minute before stirring into the egg mix.

Get the tin from the fridge. Pour in half to two-thirds of the mix. Smooth to the edges of the tin using a spatula or back of a metal spoon. Drizzle the raspberry purée over the top in irregular lines or swirls. Spoon over the remaining mix and smooth it gently to the edges.

COOK Bake in the oven for 35–40 minutes until firm-ish at the edges but only just set and still wobbly in the centre when the tin is shaken a bit. Turn off the oven, leaving the cake in there for an hour as it cools down. (Take it out now and it will crack and won't firm up enough.) Remove from the cooled oven and place on a rack for 10 minutes to rest. Carefully run a thin blunt knife between cake and tin to loosen, then pop the cake back in the oven with the door open and leave for another hour. Take the cheesecake from the oven and leave to cool before removing the sides of the tin and chilling in the fridge for 2 hours.

PLATE Serve plain, or dot with a layer of raspberries or summer berries.

Puddings

The 'pudding' - a word normally followed by the phrases 'oh I shouldn't', 'oh go on then', 'why not?' and, finally, 'mmmmm'. The world of the dessert tends to divide people. Some have savoury palates while so many others have sweet. It's much the same in the kitchen. There are some people out there who go crazy for making puddings and others who could do without. In this section,

I promise you that whatever your taste and preference, you'll find some absolutely gorgeous treats. From the humble crumble to a sinful triple chocolate tart this section ain't light on the skill set. So pick up your fork, your spoon, your whisk and rolling pin. Wherever your palate is coming from, this chapter will sort you out with some classic techniques.

THE PUDDING ROOM
BASIC INGREDIENTS

You need the proper stuff to make a proper pudding; from your supermarket or your farmer's market it's all out there and easy to get hold of.

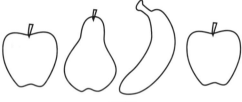

FRUIT

Get in season and locally if you can. Select by touch, smell and looks (though this final test can be deceptive – it's often the prettiest fruit that don't taste as good). Get loose rather than bagged so you can check the state of it. Get berries off-season in frozen packs for purées, ice-cream and sorbets. Look out for other fruit in the freezer cabinet or freeze your own if that's what you're into.

CHOCOLATE

70% cocoa solids are best for cooking. Shop around for a brand you trust. Go fair trade.

•••• *Melting* CHOCOLATE ••••

Break chocolate into a bowl. Sit it into the top of pan which is a third full of gently simmering water. Don't let the base touch the water. Chocolate melts at a low temperature so will seize and solidify if too hot. Contact with a single drop of cold liquid has the same effect. Leave it to melt. Stir with a chopstick to avoid wasting it. If you're adding liquids to chocolate to melt, they must be warm.

LEMONS

Buy unwaxed if you need to zest them. Always have some in.

CREAM

Get one that's fit for purpose. **SINGLE**: for pouring only. It splits if boiled and won't whip. Swirl into soups and pour on puddings.
DOUBLE: here's your best cooking cream as it boils without splitting; downside is it's fattier. It whips well. **WHIPPING** cream does what it says on the tin and tastes less fatty (it is). You can substitute for double cream in some cooking. **CRÈME FRAÎCHE**: has a slightly sour taste. Serve it with tarts and fresh fruit – it won't split when heated. **CLOTTED CREAM**: rich and thick and can transform the simplest pudding.

EGGS & SUGAR
see p198

BUTTER

Comes in salted and unsalted form. Chefs swear by unsalted butter for baking. It's got a fresher taste, is healthier and affects the quality of your pastry.

FLOUR

Supermarkets sell a whole range of different flours from independent mills and with different blends of grain and organic options. Experiment and find a good one.

VANILLA

Comes in different guises. Buy natural vanilla extract for ease and value – find a brand you love. Vanilla paste contains seeds. A vanilla pod is the real deal. Keep one in for special occasions. Split and scrape for ice-creams and puddings.

SYRUPS

Honey, maple, golden. They're all useful sources of sugar, particularly in old-school puddings.

Golden Syrup

Weighing out golden syrup can be a challenge. But 1 tablespoon is equivalent to 25g. To be accurate, sit the tin on your scales and note the weight. Spoon syrup out until the weight is reduced by the designated amount.

Make Your Own
VANILLA SUGAR

Keep used vanilla pods. Wash and dry them well. Store in a jar of caster sugar.

GELATINE

A must for jelly makers. It comes in leaf or powder form. Vegetarians can use agar-agar instead.

CINNAMON

Use sticks for flavouring compotes. Ground is convenient.

CARDAMOM

Keep a stock for partnering with fruit and sweet things.

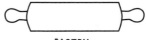

PASTRY

FILO Too epic to make at home so buy it in packs – it comes in long rectangular or square sheets.
PUFF Keep a good all-butter puff pastry in the freezer for when you feel a pie coming on. All-butter means no unhealthy trans-fats.

PUDDING NUTRITION

Let's not pretend this is the healthiest chapter but there's valuable stuff in here still. YOGHURT PACKS LOADS OF

Calcuim

FOR BONE BUILDING AND MAINTENANCE. BLUEBERRIES ARE PACKED WITH

VITAMIN C

WHICH STRENGTHENS THE IMMUNE SYSTEM APPLES ARE RICH IN

FIBRE

which lowers cholesterol and are a good source of

CHROMIUM & QUERCITIN

PISTACHIOS & ALMONDS ARE A GOOD SOURCE OF

COPPER

which is good for skin, hair eyes, WHILE RASPBERRIES ARE LOADED WITH **CALCIUM** AND

SULPHUR

which helps regulate blood sugar levels and boosts hair and skin and nail health. GRAPEFRUIT CONTAINS

FOLIC ACID, VITAMIN C

AND HIGH LEVELS OF

Bioflavonoids

which boost the immune system.

PLUMS CONTAIN

POTASSIUM

helping control blood pressure and regulating fluid in the body WHILE CHOCOLATE RELEASES

MOOD-ENHANCING ENDORPHINS

with the dark stuff high in

IRON and ANTIOXIDANTS

BUTTER UNSALTED lasts 3 months in the fridge and SALTED lasts 6 months.

SPICES Keep them in the dark with the tops firmly on or they lose strength.

CHOCOLATE Has a shelf life in theory although that's never an issue in my house...

FRUIT BERRIES have a very short shelf life. Get them straight into the fridge. BLUEBERRIES last longer than others. BANANAS emit ethylene gas which causes other fruit and vegetables to rot quickly so store them separately.

APPLES Best kept in the fridge. PEARS Best bought under-ripe and stored in the fridge. SUPERMARKET FRUIT Often seems to be on the edge so check it frequently and throw rotten stuff away before it contaminates anything else.

PUFF PASTRY Keep some in the freezer.

OWN PASTRY Freeze it uncooked wrapped in freezer bags for a month or store uncooked but wrapped in the fridge for 1 day. BAKED TARTS can be stored in airtight containers for 3 days.

CREAM – *Whip it*

Some people over-whip cream and it goes grainy. Or it won't thicken at all. Check this out: keep cream refrigerated always. Even a few minutes at room temperature or near a heat source can inhibit it. Whisk it in a large wide bowl so it's got air to feed on. Do it with a metal balloon whisk so you can sense the feel of your cream as it thickens and you'll know when to stop (not possible with an electric machine). Hold the bowl at an angle as you whip. Softly whipped cream holds in a soft peak. Use this for spooning onto your puddings. Stiffly whipped cream is better for piping.

SUGAR SYRUP
FOR FRUIT SALAD

Use this simple little sugar syrup to jazz up a fruit salad.

Put 250g sugar and ½ litre of water in a heavy-based pan. Heat very slowly, stirring, so the sugar dissolves completely. Only then let it boil. Stop stirring. Boil for 2 minutes. Leave to cool. Chill it and pour over your fruit. If you like you can add aromatics.

MAKING PASTRY
COOL TIPS *(for hot hands)*

COOL your hands in very cold water

AVOID making pastry on a hot day or close to a heat source

FLOUR everything in sight

Use **CHILLED** butter

MEASURE the ingredients accurately – proportions matter

Work **QUICKLY** and gently or the pastry will toughen up as you stimulate the gluten

Use the right **SIZE** tin

ROTATE the pastry as you roll it

RUN a floured spatula under it if it sticks to the pastry board

To transport, **ROLL** over your rolling pin and gently lay it down

PATCH it up with extra pastry or the filling may leak

Use a bit of **EXCESS** pastry to press the rest into the sides of the pastry tin

Leave a pastry **OVERHANG** so if the pastry shrinks a bit you're safe

PRICK the base so it doesn't rise

CHILL your pastry for the required time so it cooks properly

Buy some ceramic **BAKING BEANS** (or use dried beans)

Check out the recipes for how to bake **BLIND**

Get your oven **TEMPERATURE** right – too low and it may slide down the tin and flatten, too hot and it may catch

PASTRY *secrets*
To calculate the size of pastry needed to line a tin, use the string test. Lay a piece of string down into and across the widest part of your tin. Measure it. Add extra for the overhang. There's your dimension.

GELATINE
Handler

Gelatine is a tricky beast to master. It comes in granule form (see packet instructions) and leaf form – my choice. To tame it, use 4 gelatine leaves to set 600ml of liquid (use 5 sheets for fruit terrine or a firmer set). Snip each leaf with scissors and put it into a bowl with 3 tablespoons of your cool liquid. Leave it to soak for 10 minutes. Sit the bowl over a pan of simmering water. Let it melt. Add it to the rest of your liquid. For jelly: pour it into wetted moulds (for turning out) or into glasses. Cool. Chill until set.

LOOKING SWEET
A FEW POINTERS FOR ARTISTIC PRESENTATION

Serve simple things in **PRETTY DISHES**

FROST GLASSES: chill in the fridge or quickly in the freezer. Cool for ice-cream

STEAM GLASSES upside down over a kettle. Dust with sifted icing sugar

DUNK STEMMED BERRIES strawberries and physalis into melted chocolate

GRATE CHOCOLATE or crumble chocolate flake over an ice-cream, meringue or creamy pudding

DUST THE DESSERT world in icing sugar

MAKE SHATTERED CARAMEL
Melt 50g sugar slowly, no stirring, in a heavy pan until a light caramel colour. Remove. Cool for a minute then pour onto silicone baking paper. Let it set. Shatter it. Use over ice-cream, sundaes or meringues.

BLUEBERRY, BLACKBERRY AND STRAWBERRY CRUMBLE

FEEDS 4-6

INGREDIENTS

CRUMBLE MASTER TOPPING

175g butter
160g white self-raising flour
a pinch of salt
75g ground almonds
60g caster sugar
40g demerara sugar
a few drops of water to finish

FILLING

450g strawberries
400g blueberries
300g blackberries
3–4 tsp caster sugar

········· **TIME SAVER** ·········

1. Make crumble topping up to a day ahead and chill. Add the water before adding to the dish.
2. Use the normal rubbing in method with cold butter rather than frozen.

──── **BONUS BITE** ────

BAKED FRUIT MERINGUE

Make up a batch of basic white meringue (p240). Pack 4 small greased dishes with your choice of fruit base and pipe or dot the meringue over the top. Bake at 180°C/Gas 4 for 20–30 minutes until the fruit is cooked (test with a skewer in the centre) and the meringue top has crisped up.

A lovely buttery summery crumble; this one's perfect for a crowd. Give it a go then try out the other seasonal options. For crumble for one: make and freeze a batch of topping. Prep an individual dish of any fruit combination you fancy. Throw on as much crumble as you need. Bake for 15–20 minutes. Always make custard….

PREP

For the topping: Wrap the butter in foil and put it in the freezer at least an hour before you want to cook (or the night before) so you can grate it easily. Sift the flour, salt and ground almonds into a large bowl. Add any nutty sediment left in the sieve. Grate the frozen butter coarsely onto the mix in big loose curls. Add the sugars. Mix everything together very lightly with a fork. Set aside.

Preheat the oven to 200°C/Gas 6. Grease a large rectangular ovenproof dish (25 x 19 cm). Wash and dry the fruit. Hull the strawberries. Halve any large ones. Tip the fruit into the dish and mix it up. Sprinkle with sugar.

Finish the topping: Flick just a few drops of very cold water over the mix and run a fork through it to make it even crumblier. Top the fruit: scatter the mix lightly and evenly over the top without pressing it down.

COOK

Bake in the oven for 30 minutes, reducing the heat to 190°C/Gas 5 halfway through cooking. The crumble should be golden-topped with hot fruit bubbling at the edges – cover with baking paper/foil if it starts to darken. Stick a metal skewer into the centre for 5 seconds then hold it against your wrist to check it's properly hot in the middle.

PLATE

Remove from the oven and leave to settle for 5 minutes. Sit the dish on the table. Spoon out onto plates. Serve with custard (p236), clotted, Chantilly or cinnamon-spiced whipped cream, vanilla ice-cream (p236) or thick Greek yoghurt with vanilla and honey.

──── **CHANGE IT UP** ────

1 APPLE AND BLACKBERRY CRUMBLE
Peel, core and roughly chop 700g sharp eating apples. Tip them into an ovenproof dish with 110g blackberries. Sprinkle with sugar. Top and bake as above for 30–40 minutes.

2 PLUM, PEACH AND RASPBERRY CRUMBLE
Grease an ovenproof dish. Cut 6 peaches and 6 plums around their centres down to the stone. Twist the halves in opposite directions to separate. Remove the stones. Chop the flesh roughly. Throw into the dish with 200g raspberries. Sprinkle with 3 tsp sugar. Top and bake as above.

3 RHUBARB AND GINGER CRUMBLE
Grease an ovenproof dish. Trim the ends off 750g rhubarb. Wash, dry and slice into 2.5 cm lengths. Tip into a large pan with 4 tbsp water and 3–4 tsp sugar. Cook gently on low heat for 3–4 minutes until it just begins to soften. Taste for sweetness, adding a bit more sugar if you need to. Tip fruit and liquid into your dish. Add 10–20 pieces of chopped crystallised ginger, 110g halved strawberries and a squeeze of lemon juice. Add topping. Bake as above.

BAKED BLACKBERRY STUFFED APPLES WITH MERINGUE TOPPING

FEEDS 2

INGREDIENTS

2 eating apples
a little butter for greasing and topping
a squeeze of lemon juice
4 large blackberries
6 tbsp cider/apple juice/diluted
*   elderflower cordial/white wine*
MERINGUE TOPPING
1 egg white
50g caster sugar

—— CHANGE IT UP ——

1. Fill each apple with your choice of the following: maple syrup and butter/1 tbsp lemon curd/a small piece of marzipan and a dab of butter.

2. Stuff with a mix of 10g finely chopped walnuts, 2 chopped dates, 25g soft butter, 5g diced crystallised ginger and ½ tbsp brown sugar. Top with butter.

········ TIME SAVER ········

Leave off the meringue and make plain stuffed baked apples.

Deliciously soft and flavoursome baked fruit with a soft crispy topping; also try this with big halved peaches.

PREP Preheat the oven to 180°C/Gas 4. Butter a shallow ovenproof dish.

Core the apples but leave the base intact so the filling doesn't leak out. Score a thin line around the centre of each fruit so it won't burst during cooking. Squeeze a few drops of lemon juice into each cavity. Add 2 blackberries to each and top with butter.

COOK Sit the apples, open-end upwards, in the dish. Spoon in the cider or other liquid. Bake for 20 minutes or until the fruit is well on its way to being tender (squeeze to get an idea). Baste them once or twice, spooning over any juices.

Make the meringue topping ten minutes into cooking. Whisk the egg white in a grease-free bowl for a few seconds till white and frothy. Add a teaspoon of sugar. Whisk to amalgamate. Add another. Repeat. When it's all in, whisk for about 4 minutes until the mixture is glossy, thick and stands in stiff peaks.

Remove the apples from the oven. Heap meringue onto the top of each one like a hat or pipe it from a piping bag fitted with a large nozzle into a stylish swirl. Bake for another 15 minutes plus or until the fruit is tender inside, crisp and browning on top.

PLATE Eat straight from the dish to enjoy the lovely juices. These are great with chilled Greek yoghurt and honey or low-fat crème fraîche whipped with icing sugar.

BONUS BITES

BAKED CINNAMON APPLE
Stew 4 peeled chopped apples with a good pinch of cinnamon, 2 tsp caster sugar, 2 tsp lemon juice, 1 tsp butter and 2 tbsp water (you may need a bit more). Stir over a low heat to get a thick puree. Pour into an ovenproof dish and leave to cool. Make up meringue as above and cover. Bake in a preheated oven at 180°C/Gas 4 for 15 minutes.

FIGS ON FRENCH TOAST
Cut 4 large or 8 small figs in two lengthways. Beat 2 small eggs in a wide shallow bowl with 2 tbsp sour cream, ½ tsp vanilla extract, a pinch of cinnamon and ½ tbsp sugar. Sit 4 brioche slices in the mix for 1–2 minutes a side. Put them on a rack. Heat a little butter in a small frying pan on a gentle heat. Add the figs to heat through for 1–2 minutes. Set aside. Increase the heat a bit and add the brioche. Fry for 2–3 minutes a side until hot and golden brown. Dust with a little sifted icing sugar, top with the figs and drizzle with a little honey or maple syrup.

SUMMER ROAST PEACHES

FEEDS 1

INGREDIENTS

a little butter for greasing
1 large peach per person (size and appetite dependent)
a squeeze of lemon juice
4 tbsp white wine/fruit juice/amaretto
TOPPING 1
½ tsp cinnamon
1 tsp caster sugar
1 tsp butter
TOPPING 2
1 tsp maple syrup or runny honey
1 tsp butter
TOPPING 3
1 tsp demerara/vanilla sugar
1 tsp butter

—— CHANGE IT UP ——

Use raspberries to make up a fresh berry sauce (p239). Pour over the warm peaches.

—— BONUS BITES ——

BAKED PEACH MERINGUE
Sit a fresh or frozen raspberry in each peach cavity. Make up a white meringue topping (p240) and use this to cover the fruit. Bake for 20 minutes or till the fruit is cooked and meringue crisp. Serve surrounded by a raspberry fresh berry sauce (p239).

FRYING PAN BAKED PEARS
Preheat the oven to 180°C/Gas 4. Melt 15g butter in a metal handled pan. Add 2 tsp caster sugar, a pinch of cinnamon and a good squeeze of lemon juice. Stir. Halve 4 small pears lengthways. Sit them, cut-side down in the pan. After 3 minutes, transfer to the oven to cook for a further 15 minutes or until tender.

Slap these in the oven for a luscious summer pudding. When peaches aren't about, use apricots or nectarines instead. Plums are usually around through the winter. The quantities given below are for 1 peach so adjust accordingly.

PREP Preheat the oven to 180°C/Gas 4. Lightly butter a shallow ovenproof dish or tin.

Cut the peaches in half lengthways. Twist to separate the halves. Remove the stones. Sit them cut side up in the dish/tin. Squeeze a little lemon juice over each one.

Topping 1: Mix the cinnamon and sugar with the butter. Stuff into the cavity and coat the top. Topping 2: Fill the cavity with maple syrup or honey. Top with butter. Topping 3: Dredge with demerara or vanilla sugar. Top with butter.

Add your choice of liquid to the dish or use a bit more butter on your fruit.

COOK Roast the fruit until soft, bubbling and slightly caramelised (20–40 minutes, size and ripeness dependent). Check and baste with their juices every so often.

PLATE Rest the fruit for a minute or two before eating. Sprinkle with flaked almonds or pistachios if you want. Eat as they are with their juices or top with clotted cream or vanilla ice-cream. Alternatively, enjoy with French toast (p231). Good warm or cold.

RHUBARB JELLY

FEEDS 4

INGREDIENTS

900g rhubarb, cut into 5cm lengths
110g caster sugar
½ tbsp elderflower cordial
5cm piece of fresh ginger, sliced
1.2 litres water
6 sheets gelatine
½ pint chilled sparkling white wine/
    pear cider/elderflower pressé/
    champagne

✳✳✳✳ **CASH SAVER** ✳✳✳✳

Use the poached fruit as the base for a
crumble or mix it up with yoghurt and
muesli and banana for a healthy breakfast.
Use any leftover juice in cocktails or
smoothies.

········· TIME SAVER ·········

Make the rhubarb juice the day ahead.

Who would have thought this would work? Sticks of bog standard rhubarb transformed into an elegant dessert. Get your gelatine skills sorted and team it with custardy vanilla ice-cream for a reworking of a childhood classic.

PREP Preheat the oven to 200°C/Gas 6. Cut the rhubarb into 5cm lengths, cutting off and discarding any leaves. Bang it into a roasting tin with the sugar, cordial, ginger and water. Cook for 20 minutes until tender. Or put it all in a pan and bring to the boil. Reduce the heat to a minimum and barely simmer until the fruit is soft and the flavours infused. Remove and leave to cool.

Sit a fine sieve over a bowl. Line it with muslin if you have some. Pour the cold fruit and its juice in and leave it to drip through. Don't mess with it or press the fruit – a pure drip means a clear jelly. Measure out a pint of the liquid. Recycle the poached fruit/jelly (see left).

Cut the gelatine sheets into large, rough bits. Sit them in a dish and cover with cold water. Leave to soak and soften up for 10 minutes, or as the pack instructs.

COOK Put a third of the juice into a pan on a very low heat. Pour the water away from the soaked gelatine and squeeze out any excess. Add the softened gelatine to the warm liquid in the pan, stirring with a wooden spoon as it dissolves. It should take a few seconds only and you'll see it's suddenly clear. Remove from the heat and add to the remaining two-thirds of the juice immediately. Leave to cool for 10 minutes.

Add your bubbles of choice. Rinse a serving bowl or jelly mould with cold water. Pour the jelly in. Shake it. Or pour it into individual glasses. Chill for a few hours or overnight.

PLATE Serve the glasses as they are or top with vanilla ice-cream. To unmould a jelly, run a blunt knife down one side to release the air. Invert it onto a plate and shake to release. Remove the mould. This jelly's good with a crisp tuiles biscuit (p251) or brandy snap (p213).

VANILLA
ICE-CREAM

MAKES 700G ICE-CREAM

INGREDIENTS

250ml milk
1 vanilla pod or 4 drops of natural
   vanilla extract
4 egg yolks
110g caster sugar
250ml whipping/double cream

—— BONUS BITE ——

HONEYCOMB ICE-CREAM

Make the basic vanilla ice-cream as right.
Put it into your machine to churn or into
the freezer if making by hand. Chop 1–2
chocolate-coated honeycomb bars into
smallish bits. By machine: Stop the ice-
cream maker just as the mix has set, add the
honeycomb pieces and churn for another 30
seconds to distribute. Transfer to a chilled
plastic container and freeze. By hand: Stir
the honeycomb pieces into the ice-cream
after the final beating process.

—— CHANGE IT UP ——

1. Add chunks of homemade or
bought meringue or bits of your favourite
chopped chocolate bars to the ice-cream
before freezing.
2. Fold in ripples of lemon curd,
butterscotch or fresh berry sauce just
before freezing
3. For fruity ice-creams, blitz up 250ml
thick mango/raspberry/banana/blackcurrant
purée and add to the basic custard before
churning.

TIP
The base you make here (before cooling)
is the classic custard sauce in its own right.
Enjoy with everything from apple pie to
crumble to Bakewell tart.

*Where would the world be without ice-cream? I'm guessing a much
sadder place. Desserts would be incomplete. Wafer cones would be
redundant. Ok it may be easier to pick up a tub from the shop but it's
nowhere near as special. This vanilla is the mother of them all. But feel
free to add other bits and pieces, and purées.*

PREP
Pour the milk into a heavy-bottomed pan. Split the vanilla pod
lengthways down the centre. Scrape out the seeds with the blade of
a knife. Add to the milk with the pod. Or use extract. Bring the milk almost to
boiling point, watching, so it doesn't boil over. Remove from the heat. Leave it
for 20 minutes so the flavour can infuse.

Pour some cold water into a bowl or a sink for cooling the custard later.

To make the custard: Tip the egg yolks and sugar into a large bowl. Beat with a
balloon whisk until the mix is frothy enough to leave a trail on the surface.

Reheat the milk until almost boiling. Remove from the hob and pour over the
sugar and egg mix in the bowl, beating continuously with a wooden spoon.
Pour it back into the pan and return to a very low heat. Stir continuously
until the sauce is thick enough to coat the back of a wooden spoon. Don't be
tempted to rush this process or the mix may split. Beat hard and dunk the pan
in your cold water if this happens.

Sit the pan in the cold water to cool. Stir occasionally. When it's cold, add the
cream. Put a freezer-proof plastic container into the freezer to pre-chill.

FREEZE
If you're using an ice-cream machine, pour the mix in and
churn as per your machine's guidelines (usually 20 minutes).
Once set, spoon it into the chilled container and freeze. By hand: chill your
shallow container in the freezer for an hour. Add the cold mix and freeze for
3 hours. Remove. Bang the ice-cream into a bowl or processor and beat to
break down the ice crystals. Return to the container and freeze for another
hour. Repeat this process twice or even 3 times, beating each hour, until the
ice-cream is wonderfully creamy. Store to freeze until you need it.

PLATE
Remove from the freezer 10 minutes before you need it. Use an
ice-cream scoop or tablespoon dunked in very hot water to scoop
it out into neat balls. Sit alongside a piece of hot fruit tart or crumble. Use in
meringue sundaes. Or drizzle with fresh berry, hot chocolate or salted caramel
sauces (p238–9) and enjoy.

GRAPEFRUIT WATER ICE

Cut 4–5 fat juicy grapefruit in half on a board. Save any stray juice. Juice them with a juicer or by hand, squeezing out every bit. Measure out 500ml grapefruit juice and strain through a fine sieve into a bowl. Add 110g caster sugar and stir to dissolve. By machine: Churn for 30 minutes or until set. Transfer it to a pre-chilled plastic container. Freeze until needed. By hand: pour into a shallow container and freeze. Remove every 30 minutes over a 2-hour period and break the ice crystals up with a fork. Once smooth, leave it frozen. Let the ice relax for 5–10 minutes before serving. Shape into balls with an ice-cream scoop to serve in a dish or scrape it out and serve in shot glasses with a spoon – this is strong stuff!

RASPBERRY VODKA SORBET

Tip 200g caster sugar and 200ml cold water into a small heavy-based pan. Heat slowly to dissolve the sugar, stirring a couple of times until it looks clear. Increase the heat and bring to the boil. Simmer for 1 minute then remove from the heat and leave to cool. Tip 450g raspberries, 2 tbsp lemon juice and 2 tbsp vodka into a processor and blitz to a smooth purée. Push the puree through a sieve into a bowl with a wooden spoon. By machine: Add 2 beaten egg whites to the purée and cold sugar syrup and churn until frozen. Transfer to the freezer in a pre-chilled plastic box. By hand: Mix together the fruit and cold syrup and pour into a shallow freezer-proof container. Freeze it for an hour plus or until large crystals are forming. Tip it into a processor or bowl and beat until it breaks up. Add the beaten egg whites to the mix and return to the freezer. Remove every 30 minutes over a 2-hour period and break the ice crystals up with a fork. Freeze until needed.

HONEY, LIME AND LEMON FROZEN YOGHURT

Wash, dry and grate 3 large unwaxed lemons and 1–2 limes. Tip the zest and squeeze the juice into a large bowl with 1 tbsp honey, a few drops of vanilla essence and 110g sifted sugar. Spoon 300ml plain Greek yoghurt, 175ml whipping cream and 2 tbsp ice cold water into another bowl. Whisk until it starts to thicken. Add to the juices and stir in gently. Pour the mix into a shallow plastic freezer-proof box. Freeze until needed.

CHOCOLATE SAUCE

Fit a heatproof bowl into the top of a pan that's a quarter full of water. Check that the base of the bowl doesn't touch the liquid. Break 250g good quality dark chocolate into squares. Drop them into the bowl with 1 tsp vanilla extract, 6 tbsp water and 170g golden syrup. Put the pan on to a very gentle heat. Let the contents melt slowly, stirring sometimes until the mix is liquid and smooth. Take the bowl off the pan and leave it to cool completely. Stir in 150ml single cream. Use now or store in a clean jam jar and chill till needed. The sauce will solidify, so reheat it very gently to return to pouring consistency.

SALTED CARAMEL SAUCE

Put 25g butter, 2 tbsp golden syrup, 175g soft brown sugar, 1 tsp vanilla extract and a pinch of vanilla or sea salt into a pan. Bring to the boil for 30 seconds. Remove from the heat and stir in 4 tbsp single cream. Use straight away or store in a jar until needed.

FRESH BERRY SAUCE

Tip 225g raspberries/strawberries/blackberries into a processor with a squeeze of lemon and a splash of water. Sieve over ¾ tbsp icing sugar, then blitz in the food processor or with a stick blender until smooth. Tip the purée into a sieve over a bowl and push it through with the back of a spoon. Taste and adjust the sweet/sour balance. A tablespoon of crème de cassis adds a nice note, if you've got any about. Chill till needed.

SAUCES

BOUTIQUE MERINGUES

MAKES UP TO 50 MINI-MERINGUES OR 12 SHELLS

INGREDIENTS

WHITE MERINGUE MIX
4 eggs
225g white caster sugar
BROWN MERINGUE MIX
4 eggs
110g light soft brown sugar
110g caster sugar

1 x chantilly cream (p216, optional)

―――― **CHANGE IT UP** ――――

1. For glazed meringues, sprinkle a little caster sugar over the meringues before cooking. **2.** For chocolate meringues, coarsely grate 225g dark chocolate and fold gently into the white meringue mix before shaping into large shells. **3.** For mocha meringues, whisk 1 tsp coffee granules into the white sugar mix. Dip the cooled cooked meringues in melted chocolate to finish.

Style it up or style it down – meringue's got everything going for it: taste, looks and wow-factor. Go for the classic white option or the brown alternative.

PREP Start by de-greasing your equipment. Dunk a large bowl (glass or metal preferably) and the beaters from your whisk into boiling water. Dry them well. Preheat the oven to 150°C/Gas 2. Separate your eggs with grease-free hands (p153) putting the whites into the dry bowl. If any yolk escapes into it, start again. For white meringues: Measure the caster sugar out into a cup. For brown: Mix the two sugars together.

Whisk the egg whites for a few seconds. As soon as they've reached the white and foamy stage, add a teaspoon of your chosen sugar. Whisk it in for a minute. Add another spoonful. Whisk it in. Repeat. Once it's all in, continue to whisk until the mix is glossy, thick and stands in stiff peaks when flicked. It could take 5 minutes.

Line 2 large baking trays with greaseproof or silicone-coated baking paper. Dab a bit of meringue in each corner and centre to stick down. For big shells: Spoon one or two heaped tablespoons of mix onto the trays, keeping it smooth or teasing it into peaks. Leave space between each. For mini-meringues: Dot teaspoons of mix onto the trays or fit a piping bag with a large/medium nozzle. Pipe it in small rounds. Reduce the oven to 140°C/Gas 1.

COOK Bake the white or brown meringues for 1½ hours for larger shells, 45 minutes to 1 hour for small ones. If they lift easily off the baking paper they are done. For chewy centred meringues, remove and sit the tray on a rack (not a cold surface – they crack). For crisper meringues, turn the oven off and leave them inside to dry for 1 hour or until they're cold. Sit them on a rack to cool completely. Make up your chantilly cream, if using, and use to sandwich the cooled meringue shells together (below).

PLATE Pile your single or sandwiched white or brown meringue shells onto a plate and serve as they are or with fruit soup.

・・・・・・・・・・・・・ **TO GO WITH** ●━━
FRUIT SOUP

Make 6 hours before eating. Tip 675ml water into a pan, add 180g caster sugar and a 5cm strip lemon zest. Stir over a low heat until the sugar dissolves. Add a sprig of rosemary and 1 large glass of rosé/beaujolais/perry. Increase the heat and simmer for 3 minutes. Remove. Chill. Just before eating, mix 110g each of hulled quartered strawberries/raspberries/blueberries/diced nectarine into the syrup. Ladle into 6 soup plates. Scoop out the zest and rosemary.

WHITE MERINGUE BASKETS WITH MANGO PASSIONFRUIT SAUCE

MAKES 4-6 MERINGUE BASKETS

INGREDIENTS

1 x white meringue mix (opposite)
200ml whipping double cream
SAUCE
1 mango
juice of 1 plump lime
1 tbsp caster sugar
3 large passionfruit

—— CHANGE IT UP ——

1. Fill the baskets with a handful of mixed sliced and whole fruit (raspberries/blueberries/sliced strawberries/physalis). Dust with icing sugar to finish. **2.** Fill with lemon passionfruit curd. **3.** Make a big basket by piping or spooning half the mix into a flat, circular basket base (20cm). Build the rest round the sides to make a steep wall. Cook as before for 1½–2 hours. Turn off the oven and leave to cool inside.

—— BONUS BITES ——

PAVLOVA For a softer-centred basket follow the recipe above to the point where half the sugar has been whisked into the egg whites. Fold the remaining sugar in, adding 1 tsp each of lemon juice, vanilla extract and sifted cornflour. Pipe or shape into one large basket as above. Cook at 140°C/Gas 1 for an hour or until hard outside. Turn the oven off but leave to cool inside. Fill with your choice of fresh fruit, whipped cream and fresh berry sauce (p239).

A classic white meringue WLTM exotic fruity flavours for friendship... maybe more.

PREP Preheat the oven to 150°C/Gas 2. Line 2 baking trays with baking paper.

Make the sauce: peel the mango over a bowl to catch the juices. Slice the flesh off and scrape it from the stone. Blitz the flesh and juices to a purée in a processor or blender. Tip it back into the bowl. Add the lime juice and sugar. Halve the passion fruit. Scoop the seeds and pulp into the mix. If it's very sweet, add a little extra lime juice. Chill it.

Make a quantity of white meringue following the basic method opposite. Spoon or pipe it onto the prepared trays to make baskets. To spoon: Heap 2–3 tablespoons of mix per basket. Using the back of a spoon, flatten each one out a little in the centre to make a space to hold the fruit. Tease the mix up steeply around the sides. The meringue may rise as it cooks so make a distinct shape. To pipe: Draw 6 x 8 cm circles on the paper. Fit a thin or star nozzle to a piping bag. Pipe a base, working from the centre outwards in a continuous spiral until complete. Pipe a wall around the edges. Or pipe a few big blobs onto the circle. Spread them flat with a palette knife. Pipe blobs around the outside to make a wall to hold the filling in later.

COOK Bake for at least an hour or till crisp. Turn off the oven and let the baskets dry out. Peel them off the paper. Sit them on a rack to cool. Pour the cream into a cold bowl. Whisk it until it just holds its shape and before it hardens up.

PLATE Spoon a little sauce into the baskets. Pile in the whipped cream and spoon over more sauce to finish.

CINNAMON BROWN SUGAR SHELLS WITH PISTACHIOS AND RASPBERRIES

MAKES 12 MERINGUE SHELLS

INGREDIENTS

1 x brown meringue mix (p240)
1–2 tsp ground cinnamon (to taste)
12 shelled pistachios
200ml whipping/double cream
1 tsp icing sugar, sifted
a small pinch of ground ginger (optional)
300g fresh raspberries

—— CHANGE IT UP ——

1. For hazelnut shells, add chopped hazelnuts instead of pistachios and don't include the spices. **2.** For chocolate shells, sift a bit of cocoa powder into the mix with the cinnamon.

—— BONUS BITE ——

BLACKBERRY STACKS

Make the meringue mix as above without the spice. Pipe into individual discs on greaseproof paper (tracing circles onto the paper then piping from the centre in an outwards spiral). Cook as above then pile with whipped cream and fresh blackberries. Leave open or top with another disc. Make a fresh berry sauce with blackberries (p239) and drizzle over to finish.

A decadent mix of spice, nuts and brown sugar with a fresh lift of tangy raspberry.

PREP Preheat the oven to 110°C/Gas 1/4. Line 2 baking trays with paper.

Make up the brown sugar meringue following the method on p240, whisking in the cinnamon at the end or folding it in lightly with a large metal spoon.

Spoon or pipe the mix into shells/large blobs. Spoon it: Use 2 tablespoons. Scoop the mix up in one spoon and use the other to ease it off onto the tray. Keep the surface smooth for a neat look or rough it up a bit. They will expand, so leave space between them. Pipe it: Fix a plain or medium nozzle onto a piping bag. Hold the bag in one hand. Fold the sides down over your hand then spoon the mix into the bag. Pull the sides up then twist it to close at the top, squeezing the meringue down to the nozzle. Point it at the paper and squeeze to release as much as you need for each meringue.

Chop the nuts roughly. Sprinkle sparingly over the meringues.

COOK Bake for 2 hours for a crisp result or 1 hour for chewy meringue. Carefully peel the paper away from one or two to check the base is crisp. Give them extra time if needed.

Peel the paper off the bases. Cool on a rack (not a cold surface) to avoid cracking.

Whip the cream in a cold bowl with a hand or balloon whisk so you can feel how it's thickening up. Add the icing sugar to taste and a little ground ginger, if you like.

PLATE Pile the meringues up on a big plate. Bang the cream into a dish and raspberries into another. Serve at the table so people can help themselves. Alternatively, sandwich the raspberries and cream between the meringues for neat eating.

A PROPER ENGLISH APPLE PIE

FEEDS 4

INGREDIENTS

PASTRY
350g plain white flour
a pinch of salt
175g cold butter, plus extra for greasing
60g caster sugar
½ tsp grated lemon zest
1 large egg

FILLING
675g tasty eating or cooking apples
    (peeled, cored weight)
15g butter
a squeeze of lemon juice
1 tsp lemon rind
3 cardamom pods/3 cloves/a pinch of
    cinnamon
60g caster sugar
180ml water

FINISH
1 small egg, beaten with 1 teaspoon
    water
caster sugar to sprinkle

— CHANGE IT UP —

For a tutti frutti pie, add small chunks
of summer fruit such as peach, apricot,
nectarine, plum to the softened apple just
before filling and omit the spices.

— BONUS BITE —

APPLE PLUM PUDDING CAKE
Prep the apples as above. Chop 2 plums.
Cream together 175g caster sugar and 75g
soft butter until light. Gradually beat in 2
beaten eggs. Sift in 225g plain flour,
2 tsp baking powder and 1½ tsp powdered
cinnamon. Add the grated zest of 1 lemon
and fold the mix lightly together. Stir in the
fruit plus 1–2 tbsp milk until the mix is soft
enough to drop off a spoon. Put into a lined
20cm round tin and bake in a preheated
oven at 180°C/Gas 4 for 1 hour.

Here's a very relaxed apple pie and an easy introduction to a sweet shortcrusty pastry: it's great with cheese, cream or ice-cream.

PREP Make the pastry. By hand: Sift the flour and salt into a bowl. Cut the butter into small cubes. Drop them into the bowl. Rub the fat and flour between your fingers until they amalgamate. Add the sugar and lemon zest. Beat the egg then dribble it in gradually, mixing with a fork as you go, until you have a pliable pastry that's neither sticky nor dry (you might not need it all). Roll it lightly into a ball and wrap in cling film. Chill for 30 minutes. By machine: Pulse everything except the egg in a processor. Pour the egg gradually through the funnel. Pulse till it comes together. Wrap and chill.

For the filling: Peel the apples. Core or quarter then cut out the pips with a sharp knife. Slice or chop them roughly then throw into a pan with the butter, lemon juice and zest, spice and a splash of water. Cook and stir on a very gentle heat until almost tender but holding shape. (Smaller pieces of watery apple will take 5 minutes, others will take longer). Set aside to cool. Taste; if the apple is very tart add a bit more sugar.

Preheat the oven to 170°C/Gas 3. Grease a shallow circular 18cm enamel pie dish or similar.

Sit your chilled pastry on a lightly floured board. Cut one third off to make the lid. Roll the larger two thirds out using a floured rolling pin, turning it 45 degrees after each roll to keep a regular shape. Create a large thin circle wide enough to line your dish, with some left over. Do this by eye or use the string test for accuracy (p229). Roll the pin under the pastry. Lift it over and into the tin then manipulate it to fit, pasting any cracks or holes as you go. Now, roll out the other piece in a circle big enough to cover the top of the pie plus a bit. Don't worry if you need to re-roll during any part of the process. It's normal. Roll any extra bits out and cut out leaves for decoration, if you like.

Spoon the cooled filling into the dish. Lift the pastry lid over it using the pin, lay it down and pinch/crimp the edges together to seal them. Brush it lightly with the beaten egg/water to give it shine. Cut a couple of slits in the centre. Stick your leaves on top if using. Sprinkle with sugar.

COOK Bake the pie for 30 minutes or until the crust is golden, crisp and buttery. Remove and sit it on a cooling rack. Leave it in its tin.

PLATE Bang the pie on the table. Serve with a wedge of strong or crumbly cheese, (like cheddar or Wensleydale) a jug of cream, yoghurt or ice-cream. It reheats well. Take it into work to warm in the microwave or take it out in the tin for a picnic.

PLUM, PEACH, BANANA AND APPLE TARTE TATIN

FEEDS 4

INGREDIENTS

1 x 500g pack puff pastry
2 plums
2 apricots
1 large cooking apple
3–4 eating apples
1 banana
4 cardamom pods
90g caster sugar
100g pear cider (perry)
40g soft butter

——— BONUS BITES ———

FAST APPLE BUTTER TART FOR 2.
Roll 110g puff pastry out very thinly. Rest it in the fridge. Cut into 2 x 18cm circles. Peel, core, quarter and thinly slice 2 apples. Arrange the slices concentrically on each tart, overlapping slightly. Dot with a few knobs of butter, sprinkle with a little caster sugar then bake at 230°C/Gas 8 for 10–15 minutes. Melt 2 tbsp apricot jam with a little water and brush over the hot tarts. Eat with vanilla ice-cream.

Here's one of the great French classics made simple; crisp pastry, gorgeous soft fruit, sticky caramel. Make it upside down in the pan then bang it in the oven. It looks and tastes ridiculously gorgeous.

PREP Sit the puff pastry on a lightly floured board. Roll it out until it's about 5mm thick and big enough to cover the top of a 20 x 25cm iron-handled frying pan with 3cm extra all round the sides. Invert the pan onto the pastry and cut round it, allowing for the extra 3cm, using a sharp knife. Lift it onto a plate. Chill it.

Prepare the fruit: Cut the plums and apricots in two. Twist the halves to separate. Remove the stones. Peel and core the apples. Cut one of the eating apples in two horizontally. Retain one of the halves to make a centrepiece. Quarter the other half and cut the remaining apples into eighths. Slice the banana. Toss the fruit in a little lemon juice. Preheat the oven to 190°C/Gas 5.

Make the caramel sauce. Bash the cardamom pods lightly to expose the seeds. Fling them into the centre of your pan. Add the sugar and cider. Stir a couple of times. Boil for 2 minutes or until it turns golden brown. Don't burn it. Add the butter, stirring. Remove from the heat as soon as it melts.

Working with care, place the halved apple, cut side down, in the centre of the pan. Arrange the other fruit around it, either randomly or in a pattern, fitting pieces tightly together. Return the pan to a very low heat for 4 minutes so the fruit starts to cook and the sauce to caramelise. Remove from the heat.

Cover the fruit with the pastry. Slip your rolling pin under the circle. Lift it over the pan then lower it down. Using a wooden spoon or fork handle, gently tuck the edges down the sides of the pan.

COOK Shift the tart to the oven. Bake for 30 minutes or until puffed, crisp and golden. Remove and leave to rest for 5 minutes (the pastry will sink but that's fine). To turn it out: place a large plate (wider than the pan) over the pastry. Holding pan and plate firmly, invert the pan so the tart and any extra juice will slip out.

PLATE Serve this impressive looking tart at the table. Enjoy it warm or cold with whipped cream, yoghurt, clotted cream or good thin custard (p236).

DELICIOUS APPLE AND PISTACHIO STRUDEL WITH SPICED CREAM

FEEDS 4

Autumn embodied in a delicious apple-packed crisp filo parcel; beat the spiced fruit juices into some softly whipped cream for the perfect accompaniment.

INGREDIENTS

125g butter
75g raisins
2 tbsp rum
2 large cooking apples
1 tbsp lemon juice
50g caster sugar
1 tsp ground cinnamon
4 large sheets filo pastry
75g dried white breadcrumbs (p201)
25g pistachio nuts, shelled weight
300ml whipping/double cream
a bit of icing sugar, sifted

PREP Melt the butter gently in a small pan on a low heat. Brush a little over a large baking sheet with a pastry brush. Set the rest aside.

For the filling: Tip the raisins and rum into a small bowl to soak. Peel and core and slice the apples thinly. Chuck them into a larger bowl with the lemon juice sugar and cinnamon, stirring to coat the fruit so it doesn't brown.

Sort the pastry: Lay a large sheet of greaseproof paper or a tea towel on your kitchen surface. Unwrap the pack of filo pastry. With great care (it's delicate), peel away the first sheet. Lay it flat on the greaseproof paper. Cover the rest.

Quickly brush the sheet of filo all over with butter so it doesn't dry out. Scatter a third of the breadcrumbs over it. Lay a second sheet of filo directly on top. Brush all over with butter again and scatter over another third of the breadcrumbs. Repeat till you have 4 layers of pastry together. Finish with more butter (no crumbs).

Mix the rum, raisins, pistachios and apples. Drain off and save their juices. Spoon/pile the filling onto the edge of the pastry nearest to you, leaving a bit of space at the end and on the two long sides for folding. To roll: Pull the edges of the long sides of pastry up onto the filling then fold the close end up and over the apples, pushing gently as you go and using the paper to help. Roll up, keeping the long edges tucked up so it's enclosed well. Place seam down on the baking sheet.

COOK Brush the strudel with more butter and bake for 25–30 minutes until golden brown. Test for doneness with a skewer. It should be hot inside. Remove and brush with more butter. Cool on the sheet for 5 minutes. Transfer to a serving dish for eating hot or at room temperature. Meanwhile, whip the cream, adding the reserved rum and spice juice.

PLATE Dust the strudel with icing sugar. Slice and enjoy with your whipped cream, or serve with ice-cream or honey with yoghurt.

SINFUL TRIPLE CHOCOLATE TART

FEEDS 6-8

INGREDIENTS

PASTRY

225g plain white flour
20g icing sugar
a pinch of salt
35g caster sugar
110g cold butter, cubed
1 small egg, beaten

FILLING

100g milk chocolate
150g dark chocolate (70%)
150g white chocolate
100g butter
3 whole eggs, plus 4 extra egg yolks
100g caster sugar

TIPS

1 When rolling out your pastry to fit the tin, either judge the size by eye or use the string technique (p229) to be really accurate.
2 If your tart starts to turn a darker brown while cooking, cover the top with baking paper.

Here's my favourite chocolate tart of all time. It's more subtle than most, smoothly intense, yummy. Put it out there with a sorbet.

PREP Make the pastry. By hand: Sift the flour, icing sugar and salt into a bowl. Stir in the caster sugar, add the butter and rub together between your fingertips until the mix resembles fine breadcrumbs. Add the beaten egg gradually, mixing it with a fork until you get firm dough which is neither too dry nor sticky. (Add a drop of cold water if you need to or a little extra flour). Roll it into a smooth ball. By machine: Put the flour, sugar, butter and salt into a processor. Pulse until it amalgamates. Add the egg a little at a time, pulsing, until the dough is right. Roll it into a ball. Flatten it slightly. Wrap it in cling film. Chill for 30 minutes.

Roll the pastry out on a lightly floured board as thinly as you can to fit the base and sides of a 23cm tart tin, allowing a bit extra for overhang. Reserve any extra pastry. Line the tin: Run a metal spatula under the pastry. Lift it up on the pin and lower into the tin. Ease it down to fit the sides and base, leaving a wide overhang. Mould and mend any cracks with the extra pastry. Chill for 30 minutes. Preheat the oven to 180°C/Gas 4.

Bake it blind: Prick the base lightly with a fork and lay a large piece of baking paper into the case. Fill with a layer of baking beans. Bake for 15–20 minutes till pale and firm. Remove. Lift the paper and beans out. Return it to the oven for a few minutes. Remove. Once it's cooled slightly, take a sharp knife and remove the overhang.

Make the filling: chop the milk chocolate randomly into fine and larger dice. Scatter them evenly over the baked cooled tart base. Break the dark and white chocolate into a heatproof bowl. Add the butter. Sit the bowl over a pan of gently simmering water, keeping the base of the bowl clear. Once the chocolate has melted, remove from the heat, stir till smooth and set aside to cool.

Increase the oven temperature to 220°C/Gas 7. Put the eggs and sugar into a large bowl. Whisk for a few minutes using a balloon or electric hand-held whisk until you get a white fluffy mousse. Pour the cooled chocolate onto the mousse. Using a large metal spoon, cut into the mix and lightly fold it together with figure-of-eight movements until just amalgamated. Pour into the pastry case.

COOK Bake for 7–10 minutes until the chocolate is just set and is a bit firmer than a mousse. The skill is to know when it's done – shuffle the tin to check that it's firm in the centre. If there's a gap between filling and pastry, it's very well done. Remove. Sit it on a rack for 5 minutes. Lift it out of the tin. Leave to cool.

PLATE Sit the tart on a serving plate to slice at the table. Dust with a bit of cocoa or icing sugar if you like and serve with shot glasses filled with grapefruit water ice or raspberry vodka sorbet (p237).

BAKEWELL TART

FEEDS 6-8

INGREDIENTS

PASTRY

225g plain white flour
a pinch of salt
110g cold butter, cubed
35g caster sugar
1 medium egg, beaten

FILLING

3–4 tbsp raspberry jam
125g soft butter
125g caster sugar
3 eggs plus 1 extra yolk (at room
   temperature)
160g ground almonds
1 tsp almond extract
1 tsp amaretto (optional)
a few flaked almonds

—— CHANGE IT UP ——

Switch the raspberry jam for strawberry,
plum or black cherry jam instead.

BONUS BITE

CUSTARD TART

Make up a batch of sweet pastry as above,
adding a pinch of nutmeg with the flour.
Chill for an hour. Preheat the oven to 180°C/
Gas 4. Roll the pastry out thinly and use to
line a 22cm tart tin and blind bake as above.
(This is a very wet filling, so be sure to repair
any cracks or holes in the base and sides
before cooking). Make the filling by putting
50g caster sugar and ½ tsp vanilla extract
into a bowl. Add 4 eggs and beat till mixed.
Add 400ml milk and mix again. Strain the
mix through a sieve and pour into the tart
case. Sprinkle over lots of freshly grated/
ground nutmeg and carry very carefully
to the oven. Bake for 15 minutes or until
the custard sets. Judge it by the amount of
wobble (shuffle the tin); it should look set.
Remove and leave to cool before eating.

An easy-to-make old-school pudding; this may look a bit safe on taste but trust me, it's not. It's soft, jammy, heavy on the almond frangipane, absolutely gorgeous.

PREP Make the pastry: Sift the flour and salt into a bowl. Add the butter. Rub them together between your fingertips until the mix resembles fine breadcrumbs. Stir in the sugar. Add the beaten egg gradually, mixing with a fork until you get a firm dough which is neither dry not sticky. Add a drop of cold water or flour if you need. Pull it into a smooth ball.

By machine: Pulse the flour, salt and sugar. Add the butter. Pulse. Add the egg gradually until the dough is right. Roll into a ball. Flatten it. Wrap it in cling film. Chill for 30 minutes. Preheat the oven to 180°C/Gas 4.

Roll the pastry out on a lightly floured board to 3mm thickness. Line the sides and base of a 22cm tart tin, allowing extra for an overhang.

Line with baking paper and fill with baking beans. Bake the case blind for 20 minutes. The sides should feel crisp and start to look a pale brown. Remove. Lift out the paper and baking beans. If the base is very pale and soft give it a few extra minutes. Remove. Carefully cut away the pastry overhang after a few seconds.

For the filling: Spoon the jam into the part-cooked case and spread it evenly to cover. Tip the butter and sugar into a bowl and cream the mix together by beating hard with a wooden spoon for a few minutes until it's light, white and smooth. Beat the eggs and yolk together in a bowl and add to the creamed mix a little at a time, beating constantly to stop the mixture curdling. Add the ground almonds, almond extract and amaretto, if using, folding everything together very gently with a large metal spoon.

Spoon the mix into the tart in large blobs, then join them up so you don't disturb the jam. Scatter flaked almonds over the top.

COOK Bake for 25–30 minutes. It's done when the centre looks firm but springy and it's a lovely golden brown. If it browns up early, cover with baking paper. Remove.

Leave to cool on a rack. Remove the sides of the tin after 5 minutes.

PLATE Slice your tart at the table. Eat on its own or serve with vanilla ice-cream or custard (p236), fromage frais or whipped cream. It's also great with a cuppa and keeps well.

LEMON POSSET
AND CRISP TUILES BISCUITS

FEEDS 4

INGREDIENTS
400ml double cream
85g caster sugar
2 lemons

The Elizabethans got it right with this one; just the three ingredients, very little effort and a beautiful thick creamy lemon outcome. Make it a day ahead or several hours before serving.

PREP Get your containers organised (small cocktail or wine glasses, cups, small dishes). Zest one lemon and juice two. Tip the zest and juice into a small bowl.

Pour the cream and sugar into a large pan (the mix will boil up).

COOK Put the pan on to a very gentle heat. Stir to dissolve the sugar. Let it come to the boil very slowly. Regulate the heat so it won't boil over.

Boil the mix for just 3 minutes. Remove. Stir in the zest and juice. If it starts to look a bit lumpy, that's ok. Taste and if it's not sharp enough (don't let the cream or sugar dominate) add a bit more juice. It should taste like a really good cheesecake.

Leave to cool. Pour into your glasses of choice. Put them into the fridge to set. Chill for at least 4 hours.

PLATE Serve topped with a handful of sliced berries and accompanied by crisp tuiles biscuits (below).

TO GO WITH
TUILES BISCUITS

Preheat the oven to 190°C/Gas 5. Grease and line 2 large baking trays. Melt 55g butter in a pan over a low heat. Tip it into a bowl to cool. Put 2 egg whites and 110g caster sugar into a clean bowl. Beat with a fork for 3 minutes. When the mix is thick and frothy, sift over and beat in 55g flour and 4 drops of vanilla extract. Once the batter is smooth, slowly beat in the cooled butter. Use a teaspoon to put 4 blobs of mix well apart on each tray (they expand). Using a metal spatula, spread them into very thin circles. Bake for 5–6 minutes until pale tan in the middle and browned at the margins (check after 4 minutes). Remove from the oven. Leave for 5 seconds only. Slide a clean spatula under each one to loosen then lift them off. Mould them into large curls over a rolling pin or back of a wooden spoon, holding them there for 5 seconds. Rest on a rack to crisp up. Repeat with the rest of the mix. Store them in an airtight tin.

INDEX

A HUGE THANK YOU TO ALL THESE LOVELY PEOPLE...

My editor Simon Davis for all his superhuman efforts, patience and making things fit; Claire Peters for making it look beautiful; Chris Terry for the amazing photographs; Emily Jonzen for great support; Jane O'Shea for believing in me; Felicity Blunt for being a brilliant agent; my brother Tom and sister Polly for always being there for me; the rest of the family; Louise for helping out; Dad for being chief taster and always supporting; Mickey (who always picks up the scraps) and Mum – for being her usual perfect self, for all her help and inspiration, and for putting up with me.

Editorial Director Jane O'Shea
Creative Director Helen Lewis
Project Editor Simon Davis
Designer Claire Peters
Design Assistant Jim Smith
Photographer Chris Terry
Food Stylist Emily Jonzen
Stylist Iris Bromet
Illustrator Claire Peters
Editorial Assistant Louise McKeever
Production Director Vincent Smith
Production Controller Leonie Kellman

First published as *Virgin to Veteran* in 2012
by Quadrille Publishing Limited
Alhambra House
27-31 Charing Cross Road
London WC2H 0LS
www.quadrille.co.uk

Text © 2012, 2013 Sam Stern
Photographs © 2012 Chris Terry
Design and layout © 2012
Quadrille Publishing Limited

Cataloguing in Publication Data: a catalogue record for this book is available from the British Library.

ISBN 978 184949 342 0

Printed in China